MW00855814

Context and Pretext in
Conflict Resolution

Context and Pretext in Conflict Resolution

Culture, Identity, Power, and Practice

Kevin Avruch

Routledge
Taylor & Francis Group

LONDON AND NEW YORK

First published 2013 by Paradigm Publishers

Published 2016 by Routledge
2 Park Square, Milton Park, Abingdon, Oxon OX14 4RN
711 Third Avenue, New York, NY 10017, USA

Routledge is an imprint of the Taylor & Francis Group, an informa business

Copyright © 2013, Taylor & Francis.

All rights reserved. No part of this book may be reprinted or reproduced or
utilised in any form or by any electronic, mechanical, or other means, now
known or hereafter invented, including photocopying and recording, or in any
information storage or retrieval system, without permission in writing from
the publishers.

Notice:
Product or corporate names may be trademarks or registered
trademarks, and are used only for identification and explanation without
intent to infringe.

Avruch, Kevin.
  Context and pretext in conflict resolution : culture,
identity, power, and practice / Kevin Avruch.
     p. cm.
  Includes bibliographical references and index.
  ISBN 978-1-61205-060-7 (paperback : alk. paper)
  1. Culture conflict. 2. Social conflict. 3. Conflict management. I. Title.
  HM1121.A88 2012
  303.6—dc23

                                                                    2011042235

Designed and Typeset by Straight Creek Bookmakers.

  ISBN 13 : 978-1-61205-059-1 (hbk)
  ISBN 13 : 978-1-61205-060-7 (pbk)

For Dennis J. D. Sandole
and in memory of
Wallace Warfield

Contents

Foreword

The Return of Culture to Conflict Analysis and Resolution

In the mid-1980s the idea that culture was important for understanding and responding to conflict was largely dismissed by policy makers, practitioners, and scholars outside of anthropology. It hadn't always been this way. At the mid-twentieth century, the idea that cultures mattered was prevalent. In the United States, regional differences in beliefs, behaviors, and values were widely acknowledged and provided material for radio and movie entertainments. During World War II, the U.S. military produced handbooks and guides to help its expeditionary forces understand and engage the island cultures they would encounter in the Pacific, and cultural guidance helped define the ways that the victorious allies dealt with Germany and Japan.

But as the Cold War deepened, this awareness of culture was eclipsed by the belief in the power of the melting pot and the rise of faith in technical knowledge. In international relations, the approaches that rose to prominence during this period stressed state actions and treated states as acultural rational actors that could most effectively be dealt with through coercive means, especially military force and economic sanctions. The idea that cultures mattered got pushed aside as it became common wisdom that cultural difference was dissolving in the face of greater interpersonal contacts spurred on by remarkable developments in travel and technology. Airplanes traversed distances in hours that previously took weeks to travel. Television and telephones brought people together in ways, often quite intimate, not possible before. As well, domestic differences and international activities all came to be refracted through the grand contest between East and West, which envisioned a great struggle between only two different value systems vying for supremacy. Then too, the very real possibility that this competition would lead to a nuclear holocaust ending human life as we knew it and the desire to avert such destruction were seen as amendable to technical solutions, making concerns with culture seem inconsequential.

It is not surprising, perhaps, that in such a context conflict analysis and resolution too should be seen as in need of technical expertise, not cultural understanding and interpretation, which was often derided as a naïve waste of time, if not soft-headed or morally mistaken. Game theory models were elaborated to guide the conduct of international strategy, even including finely calibrated scenarios for nuclear war, in which escalation would be limited by the use of nuclear bombs of varying destructive force to send finely calibrated messages about national intentions. Overtaxed court systems were to find relief in the creation of an alternative dispute resolution system that relied on technical skills in negotiation and mediation to efficiently process a myriad of disputes that were said to be clogging the court system.

By the early 1980s, the view that most any conflict—domestic or international, intergroup or interpersonal—could be reframed and negotiated to a satisfying conclusion if only the right technical skills were brought to bear on it had become part of the popular imagination. Books championing such technical approaches regularly appeared on bestseller lists. This was soon followed by the growth of a cottage industry promoting those approaches. Quickly, the cottage industry gave way to larger enterprises consuming millions of dollars in executive seminars, policy advisory groups, and training programs promoting and prescribing these technical approaches to conflict management throughout the world, all largely without concern for how cultural differences might affect those activities.

Yet even as the possibility that all conflicts might yield to skilled application of technical knowledge assuaged the popular imagination, some scholars and analysts were sounding alarms about the dangers of a culture-free conception of conflict. And we began to push back against the received view that conflicts required only mechanically technical solutions.

Internationally, in the late 1980s and 1990s as the Cold War came to an end, conflicts that had been controlled by the power and patronage of the Soviet Union or the United States reemerged, sometimes with the most deadly consequences. Countries shattered; Yugoslavia split apart; Somalia became a "failed state." "Ethnic cleansing"—a polite euphemism for genocide—ravaged places as different as Rwanda and the former Yugoslavia. Within the United States, the reassertion of cultural difference was evident in the rise of "value politics," often revealing sweeping and stunning antipathies within our society.

These changes led analysts to see that culture is important. Yet, the approach to culture that got taken up was itself a mechanical and outdated one. Those of us who had urged the importance of culture for understanding and responding to conflicts pointed out the dangers of treating dynamic cultural systems as stable, unchanging things that could be given mechanical treatment. The critiques took issue with the mechanical use of culture and the many ways in which it resulted in distorted understandings of events. A good deal of this work was being done by anthropologists writing on peace, conflict, and security under the auspices of the Commission on Peace and Human Rights of the International Union of Anthropological and Ethnological Sciences, of which I was the executive secretary. It was in that context that I first came to know and admire Professor Kevin Avruch and his contributions to these debates. After a sabbatical year at the United States Institute of Peace, Kevin published his 1998 book, *Culture and Conflict Resolution,* which crystallized and extended those critiques in a way that made them accessible and relevant to policy makers, analysts, and scholars alike.

Culture and Conflict Resolution not only marked the crystallization of an intellectual movement that had been taking place throughout the 1980s; it announced Professor Avruch as a commentator of great potential on the role of culture in conflict and its management. Over the dozen years since the publication of *Culture and Conflict Resolution,* Kevin and I have often been in contact, which has been a personal and professional pleasure for me, as Kevin has exceeded the promise of that book; he has emerged as an analyst of keen insight and unique ability.

In the present book, *Context and Pretext in Conflict Resolution,* Professor Avruch succeeds in the ambitious goal of exploring the vibrant and multifaceted roles that culture plays in conflict analysis and resolution. He unites a dynamic, cognitive-affective model of culture with the sensitive analysis of structure and politics, no easy accomplishment. In doing so, *Context and Pretext* leads us through the understanding of just how important it is to recognize culture as an element of conflict, a source of identity and power, and a shaper of our own practice. He applies this model to human rights, to post-conflict reconstruction, and to the modeling of conflict resolution practice. Power, representation, and identity emerge as important categories of analysis. In all of these excursions, *Context and Pretext* is a closely reasoned and highly accessible. Culture is indeed back as an important area of work in conflict analysis and resolution, and it is back in no small measure because of the wonderful work that Kevin Avruch presents here in *Context and Pretext,* which is a model of how cultural analysis can be applied thoughtfully and consequentially to conflict analysis and resolution.

Robert A. Rubinstein
Professor of Anthropology and
International Relations
The Maxwell School of Syracuse University

Acknowledgments

I began work on the book during my semester as the Joan B. Kroc Peace Scholar in the new Kroc School of Peace Studies at the University of San Diego, in 2009, in a lovely office with a view of the Pacific Ocean. I thank Dean William Headley, C.S.Sp., for extending the invitation to join the School for a term so early in its existence and, along with colleagues, students, and staff at the School and the Institute for Peace and Justice, for offering me splendid hospitality. The book was completed at my home institution, the School for Conflict Analysis and Resolution (S-CAR) at George Mason University. (Called the Institute for Conflict Analysis and Resolution, ICAR, for more than twenty years, ICAR became a school in July 2011.) I want to thank S-CAR's dean, Andrea Bartoli, and ICAR's past director, Sara Cobb, for their support over the years.

The original versions of the essays on which the following chapters are based were written over a number of years, and therefore I acknowledge friends and colleagues who contributed to my thinking, roughly in order of the chapters themselves. I thank Peter W. Black, Sandra Cheldelin, Carrie Menkel-Meadow, Julie Mertus, Jeffrey Helsing, Carlos Sluzki, John Stone, Rutledge Dennis, Howard Gadlin, Tricia Jones, Ingrid Sandole-Staroste, Andrea Kupfer Schneider, Christopher Honeyman (to whom I owe the title "The Poverty of Buyer and Seller"), Dan Rothbart, Marc Gopin, Steve Wolin, Laurence J. Kirmayer, Antonius Robben, Nadim Rouhana, Morgan Brigg, Jamie Price, Solon Simmons, Mark Goodale, Alex Scheinman, and Maneshka Eliatamby.

I owe special thanks to Professor Louis Kriesberg and Robert A. Rubinstein for their careful and critical reading of the manuscript, which greatly improved it, and Robert for graciously agreeing to write the Foreword.

I have been very fortunate to be part of the community of scholars and practitioners at S-CAR—students as well as faculty—and want here to acknowledge several friends whose contributions exceed that of any single chapter. Richard Rubenstein, Christoper Mitchell, Dennis Sandole, and the late Wallace Warfield were all part of my intellectual growth in the field. In 1980, I sat on the faculty committee that hired Dennis as the first dedicated faculty of the (then) Center for Conflict Resolution, but it was Dennis's invitation to Peter Black and I to contribute a critique of the theory of basic human needs, in response to an article he and John Burton wrote for *The Negotiation Journal,* that marked my first publication in conflict resolution. To Rich Rubenstein, I owe reminders of the base truth that around all the sometimes numinous talk of culture, discourse, and symbols there are hard materialities and regimes of unequal and maldistributed life chances. Chris provides me an exemplar of what being a scholar-practitioner in our field means, and I could not have begun to untangle for myself the many riddles of power and conflict resolution without his own writings on the subject. Wallace afforded me a decades–long course of study on the ethics of practice and the risks and responsibilities created by our intervention in other people's misfortunes. I dedicate the book to Dennis and Wallace.

John W. Burton died in June 2010, while the book was in press. Rereading the book now, I see his spirit inhabiting many of the chapters like some stern Methodist (his father, a socially activist, reformist pastor in Australia, must have been formidable indeed), and I find myself continuing discussions (and, of course, arguments) that I began with him a quarter-century ago. These have been valuable to me.

To Sheila, I owe a life of love and companionship, and our two daughters.

Part 1
Culture and Conflict Resolution

1

Introduction
Culture, Conflict, and
Conflict Resolution

Air Florida: The Ubiquity of Culture

The January 12, 2007, edition of *The Washington Post* carried on its front page a story commemorating the tragic crash, twenty-five years earlier, of Air Florida Flight 90.[1] The Boeing 737 took off from Washington's National Airport in a snowstorm and crashed almost immediately into the icy Potomac River. Seventy-eight passengers, crew members, and motorists on the ground died. The subsequent National Transport Safety Board (NTSB) investigation, examining voice transcripts of preflight procedures by the pilot and copilot, focused on faulty de-icing and pilot error in causing the crash, and particularly on the failure of the pilot to heed warnings by the copilot that some instrument readings didn't "seem right." The communicational breakdown, safety experts decided, stemmed from the resistance of the copilot to be (or act) more assertive with the aircraft's captain. The article went on to detail some safety reforms implemented after the crash, as part of pilot training and industry standard operating procedures. "Though some of the lessons may seem simple, such as communication and management skills," the article noted, "it helped break down an authoritarian cockpit culture dominated by captains." The article continued: "Safety experts said evolution in the cockpit's culture, which now also includes listening more attentively to advice from flight attendants, has made aviation far safer." The article ended by noting that similar communicational reforms have even been extended to other multi-actor high-risk settings, such as the hospital: "A similar ethos has moved into the hospital operating room," where the surgeon, traditionally the authoritarian "captain" of the surgical team, must now also be willing to listen to other team members who might raise "red flags" but in the past were reluctant to do so. Now, presurgical checklists (modeled on preflight checklists) are common ("Do we have the right patient? The right procedure? The correct limb?"), and surgical team members are encouraged to speak up if something seems amiss.

The notion of culture is used, explicitly, twice in the article—perhaps three times if its semantic first cousin ethos is counted. The first time it is linked to the notions of power and hierarchy through the modifier "authoritarian (... cockpit culture"). The second time it is linked to the idea of change by speaking of "evolution in the cockpit's culture." Implicitly, at least, some idea of norms and values ("it's right and good for the captain to be unquestionably in charge—until it isn't") is also present here, in both uses of the term *culture*. If we count as well the explicit connection made throughout the article between interpersonal communication and culture, we have in this piece a fair beginning of an understanding of the term. Culture, we learn, somehow connects to communication, to power or authority, to norms and values—and is susceptible to change.

A deeper reading can also connect culture to conflict, mainly though the dynamics of power, authority, and hierarchy. This is because "cockpit culture" implies that pilot and copilot—if not as individuals, then through their *roles*—even as their goals (the safe operation of their aircraft) are identical, are in potential conflict via any threat to their hierarchical relationship, such as the copilot questioning the captain. Indeed, authoritarianism as a social modality is one way of managing potential conflict by defining and delimiting social relationships along relatively clear dimensions of dominance and subordination: Everyone knows where they stand. In this sense, safety reforms, whether in the cockpit or the operating room, can be seen as modifying, even subverting, authoritarian limits on overt role conflicts, in the service of achieving overarching shared goals—safe flights and successful surgeries. The requirement for achieving these goals, in fact, is to defuse authoritarian and hierarchical strictures that previously managed potential role conflicts by keeping actors in their appropriate place. In a way, potential conflict is now brought into the open—the copilot contradicting the captain, the surgical nurse questioning the surgeon—and is encouraged. Conflict is transformed into collaboration in the service of the team's shared goals. There is a phrase in our field for this process; after Kriesberg (2007b), we say that conflict is now "constructive."

There is, finally, the reporter's use of the notion of (cockpit) culture to begin with. Without bothering to define it as a technical term, the article's author presumes it to be a colloquial word whose meaning (even when modified by the unlikely "cockpit") will be understood by his readers. And note how he uses the word as a way of talking about, and bringing together, a number of different aspects—communication, power, norms, values, role expectations, change—of the social setting of the cockpit. He uses it, that is, as sort of shorthand with which to talk about *context*. Indeed, if we think of the NTSB experts reviewing the pilot–copilot transcript as the close study of a text, then, literally, the idea of context—of culture—is how *they* came to frame their understanding and interpretation of the various communicational impedances or dysfunctions that ended in tragedy. The idea of culture thus appears protean and ubiquitous. It is used to make sense of *communication*, the interlocutory dynamics of encounters, and of the larger *context* in which these encounters take place. This makes culture, as Raymond Williams (1983:87) remarked, a very complicated idea.

Conflict Resolution, Transformation, and Peace: Introductory Remarks

This introductory chapter reviews some of the major conceptions of culture that have developed in the past couple decades in the field of conflict resolution, while touching briefly on some themes that are the main topics of the chapters that follow. In this chapter, I use the term *conflict resolution* broadly to encompass a variety of discourses in an emerging field, including dispute resolution, conflict transformation, and peace studies among them. The relationship between *conflict* and *dispute* (particularly in the guise of alternative dispute resolution [ADR]) is the topic of Chapter 2. Advocates of the other two terms, *transformation* and *peace*, base the distinction on what they consider serious limits in the goals of resolution. Some regard transformation as an evolved version of conflict resolution, an advanced form that aims at deeper change in the relationship between the parties than mere resolution aspires to, and points the way toward true reconciliation between the former adversaries (Kriesberg 2008). In contrast, I agree with Ramsbotham, Woodhouse, and Miall (2005) that conflict resolution "properly perceived," in the sense of getting to the root causes of serious, deeply rooted conflict, implies notions of transformation (see Chapter 2). The ambitious promise of reconciliation, seen nowadays by some as the ideal endpoint in the process of building peace to replace enmity is, I agree, perhaps less adequately covered by conflict resolution, and it is on this basis that advocates of conflict transformation as an advanced form most strongly make their case.

The connection between conflict resolution and peace studies is more complicated, and the tension between them, of longer duration (see Schmid 1968; Reid and Yanarella 1976). As noted in Chapter 2, when the first postgraduate degree in the field in the United States was envisioned at George Mason University, the word *peace* was purposely left out of the title. In those early days, the gulf in the academy between the conflict resolution camp and the peace camp was wide. Some scholars in the peace camp thought conflict resolution reflected a cold, technocratic, and even amoral view of the world; it seemed unconcerned with questions of social justice and deeper structural change. (The emphasis here is on *social structural*; the sort of change epitomized by conflict transformation, in contrast, was interpersonal, in the relationship between the parties.) Although not exclusively associated with national differences—many esteemed peace scholars were and are Americans (and critics of conflict resolution)—the center of peace research remains European (particularly Swedish and Norwegian, and at Bradford University in the United Kingdom). Ramsbotham and colleagues (2005) have characterized this as the difference between a more (perhaps typical) American "pragmatic" approach toward attaining peace and a more "structural" (and consistently leftist) European one. Although I think this distinction held true for a long time, the two orientations have grown together as the field developed and expanded, first because such newer state-of-the-art terms that direct our attention to "post-conflict" (properly, post-*settlement*) issues, like "peacebuilding" (introduced in 1992 as part of Boutros Boutros-Ghali's influential *Agenda for Peace*), have broadened the purview of what conflict resolution ought to consider important—beyond, for example, drafting the formal agreement by "getting to yes." Second, many younger conflict resolution scholars and practitioners bring a (self-) critical lens to the field, and although still engaged with the mechanics and techniques of resolution—with *process*—now also agree that concerns with, say, human rights and justice cannot be set aside in favor of processual efficiency. Many of these concerns are expressed as problems in the conceptualization of *power* in conflict resolution, the theme of Chapter 9.

On the Absence of Culture in Early Conflict Resolution

Although not the case today, in the early days of the field the idea of culture—of the implications of cultural difference—was not a matter for serious concern, either in the academy or among practitioners. There were at least four reasons for this, two stemming from the conceptual biases inherent in the two main academic disciplines that fed the field and two from biases in the world of practice. The field of conflict resolution drew much of its conceptual capital from scholars in the disciplines of international relations (IR) and social psychology. IR had resonance particularly for peace studies: The peace studies perspective was conceived as offering an alternative to IR's neorealism. The work of social psychologists was influential in the development of conflict resolution as an expression of American "pragmatism." In both cases, the resistance to culture lay in the effacement of *difference*.

Political scientists and IR specialists, even when they argued against the policy implications of neorealism and *machtpolitik*, typically took power to be the only "variable" that counted; power was conceived simply as the ability to apply force or to coerce (how many submarines? how many warheads?); states were autonomous "actors" who "calculated" their interests and behaved rationally to achieve them. In this constricted sense of power (neither Hans Morgenthau nor Kenneth Waltz could pass muster as Foucauldians), culture all but disappears from view (see Chapters 6 and 9). If culture matters at all, then we understand it in its essentialized and totalized form of "national character" (see Chapter 6).

Scholars from social psychology (many with roots in Kurt Lewin's interest in social conflict) were especially influential in the study of negotiation; and negotiation was often conceived as the fundament, the "atom" of conflict resolution (see Chapter 7). The psychologists assumed that given the biogenetic unity of the human brain, we must all think and reason in the same way, and so, say, decision making (as in negotiation) must look the same everywhere. ("Everyone negotiates the same way; just speak louder and slower"). Once again, culture disappears or—if cross-cultural psychologists are heard from—is to be understood in such constricted senses as individualist versus collective cultures; high context versus low context, and so on.[2] Moreover, behind both international relations theories of states and world politics, and social psychological theories of the individual actor, the authority of rational choice theory, with its restricted conceptions of motivation and intentionality as simply interests and utilities—and in negotiation research, by the reigning heuristic of the buyer-seller—effaced all other theories of mind or sociopolitical action, but in particular culturally informed ones. In IR, rationality resided in the state; for the social psychologists, in the individual actor (see Chapter 7). The epitome of this, which brought together scholars (and their assumptions) from psychology, economics, and political science, can be seen in the amount of work devoted to game theory in general and the prisoner's dilemma game in particular, as a way to model conflict and conflict resolution processes in the real world.

As for practitioners, the absence of attention to culture had two main sources. First, many practitioners came from such fields as labor-management relations, where whatever cultural differences between the sides (based on class?) that might exist were subsumed by the strong commitment on both sides to negotiate around shared and usually narrow conceptions of interest. Communicational impedances that arise in the negotiation that might be related to cultural difference were likely attributed to individual personalities and dismissed as "atmospherics." Then too, the early practitioners themselves were not a culturally diverse group, being overwhelmingly male, white, and North American.

The other source of practitioner resistance to culture was more complex in being intentional, and involved practitioners who worked in situations different from labor management, family, or other domestic settings. For those who worked in deep-rooted or intractable conflicts around issues of race, ethnicity, religion, nationalism (the whole range of so-called identity conflicts), often marked by extreme enmity, violence, and suffering, it seemed that anything having to do with culture was part of the problem and not the solution; therefore, any attempt to bring attention to culture back to the conflict was both counterproductive of conflict resolution—and probably unethical. In several later chapters, I argue that this stance is mistaken. It reflects a sort of categorical error, conflating *culture* as an analytical term and *culture* as a political term used in identity politics (see Chapters 4, 5, and 6). This mistake can be costly. Keeping culture (in the analytical sense) out means that the practitioner is potentially self-blinded to the sorts of obstacles—say, communicational impedances or misinterpretations of key symbols by one side or the other—that may doom a negotiation or an entire peace.

As one example, consider Docherty's account of the 1993 Waco tragedy (Docherty 2001). Docherty prefers to write about significant cognitive and social *difference* in terms of worldview rather than culture. Whichever term is used, the differences separating members of the American unconventional and millennial religious community calling itself Branch Davidians from the U.S. federal law enforcement personnel who negotiated with them fruitlessly between February 28 and April 19, 1993, outside Waco, Texas, were deep and tragically fateful. Branch Davidians followed a form of Christianity that held that the End of Days was close at hand; they stockpiled weapons against the coming chaos of the apocalypse and practiced unconventional gender and familial arrangements. They also harbored a deep distrust of secular institutions like the government or state. Their variant beliefs and practices troubled some in the larger American community around them, and their possession of many weapons, some thought to be illegal, brought them to the attention of police. When U.S. federal law enforcement agents raided the settlement in force, the Davidians reacted violently, and four federal agents, among others, were killed. Thus began a fifty-one-day siege, during which federal law enforcement tried to negotiate a nonviolent surrender, but unsuccessfully so. On April 19, after negotiations had been stalled for weeks, a forceful entry was attempted, in the course of which the complex burned and more than one hundred people, including twenty-one children, died. The repercussions of this tragedy have been felt ever since in America, often expressed as continuing mistrust, hostility, and even rage, by some citizens toward the federal government. On April 19, 1995, the second anniversary of the violent end of the Waco standoff, the federal building in Oklahoma City was bombed, killing 168 people and injured more than 500 in the deadliest act of terrorism committed on American soil before September 11, 2001. It turned out that this was conceived as an act of vengeance, linked directly to the events at Waco.

Whatever religious differences separated the Branch Davidian community from mainstream American society and culture, when these differences erupted into open social conflict, the unsuccessful processing of the conflict, ending in lethal violence, was shaped primarily by the communicational difficulties bedeviling the negotiation. It was more than a matter of differences in respective negotiation styles. Docherty analyzed transcripts of the negotiations between the parties and found that that they revealed, in her words, profound differences in the respective worldviews of both sides. Police negotiators brought their own perception of the situation to the negotiations and presumed they could bargain instrumentally with the Branch Davidians. When they ran into difficulties, they assumed that the charismatic but psychopathological Branch Davidian leader, David Koresh, had brainwashed his followers, who were thus irrational. Docherty's point is that a full understanding of Branch Davidian beliefs would lead one to see not psychopathology or irrationality but another *alternative* rationality, a completely logical one in the world constituted by Branch Davidian culture. Rejecting this world out of hand, and bound by the realities of their own culture and experience, FBI negotiators and Branch Davidians faced each other for almost two months across the great cognitive and moral divide of different worldviews, and managed at the end only a dialogue of the deaf that ended in death.

It is, finally, useful to compare the Waco and Air Florida cases. Although both illustrate the importance of taking culture into account, it is obvious that the gross amount of "shared culture" was much greater in the 737's cockpit than among the interlocutors at Waco. A cultural reading of Air Florida provides us insight into the underlying texts (cultural assumptions) about power, authority, and hierarchy that impacted communication among the crew. These assumptions are by no means trivial, but neither are they ontological or foundational in nature. In contrast, Docherty writes of worldview differences (and one sees why she chooses a term differentiated from semantically overdetermined *culture*), profound differences in *context* that eventually and tragically rendered *communication* between the federal agents and the Branch Davidians mute.

Defining Culture

The argument is simple: Understanding the concept of *culture* is a *prerequisite* for effective conflict analysis and resolution. The problem of defining culture starts in recognizing that the term comes to us from the nineteenth century, with different meanings, and that these meanings came attached to political agendas of one sort or another, and do so today (see Chapter 5). Think, for example, of how some regimes resist criticism of their human rights record by saying, in effect, "Our culture's notion of 'human rights' is different from yours (in the West), and to criticize us is therefore neocolonial and unjust" (see Chapter 3). Leaving aside the political uses of the term, it is the case that even analytically *culture* is used differently (and sometimes deficiently) in the various social science disciplines that have contributed to the study of conflict and conflict resolution (see Chapter 6). Another, more recent critique has come from poststructuralist scholars who say the notion has never overcome its colonial past (e.g., Brigg 2008), and in effect the analytical and political uses are inseparable. I shall have more to say about this criticism later (see Chapters 5 and 9). In any case, noting these problems, some advocate doing away with using the term entirely, substituting for it such concepts as *discourse* (from Foucault 1978), *habitus* (from Bourdieu 1977; see Abu-Lughod 1991), or *worldview* (Nudler 1990; Docherty 2001). There are reasons for retaining the term (even the sharpest critics see its importance and indispensability) while seeking to sharpen both how we understand it and how we—and others—use it in situations of conflict. We must grapple with definition.

One of the things that all contemporary social science definitions have in common is that for none of them is culture connected primarily—as Raymond Williams (1983:92) put it—to "culcha": high art, superior knowledge, refinement, or "taste." (This, indeed, is one of the main nineteenth-century meanings of the term that has so confused contemporary, colloquial usages.) For no anthropologist, certainly, is culture something possessed only by the educated, aesthetic—and upper—classes![3] Everyone has culture. In fact, everyone has potentially *several* cultures; this is partly why (as we shall see) using the concept gets complicated. At a minimum and very generally, it is possible to think of culture as something widely *shared* by individuals in a society, namely, "the socially learned ways of living found in human societies" (Harris 1999:19) or perhaps the "socially inherited solutions to life's problems" (D'Andrade 1995:249). Notice that both of these definitions stress the idea that culture is learned and that it is passed down (reproduced or inherited) in the context of social groups. Beyond this agreement, however, many questions are raised. For example: Is culture *only* learned—is no part of it innate? Does culture refer *only* to how people think about the world, or must it refer also to how people actually behave? How widely shared are these things in any event? With regard to the second definition: Are the solutions proffered by culture always the best ones possible? If solutions differ from society to society, can we—or ought we—judge some of them better than others? And can it be that culture sometimes creates new problems in the course of presenting solutions to old ones? If it does, how can we deal with these new problems?

Even these few questions might indicate why, pushed beyond the barest minimum, definitions of culture tend to proliferate and contend with one another (Kroeber and Kluckhohn 1952). As well, neither of these definitions addresses some of the oft-found deficiencies that the culture concept is prone to, such as connotations of *homogeneity* (culture is all one thing; there is a single thing called "Mexican culture," for example); *stability* (culture is timeless or changeless); *singularity* (culture maps onto society in a singular way, so that Japanese society is characterized unproblematically by a single Japanese culture, for instance); or *entityness* (the idea that culture is a *thing* that can act independently of the persons who carry it; see Avruch and Black 1991; Avruch 1998:12–16).

To account for this complexity, in *Culture and Conflict Resolution* (Avruch 1998) I drew on Theodore Scharwtz's definition of culture. "Culture," Schwartz wrote, "consists of the derivatives of experience, more or less organized, learned or created by individuals of a population, including those images or encodements and their interpretations (meanings) transmitted from past generations, from contemporaries, or formed by individuals themselves" (Schwartz 1992:324).

In this definition, culture retains some of the traditional or customary force often associated with it—because it is transmitted from past generations—while the dynamism of contemporary influences and individual agency are recognized. This definition stresses cognitive aspects of culture, such as images, encodements, and also schemas or cognitive representations (D'Andrade 1992; Romney and Moore 1998) as well as its interpretive dimension (Geertz 1973).[4] But although culture in this sense exists in the minds of individuals, as it provides "solutions to life problems," it is also in no way disconnected from collective behavior and social practice.

Schwartz's definition must be supplemented by three other observations. First, because individuals in societies are distributed across many different sorts of social groupings—regional, ethnic, religious, class, occupational, and so on—and because each of these groupings is a potential container for culture, any complex society is very likely multicultural. Thus, *culture is socially distributed across a population.* Second, even members of the same social grouping do not internalize cultural representations or schemas equally. Some schemas are internalized very superficially and are the equivalent of cultural clichés. Others are deeply internalized and invested with emotion or affect. The more deeply internalized and affectively loaded, the more certain cultural representations are able to motivate action (Spiro 1987). In other words, in addition to being socially distributed in a population, *culture is psychologically distributed within individuals across a population.*

Finally, because culture is the derivative of experience, it is deeply connected to ongoing or past social practice. Therefore, despite its traditional or customary base, culture is to some extent always situational, flexible, and responsive to the exigencies of the worlds that individuals confront. And because human social experience is often rife with conflict, culture, far from being always identified with shared values or consensus, is often contested as well (Martin 1992).

Culture and Conflict Analysis

Given this definition, how does culture help us to understand social conflict? First, notice that for any given individual, culture always comes in the plural: Individuals carry multiple cultures, from ethnic, racial, national, or religious ones, to those contained in—or derived from experience in the practices associated with—occupational, professional, or class social categories. This point will be especially important when we turn to such conflict resolution practices as negotiation in intercultural contexts. For now, it means that a statement such as, "Juan is a Mexican," tells us quite a bit less than some think it does. Is he Zapotecan or mestizo? From the South or the North? A Catholic or a Protestant? A peasant or a university graduate? A military veteran or a victim? It also means—even if we knew the answer to all of these questions—that we should be wary of such simple causal statements as, "Juan behaved in this or that way *because* he is a Mexican." This is so because even a more or less complete listing of all the relevant *categories* would still constitute a rather blunt instrument for getting at the *specific* images, encodements, schemas, metaphors, and interpretations that Juan brings to a *particular* social encounter.

Second—notwithstanding the plural nature of culture as just discussed—note that culture is no longer *simply* a label—a name for persons aggregated in some social, often national or ethnic, grouping. (This point is elaborated in Chapter 5.) Nor is it simply a synonym for attitudes, norms, or values—the soft side of the harder (and putatively more real) materialities of social life. Instead, culture is conceived more deeply and comprehensively as an evolved constituent of human cognition and social action. It constitutes social worlds for individuals, as it is in turn constituted *by* those actors in those worlds. The dialectical nature of culture means that except in the narrow sense of a failure to communicate across cultural boundaries—not an unimportant concern to be sure!—culture is rarely by itself *the* cause of conflict. The mere existence of cultural differences is usually not the primary cause of conflict between groups (cf. Huntington 1996; and Chapter 6 in this volume). However, culture is always the lens through which differences are refracted and conflict pursued (Avruch and Black 1991, 1993).

This is so because culture frames the context in which conflict occurs. It does so partly by indicating what sorts of things are subjects for competition or objects of dispute, often by postulating their high value and relative (or absolute) scarcity: honor here, purity there, capital and profits somewhere else. It does so also by stipulating rules, sometimes precise, usually less so, for how contests should be pursued, including when they begin and how to end them. And it does so—to return to our earlier definition of culture—by providing individuals with cognitive and affective frameworks, including images, encodements, metaphors, and schemas, for interpreting the behavior and motives of others (cf. Ross 1997:46, 49).

In these terms, the important point for analysts of conflict to consider is this: When contestants (and analysts) mostly share frameworks for interpretation—share culture—then the cultural factor disappears into the background, and the actual conflict may appear (to cultural insiders, anyway) to be entirely over scarce resources or divergent interests. However, in this case culture's disappearance is only an illusion to which cultural insiders are susceptible. Outsiders, who do not share the interpretive frameworks of the contestants, may see culture at work when and if they do not understand what the conflict is about or how it is being socially processed—which often means not sharing with contestants the cultural calculus by which certain resources or interests are valued or counted: "You beat your daughter severely to protect your family's ... *honor*?" Note that such cultural nonapprehension is usually experienced and expressed ethnocentrically by outsiders in a moralizing way.

Culture (re)appears—literally in sharp relief—when contestants come into contact from significantly different cultural backgrounds and thus share few frameworks for interpretation. In that case, whatever conflict there is between them over resources or interests is potentially complicated, in part by intercultural interference or impedance to the actual processing of the conflict (What are we really fighting over? Do we share the same interests and notions of valued resources? How do we fight?), as well as to communication among contestants about the conflict (How do we negotiate?).

Of course, recalling heterogeneous nature of culture, it should be clear that usually contestants "even from the same culture" may share some, but not all, interpretive frameworks. Individuals in complex, differentiated social systems are in effect multicultural. This means that even within the same society, intercultural encounters abound and affect the processing of social conflict. In the United States, for example, African Americans and whites approach conflict differently (Kochman 1981); members of different social classes do when they interact in such institutions as courts (Merry 1990; Yngvesson 1993); workers in different occupations do (Trice and Beyer 1993); as do middle-class women and men, even within the microsociality of the family or workplace (Tannen 1994).

Culture, Ethnic Conflict, and Social Identity

Another way to further clarify culture's role in conflict is to distinguish as clearly as we can between culture and ethnicity, explored further in Chapter 5. (Insofar as they are also socially constructed categories, in the discussion that follows what holds for ethnicity also holds for class, race, and nationality.) This is not so simple, however, because usually ethnicity, race, or nationality—less often, class—is conflated with culture. This means that ethnic conflict, for example, is thought of as primarily a cultural conflict, and solutions are sought in the cultural realm. Indeed, in the preceding section we briefly mentioned African-American and white interaction as an example of an intercultural encounter (cf. Gadlin 1994). It is the case that ethnicity, or race and nationality, are always constituted by some measure of cultural content, though often (from an outside observer's perspective) exaggeratedly or even spuriously so. For instance, Hobsbawm has demonstrated that many ethnic or national "traditions which appear or claim to be old are often quite recent in origin and sometimes invented" (Hobsbawm and Ranger 1983:1; see Chapter 4).

The key point here is that social categories such as ethnicity, race, or nationality have a peculiar relationship to culture. They are culture objectified, projected publicly, and then resourcefully deployed by actors for political purposes. To complicate matters, ethnicity, for example, is also a component of an individual's social identity. Social identity refers to the social *uses* of cultural markers to claim, achieve, or ascribe group identity (Black 2007). Group identity, in turn, functions not only as a source of psychosocial support for individuals (Erikson 1959; Isaacs 1975) but equally as a sociocultural resource and *site* for mobilizing groups (sometimes ranged against other ethnic groups, but often against a state) in their efforts in one political arena or another (Cohen 1974; Horowitz 1985). This is so because the cultural markers referred to in the chapter on social identity often function to set out the social boundaries by which groups distinguish themselves from others (Barth 1969).

One way to vividly see the *uses* to which culture is put, as well as its role in conflict, is to consider the large literatures on the "invention of tradition" (Hobsbawm and Ranger 1983); "imagined" national communities (Anderson 1991); and the social construction of ethnic (Cohen 1969), racial (Dominguez 1986), or national (Malkki 1995) identities, as well as the fierce political contests among elites surrounding the production of national cultures for ideological control of a state (Gramsci 1985; see also Handler 1988; Aronoff 1989; Fox 1990; Avruch 1992; Verdery 1995). In each of these instances, cultural content—most often linguistic, racial, or religious—is infused in the making of social groups and thereby enlisted in agonistic, sometimes lethal, pursuits.

To complicate already complicated matters: Earlier, I dismissed, with Raymond Williams, the Arnold or Eliot conception of culture as (upper-class) "culcha." However, although *culture* (as analytically understood) is not isomorphic with *culcha* (as the natives use the term), it is the case, as Bourdieu (1987) argues in *Distinction*, that one can read culcha, now understood as sources of symbolic and social capital, as constituting part of the culture of elite upper classes. In other words, culcha has become ingredient to social, in this case class, identity. Some of the ways in which culture constitutes social identity, and some political implications of this for actors and potential interveners, is taken up in more detail in Chapters 4 and 5.

To return specifically to ethnicity: What makes disentangling culture and ethnicity so difficult in conflict analysis is that when conceived as a component of a total *social identity*, ethnicity is also invested by individuals with affect and thus can motivate social action. In this way, culture serves to link individual and collective identities: instrumentally (Ross 1997:47) by providing a reservoir of symbols or rituals upon which social groups may form and organize, and psychodynamically by anchoring individual identity(ies) in collective ones (Avruch 1982). Instrumentally, culture linked to identity is crucial to the formation of social groups. Psychodynamically, culture linked to identity is the source of schemas for cognizing the world and motivating social action in it. Among the most powerful examples of this double-duty work of culture, and among the most relevant for understanding conflict, is what Vamik Volkan (1988) has called "chosen traumas." These are experiences that come "to symbolize a group's deepest threats and fears through feelings of hopelessness and victimization" (Ross 1997:70). The Nazi Holocaust for Jews, New World slavery and the Middle Passage for African Americans, the Armenian massacre by Turks, mutual massacres by Hutus and Tutsis, the fourteenth-century Turkish defeat of Serbs in Kosovo, the 1948 Calamity for Palestinians, the Cherokee Trail of Tears—the list is a depressingly long one. For analysts of conflict, the key is that such traumas serve double-duty. They symbolize group distinctiveness in emotionally compelling ways and provide therefore a site for political mobilization, *and* they provide for individual members of the group, and for elite decision makers sensitive to history and public opinion, cognitive and emotional maps of the nature of the world that surrounds them. That world, needless to say, is usually perceived as hostile, uncaring, or evil—and dangerous. To take just two examples among many: Who can understand the Israelis' obsessive concerns about their national security without also understanding the searing role of the Holocaust in the Jewish experience of the twentieth century? And as well, who can begin to understand Serbian claims of victimization by the West in 1999—even as some Serbs themselves victimized Albanian Kosovars—without also understanding how many Serbs seemed able to experience *in their own generation* what happened to "them" in Kosovo in 1389? The multiple traumas, generational and individual, left behind in the aftermath of violent conflicts are partly the subject of Chapter 8, which looks at the role of truth and reconciliation commissions in reconstructing damaged identities and selves.

The relationship of culture to identity is one of the most difficult problems for students of conflict analysis, with important implications for the practice of conflict resolution. In Chapter 5, a heuristic for approaching this problem is presented. But it is fair to say now that the heuristic itself is not without difficulties, some analytical and some potentially ethical (Brigg 2008). The difficulties arise because even proposing a heuristic with a neat two-by-two division of the world as a guide for third-party practitioners to follow is, to some extent, to engage in an exercise of power, the subject of Chapter 9.

Intercultural Encounters

As our discussion of culture indicated, many more encounters, even in our everyday lives, are "intercultural" than we might at first perceive. However, insofar as these are casual or, more to the point, do not involve competition over valued resources or engage us in forms of dispute, we are likely to pass lightly over potential cultural divides. And—recognizing that culture is not homogenous, but inheres in many different sorts of social categories—we understand that intercultural in practice is always a matter of degree. Sometimes, though, the nature of the cultural divide is a great one, typically involving linguistic, religious or, in Huntington's (1996) sense, civilizational dimensions (see Chapter 6). Sometimes we do find ourselves in intercultural encounters in a competitive or otherwise conflictual context. In these latter cases, the cultural factor can loom large, and conflict analysts and especially conflict resolution practitioners must be knowledgeable and attuned to it.

Avruch and Black (1993:133–36) set out the rudiments of cultural analysis in intercultural encounters. Following a long ethnographic tradition, they encourage analysts to treat cultural analysis as "thick description" (Geertz 1973), always sensitive to social context and to seeing the world "from the native's point of view." What they aim to get at is the collection of schemas, metaphors, and so on, that characterize the natives' local common sense about the root causes and consequences of conflict, what Avruch and Black call *ethnoconflict theory,* as well as the indigenous techniques or practices used to manage or resolve conflicts, *ethnopraxes* (Avruch and Black 1991:31–34; Avruch 2000).

Examples from different cultural settings of different ethnotheories and related ethnopraxes can be found in the case studies reported in Avruch, Black, and Scimecca (1998; see also Fry and Björkqvist 1997).

Culture and Rationality

Ross (1997), in his discussion of how culture provides actors a framework for interpreting the actions and motives of others, points out that "motives," which link cognition to behavior, serve the same explanatory role as "interests" do in rational choice theory. Indeed, in shared cultural contexts interests and motives appear to be the same thing. But the difference between them—and thus between rational choice and interpretive cultural theories—is a crucial one. For rational choice theorists, interests, conceived as utilities in a cost-benefit mode, are "assumed to be more or less transparent, given," and universal, whereas "motives are knowable only through empirical analysis of particular cultural contexts" (Ross 1997:50). In fact, it is precisely in intercultural encounters—especially when the cultural divide is a large one—that the difference between interests and motives becomes important. This is so because what Ross called the presumed universal, "imperialistic," and "dominating" character of interests in rational choice accounts of action can lead to serious intercultural misunderstandings when the *culturally constituted* motivations of one party do not match the assumed universality of interests posited by the other (or by the analyst; Avruch 1998:74–76). (A more general discussion of the limitations of rational choice theory, its approach to interests, and some implications for conflict resolution in conflicts over deeply held values is the subject of Chapter 7.)

A compelling example of this mismatching is offered by Cohen (1990) in his study of Egyptian-Israeli diplomatic and political miscommunication. Cohen considers why, throughout the 1950s and 1960s, Israeli deterrence, based on massive use of force as reprisals against Egypt for terrorist attacks emanating out of Egypt against Israel, failed to actually deter. As part of a cultural analysis, he investigates the broad understandings relating to violence, vengeance, and vendetta in each society. He concludes that Israel's use of massive force violated Egyptian ethnoconflict theories relating to vengeance and retribution; in particular, Israelis misunderstood Egyptian conventions of proportionality in these matters. The cultural logic of Israeli deterrence was that the "more disproportionate the punishment, the greater the victim's compliance." Unfortunately, Cohen continues, "Egyptian rationality refused to conform to the Western, utilitarian model designed by Israeli strategists" (1990:97). What Egyptians regarded as highly disproportionate vengeance on the Israelis' part had the effect of shaming and humiliating them—a serious loss of honor in a culture where honor is deeply valued and its loss has great motivational force. To erase the shame and regain lost honor, Egypt supported further attacks against Israel. Continuing Israeli reprisals then had the effect of ensuring continuing Egyptian support. This positive feedback loop of mounting violence was ultimately predicated, as Cohen put it, on Israel's mistaken assumption that the Egyptians (and Arab confrontational states in general) "shared the same Israeli calculus of cost and benefit" (1990:99; also Avruch 1998:48–55). Israelis mistakenly projected their own understandings of interests, including the avoidance of mounting retaliatory punishment, and expected ways to satisfy them—by preventing terrorist provocations from Egyptian soil—onto their Egyptian adversaries. These interests, however, turned out to be neither as universal, transparent, nor dominating as the Israelis thought. Other interests, culturally constituted in Arab culture, were held by the Egyptians, and they served as strong motives for Egyptian responses to mounting Israeli violence that were unexpected and unsought by the Israelis—and ultimately, of course, costly in lives to both sides. This dynamic continues to operate in Israel's conflict with Hamas, and more generally with the elaboration in Palestinian culture of the notion of *martyrdom* and the celebration of martyrs as an *Islamically* valid response as a form of resistance in militarily unequal confrontations. Martyrdom legitimates the "suicide bomber" in the face of Islamic injunctions against suicide by reframing the cultural understanding of the individual act. *Martyrs are not suicides.* More broadly, it provides a powerful cultural (religious) framework for honoring every Palestinian victim (active combatant or not) of Israel's military actions.

Culture and Conflict Resolution

If the field of conflict resolution has a fundamental principle, it is that effective conflict resolution depends upon conflict analysis. This chapter proposes that effective conflict analysis, in turn, requires cultural analysis. This requirement is especially keen in cases of intercultural conflict, where one can expect that the greater the cultural divide, the more acute the requirement. However, as our discussion of the nature of culture has indicated, many more conflicts—ethnic, class, religious, occupational, gender—are more intercultural than may be initially apparent.

Most of the research and analysis of intercultural conflict resolution thus far has dealt with negotiation, rather than third-party processes such as mediation, or more specialized forms such as the problem-solving workshop (see Chapter 7). Some of this early work aims to get at "national negotiating styles" (e.g., Binnendijk 1987; McDonald 1996) or focuses by way of case study on the purported styles of particular countries—Japan (Blaker 1977), Russia (Schecter 1998), or China (Solomon 1999), for example. For the most part, these studies concentrate on diplomats and treat culture monodimensionally, only at the level of "national culture." They have been criticized for this, among other reasons (Zartman 1993; Druckman 1996).

Another genre of intercultural negotiation work has tried to be more explicitly comparative by identifying several transcultural dimensions according to which all cultures may be commensurably evaluated. The work of Hall (1976) on high-context versus low-context communicational styles is foundational here. It has been extended by Cohen (1997), who added to the basic sociolinguistic distinction (high-context language use is expressive and group oriented; low-context is instrumental and status/individual oriented) other dimensions of cultural difference that include orientations toward time (polychronic vs. monochronic); individual versus interdependent/communal ethos; and a concern with negotiating mainly for results (a prototypical American's bottom line) versus mainly for the maintenance of valued social relationships.

Another influential researcher in intercultural communication is Hofstede (1980), who investigated corporate (transnational IBM) culture and found that values across all "cultures" sampled (again, *national* culture) clustered into four underlying dimensions: power distance (the degree of inequality in a social system, from small to large); collectivism versus individualism; "masculinity" versus "femininity" (similar to assertiveness vs. compliance); and uncertainty avoidance (weak to strong). Later on, work in Asian societies prompted him to add a fifth dimension: temporal orientation (long term vs. short term). Building on this and other work (e.g., Weiss 1994a and 1994b), Salacuse (1998) has proposed ten basic ways in which culture affects negotiating style or behavior: (1) negotiating goals (for contract [outcome] or relationship); (2) attitudes toward negotiating process (win–win or win–lose); (3) personal styles of negotiators (formal or informal); (4) communication styles (direct [low context] vs. indirect [high context]; (5) time sensitivity (high or low); (6) emotionalism (high or low); (7) agreement form (specific or general); (8) agreement building process (bottom up or top down); (9) negotiating team organization (one leader or consensus); (10) propensity toward risk taking (high or low).

The overlap of dimensions for most of these schemes should be apparent. The assumption underlying all of them is that when negotiators from polar-opposite cultures (say, risk takers vs. risk avoiders) interact, the effects of the differences are powerful enough to create communicational dissonance and misunderstanding. Cohen (1990) subtitled his earlier study of Israeli-Egyptian negotiations "a dialogue of the deaf."

These studies are useful and signal a welcome change from the days when cultural factors were ignored more or less completely in the study of negotiation and conflict resolution. They serve well to remind us that even successful and widely accepted prescriptive models for negotiation—that proposed by Fisher and Ury, for instance—should be deployed cautiously in other cultural settings (Fisher, Ury, and Patton 1991; cf. Avruch 1998:77–80). Nevertheless, their reliance on transcultural dimensions, say individualism versus collectivism, puts us in danger of losing much of the rich context that actor-oriented, ethnographically based thick description provides. This context should not be thought superfluous: it is not the case, for instance, that *individualism* means the same thing for "individualist" Muslim city dwellers in central Morocco (e.g., Rosen 1984) and "individualist" Southern Baptists in central Georgia (Greenhouse 1986). In much the same way, Cohen (1997:108), paying careful attention to context, tells us that even such key negotiating terms as "compromise" may be emotionally valenced entirely differently in American English (where a problem-solving, rationalist, and legalist culture gives it a neutral or even positive gloss), and Arabic (where in fact "it" doesn't exist; and cognate words negatively connote concession, retreat, and abandonment; see also Cohen 2001).

Given enough time and resources, culturally sensitive conflict resolution would pay attention to elucidating the relevant cognitive representations and their accompanying affect—images, encodements, schemas, and metaphors—the "psychocultural interpretations," as Ross (1993) has put it, that contestants bring with them to the conflict. Such resolution would aim first to get at the relevant ethnotheories of conflict and would then try to utilize as much as possible relevant ethnopraxes—the resources of conflict resolution that the parties themselves bring to the table. This orientation to culturally attuned conflict resolution is expressed most strongly by Lederach, who compares the prescriptive models of resolution that many Western third parties bring with them and try to impose on the parties, with the elicitive model—essentially a kind of ethnographic practice that uses indigenous techniques and resources as a foundation for resolution work (Lederach 1995:29–31). Much conflict resolution work now takes indigenous conceptions of practice seriously, indeed as the sine qua non of ethical practice (e.g., Brigg 2008; Francis 2002; Trujillo et al. 2008). In this mode, the role of third parties in conflict resolution is to help the contestants reframe their psychocultural interpretations of one another and thus of part of the world: to change metaphors and schemas (see Ross 1995). This doesn't mean that material interests no longer matter or can be safely ignored. As is abundantly evident in the Middle East, it is the case that in deep-rooted conflicts (often ethnic, racial, or nationalistic ones), the parties may never be able to get to the point of negotiating interests until they recognize each other as fully human, if not yet wholly legitimate, interlocutors. Parties must recognize each other's mutual existential right to exist before they can move on to negotiating interests around water, much less the contours of a new state. Here we are in the domain of affect, language, and metaphor—of interpretation, of *culture*.

Preliminary Notes for Practitioners

Near the beginning of their *Handbook* for running problem-solving workshops for conflict resolution, Mitchell and Banks point to a key requirement of sound practice for third parties, professionalism. This "involves, as a first step, making oneself aware of one's own goals and values in undertaking any problem-solving exercise" (Mitchell and Banks 1996:6). A good part of this involves a cultural analysis of oneself: one's own metaphors and schemas, images and encodements. Such autoethnography is possible, though not easy, and the reflexivity it demands and brings forth is central to an effective, engaged, and ethical practice. Indeed, one of the key issues for intercultural conflict resolution is the extent to which our very conceptions of effective and ethical practice—negotiation, mediation, facilitation, and so on—are determined by our culturally constituted assumptions and presuppositions about the world. And because so much of conflict resolution theory has arisen from the crucible of reflective practice, as we more closely examine our practice, in the end we are also led to examine the cultural underpinnings of these theories.

This is a fundamental lesson for students, analysts, and practitioners: *You have a culture, too*—several of them, in fact. Culture is not just something "they," the "others"—the parties—possess, while you have … natural and self-evident Western rationality, goodwill, problem-solving skills, common sense, virtuous intentions—and the English language (cf. Cohen 2001). Culturally sensitive conflict analysis and resolution begins with this insight—though it hardly ends there.

Conclusion: Culture

In closing, I summarize the main ideas behind the concept of culture as follows:

- Cultures do not possess agency; individuals do.
- Cultures are not things, but analytical categories.
- Individuals are bearers of multiple cultures, not a single one.
- Individuals acquire their cultures as a part of ongoing social life; they are not eternally deep coded in the gene or *Volksgeist*.
- Cultures are passed down to individuals, and in this sense one may speak of "traditions"; but cultures, as acquired by individuals throughout their lives, are also emergent and responsive to environmental or situational exigencies.
- Cultures are not monolithic, integrated, and stable wholes, but are fragmented, contestable, and contested.
- Cultures do not cause conflict; they are, however, the "lenses through which the causes of conflict are refracted" (Avruch and Black 1993)— and none the less critical for that.

The chapters that follow reflect more deeply and critically on many of the topics touched upon in this introduction, particularly on the relation of culture to social identity, the misuses of culture, and the place of culture in understanding negotiation, mediation, and conflict resolution practice more generally. An important theme in most of the chapters is the problem of power and authority in conflict resolution (much as it emerged in the Air Florida and Waco examples). It is explicitly the focus of Chapter 9.

2

Context and Pretext
in Conflict Resolution

Introduction

In the period when practitioners were blind to the importance of culture—or, equally, convinced of the universality of application of *their* conflict resolution approach—it was possible to adopt a simple and assured attitude toward working in other places: *have process, will travel.* As "the culture question" (Avruch and Black 1991) gained prominence, such an unself-reflective approach was harder to sustain, and a number of works appeared that advised outsider third parties in the nuances of cultural difference. The more naïve of these simply listed traits or the characteristics of the "other culture" that needed attending to: individualism here, collectivism there; low context versus high context, and so on.[1] The better ones also advised a measure of humility in working abroad (e.g., Augsburger 1992; Lederach 1995). It would be a while, however, before a certain and appropriate *anxiety* in working with cultural others was also featured in this work (e.g., Cohen 2006; Brigg 2008; and Chapter 9 in this volume).

An advanced example of thoughts on working with cultural others is to be found in Carrie Menkel-Meadow's work. Menkel-Meadow has had much experience as a teacher, trainer, and practitioner specializing in mediation. In a provocative essay reflecting on teaching and practicing conflict resolution in other cultures, Menkel-Meadow (2003) manages to portray both the self-assurance of the mature scholar and experienced practitioner and (serially, if not quite simultaneously) the anxiety and doubt of the self-critical agnostic thinker. I take her anxiety to comprise the two "-texts" of this chapter. *Context matters* in conflict analysis and dispute resolution practice, says the assured scholar and experienced practitioner. And if it does, then two problems arise. The first is conceptual: As a social scientist, what can I say that is empirically valid or generalizable across cases and contexts? The second, not unrelated, problem is at root political: As a trainer-educator-practitioner coming from U.S. domestic contexts and now working internationally in other societies and cultures, what is my ostensible or professed purpose; *what is my pretext,* my excuse, as an American, Western, liberal, white, feminist, middle-class professor of law … in telling differently contextualized Others what to do with their conflicts and disputes?

The first problem—what happens to "general theory" when context is privileged—is hardly limited to the field of conflict analysis or dispute resolution. It is the dilemma of many *début de millénaire* social scientists in this postpositivist moment. Over the last two decades or so, the steady disparagement of what postmodernists called the universalizing and totalizing thrusts of "the Enlightenment project" has advantaged, for now at least, the sorters over the lumpers, and the foxes over the hedgehogs. The promise of nineteenth-century grand theory—a universal field theory of human behavior—dating back explicitly to Comte's first conception of sociology as "social physics," seems to many unfulfilled and, except to evolutionary psychologists and unreconstructed economists, unfulfillable. Clifford Geertz, poking fun at his Harvard mentor, the great sociological systems builder and synthesizer Talcott Parsons, characterized it as the moment when it is finally realized: "The Sociology is Not About to Begin"(Geertz 1973:4).

In her skepticism about general theory, Menkel-Meadow in effect addresses that founding generation of conflict resolution scholars, researchers, and practitioners—including Kurt Lewin and Morton Deutsch, Louis Kriesberg, Anatol Rapoport, and John Burton; those game theorists around Kenneth Boulding at Michigan who founded the *Journal of Conflict Resolution* in 1957; and those lawyers and economists at Harvard who distilled the essence of rational choice and bargaining theory to derive a universal model of interest-based negotiation—to express her doubts about the science of conflict analysis and dispute resolution that is (perennially) About to Begin.[2] But who can address such an august group in this way without some anxiety and doubt? And if one gives up on general theory in favor of context, what precisely has one gained—and what are some potential costs?

I will examine this postmodern (poststructuralist or anti-Enlightenment) challenge to conflict resolution in greater detail in Chapter 9. In this chapter, I want to reflect on some of the problems raised by context and pretext from a different angle, having to do with the growth of the field more generally. I first consider some aspects of the varied contexts in which *conflict resolution* and alternative dispute resolution (ADR) developed in the United States, particularly in the academy. Historically, there have been some differences between the two, partly evident in the different meanings of the notion of "dispute" adopted by theorists and practitioners.[3] I then examine some of the underlying pretexts for doing this work, and some possible consequences, especially as we more frequently engage in the "contested export," as Menkel-Meadow has put it, of American-style dispute resolution practice into the international arena or into other domestic (social and cultural) domains. Because the Institute for Conflict Analysis and Resolution (ICAR, now S-CAR) at George Mason University was the first academic institution in the United States to offer a postgraduate degree in conflict resolution, starting in 1982, some of this can be grounded in a bit of institutional and personal history.[4]

A Context and Pretext for Conflict Resolution in the United States

When I arrived at George Mason University in 1980, an assistant professor hired to teach undergraduate anthropology, a faculty group from all the various social science departments (save economics) was already in place and meeting to consider the possibility of starting the first postgraduate program in the world devoted to conflict resolution. The group was chaired by the cultural anthropologist Thomas Rhys Williams, then graduate dean, and had the crucial support of the canny chair of the Department of Sociology and Anthropology, Joseph Scimecca. The patronage of the graduate dean and the support of a key social science chair (the new program incubated and was nurtured inside Scimecca's department in its formative years), especially in a new, tradition-free and institutionally pliant university, meant that what was then the Center for Conflict Resolution—today the freestanding School for Conflict Analysis and Resolution—would grow very quickly. By 1982, a curriculum was in place (sort of: curriculum in conflict resolution has been a moveable feast from the beginning), the first cohort of master's students arrived, and some faculty began to orient their research and writing specifically toward the emergent discipline.

But if George Mason and some of its faculty provided the institutional home for the program, its motive force came from the late social psychiatrist Bryant Wedge. In addition to his clinical practice, Wedge consulted with U.S. government agencies, like the State Department and the Arms Control and Disarmament Agency, on psychological aspects of crisis management and international negotiation. He was also an activist domestically, including cochairing (with the late James Laue) from 1975 the campaign to get Congress to create a United States Peace Academy. In fact, Wedge first came to George Mason with the idea that if a master's program and matriculating students already existed, then perhaps the Peace Academy would locate itself at the University. In the event, no bricks-and-mortar academy devoted to peace was created—though as a result of the campaign the U.S. Institute of Peace was begun in 1984.

What was interesting is that although the citizen campaign Wedge co-led was directed toward the establishment of a *Peace* Academy, and the new postgraduate degree program was housed in a Center for Conflict *Resolution*, Wedge was insistent that the degree proclaim its professional *bona fides* by being an M.S. (master's of science) rather than an M.A. (master's of arts). Moreover, not only was the word *peace* conspicuously absent from the Center's name or its course titles, but the first degree was a Master's of Conflict Management (MSCM); the key course in the first curriculum (designed by Dennis Sandole, the Center's first official faculty hire) was a "Pro-seminar in Conflict and Conflict Management"; and the first publication (arising from that seminar) that in some way represented the Center's faculty's collective sensibility favored the notion of conflict *management* over *resolution* (Sandole and Sandole-Staroste 1987). None of this was accidental. In fact, we are once again in the realm of context and pretext. Wedge and his codirector, the late Henry Barringer, a retired Foreign Service officer, were (echoing here Ramsbotham and colleagues' characterization of the American approach) consummate American pragmatists and wanted the new discipline, its degree, and its graduates, to be accepted, and taken seriously, by the hardheaded neorealists of the Washington policy establishment—the State Departments and Arms Control and Disarmament Agencies of that world. In many ways, the word *peace* might compromise this. First, there was the lingering Cold War, indeed McCarthyite, suspicion that anything to do with "peace" was a communist front. Less conspiratorially but more recently, the division of America over the Vietnamese War and the identification of the "Peace Movement" with anti-Washington political dissent, made it a fraught term, especially as the Carter era gave way to the Reagan one. Wedge quite self-consciously wanted to differentiate this new field of conflict studies, fronted by a conflict management degree, from the several extant "Peace Studies" programs that existed in colleges and universities, many of them in religious or otherwise church-connected schools. Why "management" over "resolution" in the first degree's name? I suspect here Wedge's medical training and background came into play. He wanted the sort of professional and clinical, indeed *technical*, competence that medical specialists could claim, to be accorded his MSCM graduates as well. He preferred clinicians to theorists, and argued for a curricular concentration in technique and process expertise over academic model building. Finally—adverting to context—I believe that in an increasingly medicalized and pharmacological psychiatry, the notion of management was undoubtedly much closer to his own clinical experience and practice than was the notion of cure, or resolution.[5]

Although I have phrased this tension between peace and resolution, on the one hand, and management, on the other, in terms of S-CAR and George Mason's genealogy, Wedge's decision was actually very much in line with the same technical, positivist, and pragmatic impulse that gave rise to the *Journal of Conflict Resolution* in 1957. And just as the field of conflict resolution (eventually "management" disappeared from the degree name, definitively done in by John Burton's arrival in 1985—see the following page) attracted critics in the United States and Europe from Peace Studies who decried it as overly technocratic, cold, without values, and spiritualness,[6] so too did the *Journal of Conflict Resolution* group attract the fierce critique of some Europeans (especially from

Scandinavia), led by Johan Galtung and exemplified in the journal he began partly as a counterweight to the Americans.[7] The basic critique (and one that still resonates in conflict resolution circles) is that the field's preoccupation with conflict's management, and with technique and process, dominates the need to work for deeper structural change and social justice (Baker 1996; Brigg 2008; Brigg and Muller 2009).

When John W. Burton arrived at ICAR in 1985, he brought with him a conception of conflict resolution that was much closer to the European one—though Burton always eschewed what he saw as the strains of hyperspiritualized and moralizing utopianism in some peace studies approaches; he regarded himself as tough a pragmatist as the so-called realists were, and his own theories, much closer to political realities.[8] His kinship with the European Peace Research community was that, like many of them, he saw conflict as originating from deeply rooted repressive social institutions, and thus "conflict resolution" required the transformation of these institutions. He eventually coined the neologism conflict *provention* to refer to techniques for addressing the root causes of social conflict rather than their symptomologies.[9] But he was also amenable to one crucial aspect of Wedge's vision of the field: the idea that one could *engineer* social change through elaborated and rigorous techniques, and that students could be trained (*qua* technicians) to utilize them. Most of these techniques conduced to the "analytical problem-solving workshop," and Burton wrote a handbook on the proper way to run one.[10] Over the years, others who worked in this tradition (though all worked in effect with variations on Burton's theme) include Edward Azar, Tony de Reuck, Leonard Doob, A. J. R. Groom, Herbert Kelman, and Christopher Mitchell.[11]

Burton was also concerned with a very specific class of conflicts, those that Edward Azar had called "protracted social conflicts," and Burton, "deep-rooted ones."[12] According to his theory, these were conflicts created when social institutions repressed individuals' basic human needs, needs such as security or identity. (Today, some consider "deep-rooted" conflict to be virtually synonymous with "identity-group" conflict.) Crucially, such needs were literally *nonnegotiable,* and therefore any techniques for their resolution based upon simple bargaining or even facilitated negotiation (i.e., simple mediation), were bound to fail (see Chapter 7). Burton insisted on a basic division in the field coming loosely to be called "conflict resolution." Elsewhere I called this the distinction between a broad conception of the field and a narrow or restricted one (Avruch 1998:25–27). Broadly (and colloquially), *conflict resolution* refers to any strategy that brings a public dispute to a nonviolent conclusion. More narrowly, it refers to a subset of specialized techniques that address the sources or root causes of needs-based social conflict. This would be Burton's "provention" or Galtung's "positive peace." One can see now why Burton objected to the term *conflict management.* For him, when misapplied to deep-rooted, needs-based conflict, management implied the suppression of symptoms, but not the addressing of causes. Alternatively, management was appropriately called for in the sorts of disputes (say, over simple wages) that were amenable to distributive bargaining or negotiation. Perhaps the great majority of disputes were of this sort, Burton freely admitted. But the ones that interested him, and that were the source of mass violence and human suffering, were not amenable to mere bargaining, negotiation, or simple mediation. They certainly were not amenable to coerced or authoritative interventions—everything from war to arbitration or adjudication. At best, these processes would result in temporary truces—conflict management, mitigation, regulation, or settlement. Conflict *resolution* was something very different, a far more radical undertaking.[13]

One of the effects of this was to separate some forms and understandings of conflict resolution, what I called restricted conflict resolution, from the rest of the developing field—particularly from alternative dispute resolution (ADR) theory and practice, as they were developing domestically, both "in the field"—in community and neighborhood action groups, mediation centers, and programs affiliated with some lower courts—as well as in the academy, in a growing number of schools of law. Also separated out were developing conceptions of negotiation theory and practice, as they were increasingly taught in law, business, and management schools and even some schools of public policy.[14]

Conflicts and Disputes

Nowhere is this clearer than in the very definition and conception of the word *dispute*. Burton and Dukes begin their volume by decrying the fact that *dispute* and *conflict* are usually used interchangeably, as are *management, settlement,* and *resolution*. They want to restrict the meaning of *dispute* to those disagreements around clashing goals or perceptions rooted in divergent interests that are susceptible to ordinary processes of negotiation, mediation, arbitration, or adjudication: disagreements that can be *managed* and result in *settlement*. The notion of *conflict* they want to reserve for deep-rooted social discord based on repressed and nonnegotiable basic human needs (Burton and Dukes 1990:1–7).

Within our field, broadly speaking, this is not the way the terms are typically distinguished—if they are at all. Sometimes the terms *conflict* and *dispute,* as well as *conflict resolution, dispute resolution, conflict management,* and *dispute settlement,* are, consciously or not, used interchangeably (Vago 2003:247–249). Sometimes a distinction between conflict and dispute is made, but it's not the same one Burton and Dukes support. Here, the notion of *dispute* comes to us from a tradition in the anthropology of law, that is, from ethnographers who studied social conflicts in small-scale social settings. This sense was also adopted (and modified) by sociologists, political scientists and legal scholars, who joined anthropologists to form the influential Law and Society movement in the mid-1960s. For them, the key notion became dispute processing.[15]

Briefly, the anthropology of law came to dispute processing by way of the more familiar method—in legal education at least—of case analysis. Early ethnographies concerned with law, based mainly on work with Native Americans or Africans, took the case as their basic unit of analysis.[16] A succeeding generation critiqued this method for its overly static and socially isolating tendencies. They argued for a more "processual" (and less structural) approach, as well as one that paid attention to the broader social ecology of the conflict—its embeddedness in a wider matrix of social (and particularly power) relationships. In an influential article, P. H. Gulliver differentiated dispute from conflict as a "disagreement between persons" that is brought by one or both (some or all) of them "to the public arena" (Gulliver 1969:14). Laura Nader (in Nader and Todd 1978), adopting a processual approach, underlined this meaning: A dispute doesn't exist until it is made public. Therefore, a dispute is one stage in a multistaged conflict: There is a preconflict or grievance stage wherein one party sees a cause for complaint in the actions of another party; a conflict stage wherein the aggrieved party brings the grievance to the attention of the other party—thus far the conflict is dyadic. If no remedy is attained, then one or the other party may make the disagreement public, and it becomes a dispute. The analysis of these stages, as well as the analysis of remedy seeking or settlement moves that follow this (by the parties or by others representing the parties or the wider community), are collectively understood as dispute processing.[17] Because the notion of "remedy" was broadened as part of the increased concern with the social ecology of the dispute, scholars interested in dispute processing moved away from formal court or otherwise adjudicative settings (and eventually away from an overriding concern with elucidating the formal if implicit rules in exotic judicial processes) toward consideration of other forms and fora, including informal or alternative and nonauthoritative third-party forms such as conciliation, facilitation, mediation, and so on.[18]

The difference between Burtonian conflict resolution and the dispute-processing approaches to defining dispute is of more than terminological significance. Burton presumed that disputes (in his definition) are amenable to settlement, and conflicts, properly analyzed, could be resolved—indeed, *provented.* (Following him, others came who worked in the same vein toward conflict *transformation.*) Galtung too argued for the possibility of "positive peace." By contrast, many scholars working in the dispute-processing tradition argued that management or regulation—in effect the removal of the conflict/dispute from the public arena—rather than its resolution—is all that can be expected, and that the deeper, structural causes of the conflict will remain unaddressed.[19] This essential skepticism (if not pessimism) toward the claims of conflict resolution (theorists and practitioners) has underlain much of the critique, on both conceptual and political grounds, directed by some social scientists against conflict resolution, including many forms of ADR.

Critiques and Response

Burton or Galtung might consider these critiques, when aimed at ADR, unjust, because they never believed it had much to do with resolution in any case. But the critics have gone after ADR, first in U.S. domestic settings and later, after ADR and conflict resolution (as an international endeavor), on broader political terms. Early on, some have pointed to the class implications of court-affiliated ADR, even to the development of a two-tiered system of justice, one for the poor and one for the well-to-do.[20] More recently, issues of gender, especially with regard to the widespread use of mediation in divorce cases, have been considered.[21] Perhaps no one has been more outspoken over the years than Laura Nader, who once referred to the whole "harmony ideology" underlying the ADR movement as nothing more than a "cultural soma that tranquilizes potential plaintiffs" at the potential forfeit of their legal rights (Nader 1998:52). Avruch and Black summarized the objections of these critics in the following terms: "All of them argue in effect that ADR functions primarily as an instrument of social control, not social change. Concentrating on individual remedies ... it neglects macrostructural questions of power and inequality" (Avruch and Black 1996:52).

Advocates of ADR have certainly responded to these critiques. Some have sought "remedies" in improved training in process (from problem solving to active listening and appreciative inquiry) or enhanced attention to ethics, especially around the issue of mediator neutrality or impartiality.[22] Another response has been to devise mediation strategies specifically around the empowerment of less powerful parties, around such notions as "transformative" or "narrative mediation."[23] But even here, where power is addressed directly, the question of "transfer effect" arises (how does one bring empowerment out of the mediation room into the real world). On the website for its dispute resolution services run by the state courts of Virginia, the pages under "Consumer Guide" note that some kinds of cases are not appropriate for mediation, including those wherein a party wishes to establish a legal precedent, those family cases involving ongoing physical or psychological abuse, and those "where there is an extreme inequality of knowledge or sophistication of the parties."[24] Presuming the Virginia judges are up on their Foucault and know that knowledge implicates power—or more impressively, have read their Bourdieu and know that sophistication and taste comprise fungible social capital!—this seems a fair and ethical warning.[25] Meanwhile, Menkel-Meadow herself has responded in a different vein, to argue that Nader and others have perhaps overestimated the "justice" to be dispensed in many courtrooms and underestimated the costs (of all sorts) of the adversarial process to those caught up in it (Menkel-Meadow 1996).

All of these responses have their merits; I am especially sympathetic to Menkel-Meadow's, and I support heartily full disclosure for ADR's consumers. Yet the problem of power asymmetries in ADR and conflict resolution practice—part of its inherent social *context*—and the problem of the uses to which ADR and conflict resolution can be put given this context—a part of the multiple political *pretexts* of its different users and beneficiaries—remains in my view an obdurate one, and one that is centrally implicated in any discussion of the relationship between ADR, conflict resolution, and justice.

And as complex and contested as these issues are when at least some amount of social context is held constant, in the domestic U.S. sphere, they become even more problematic when the technologies of ADR and conflict resolution (and *technologies* is precisely what many in the founding generation of our field had hoped to achieve) are exported to other contexts, to other societies and cultures.

Contexts and Pretexts of Conflict Resolution in Other Places

One important context is, of course, culture itself. Earlier (Chapter 1), I wrote of the relative neglect of culture in the conflict resolution field, both in the academy and among practitioners. This is no longer the case. By the new millennium, culture was no longer neglected, and nowadays any self-respecting curriculum in ADR or conflict resolution without at least a module devoted to culture would be considered deficient. There have been two major ways in which culture has been understood, each very different. First, in keeping with the dominant positivist and behaviorist orientations of early researchers and practitioners, the "culture question" was understood pragmatically, as a technical issue, focused particularly around how culture (now an independent variable) affects communication between parties or interlocutors. Attention to communication in this way means that we understand culture in order to understand interparty communicational dynamics, in turn in order to train our conflict specialists to be *culturally competent* as part of a broader requisite communicational competence. The result of this approach was a number of studies, many sponsored by the United States Institute of Peace (USIP), focused on culturally inflected negotiating styles, rules for mediating across cultures, the differences between high and low context cultures, face-threatening acts, and so on.[26] Here, we worry about culture in order to make our practice more efficient and efficacious.

Culture *does* affect communication, and communication (whether thought of instrumentally or constitutively—say, as discourse or narrative) is at the heart of conflict resolution practice. But culture conceived as context is broader than communication and affects other things as well, including the very meaning of *interest, norm, value*—indeed, of the parties' social reality—that so many of our approaches, principled negotiation among them, grounded in *utility* talk, take for granted as given. I take up the issue of the limits of utility talk in Chapter 7.

The concern with making our conflict interventions instrumentally efficient raises—or should raise—ethical questions: efficiency for whom, in the service of what? These are questions of pretext, inquiring into our professed purposes for doing this work in other places. Is the instrumental efficiency of our processes our only or main concern? Would attention to the broader sense of culture as constitutive context, in fact, orient us beyond instrumentalities and efficacy, and toward self-critique and reflexivity? If it does, then the problem of power comes to the fore, and there is no lack of critical questions to be asked—some of them in Chapter 9.

The second main approach to culture in our field has been around the issue of culture's relation to identity. If the first approach turns culture into a variable and clearly separates the conflict analyst from the subjects of the analysis (or the objects of practice), the second understanding of culture often conflates the analyst and with the players. This occurs when "culture" is deployed by the parties in conflict, especially in conflicts built around identity politics and identity groups. Their understanding of culture, affectively and political saturated, are very different from the instrumentalist and technical understandings we or our students bring to the field. I touch on some dynamics of identity politics in issues in Chapters 4 and 5, and on the politics of conflating subject and analyst in Chapter 9.

Once conflict resolution gets connected, through the concept of culture or the desire for cultural competence, to identity (and once analyst and player can be conflated), the question of pretext arises again, now as a question critically posed in terms of the identity of conflict resolution itself.

In noting the increased presence of conflict resolution discourse and practice in approaching conflict in the post–Cold War world, the sociologist John Stone comments that, "to the more jaundiced eye," conflict resolution appears to be "a hybrid of military science and transnational social work" (Stone 2003:512). Archness aside, he seems to have captured some sense of the core tension (if not quite paradox) at the heart of this technology coming from the West, and from North America in particular, to Others out there: a combination of enlightened Christian meliorism potentially backed up by the resources of NATO and "coercive diplomacy."[27] At the very least, we should be aware, first, of how our efforts might be viewed by some of those Others; and second, of what some of the consequences, particularly the unintended ones, of these efforts might be.

As to the first, at least in much of the Arab world today, the very phrase *conflict resolution* smells of hegemony and neocolonialism. "The ideology of peace," the Lebanese political scientist Paul Salem writes, "reinforces a status quo that is favorable to the dominant power" (Salem 1997:12). Elsewhere it is sometimes viewed as simply the latest in an ever-changing menu of buzzwords and catchphrases that the World Bank, U.S. Agency for International Development (USAID), or "the Europeans" expect to see in grant applications from both outsiders (us) and local/indigenous NGOs.[28] As to the second, we must be attuned to the limitations of our interventions—here I am in complete agreement with Menkel-Meadow that grafting ADR onto an already essentially corrupted judicial system is bound to fail, and is ethically questionable to boot—and, more crucially, into what the unintended consequences of even our successful ones might be.[29]

"Can My Good Intentions Make Things Worse?" is the title of a chapter by Mary B. Anderson in a recent handbook for international peacekeeping (Lederach and Jenner 2002). The subtitle, building on her work in aid and development (Anderson 1999), is "Lessons for Peacebuilding from the Field of International Humanitarian Aid."[30] Pauline Baker (among many others) has raised the issue of trade-offs between resolving conflicts and achieving social justice—a version of older questions phrased around peace and justice, and nowadays hooked up to yet other questions in postconflict settings, of guilt and liability and impunity, say, in international tribunals or, more complicatedly, in truth and reconciliation commissions (Baker 1996; Minow 1998; Avruch and Vejarano 2001; and Chapter 8 in this volume). Once again, Laura Nader has been at the forefront of such questioning, extending her critique of domestic U.S. conflict resolution and ADR into the international arena (Nader and Grande 2002). But are all Western imports—conflict resolution included—poison pills? Menkel-Meadow thinks not, arguing strongly for the value of ADR-type mediation in other places, and Mark Goodale's work on the adaptation of a human rights discourse in Bolivia also makes the case for some positive role for "Western" and American legal imports (Goodale 2008; see also Cohen 2003). I take up the issue of "Western" culture and the importation of human rights in Chapter 3, alongside the hoary question of relativism and universalism as usually counterposed in human rights discourse.

In the end, questions about the pretext of our work are central ones, touching on ethics as well as efficiency. We need critical thinking here. In aid of critical thinking, let me pose a question suggested by the political scientist Roy Licklider in his comparative study of civil wars and their termination. We presume almost as a matter of faith that our first goal in conflict resolution work in conditions of violence and death is to stop the killing and ameliorate the violence. Licklider writes: "Of course it is not necessarily desirable to end all civil wars; it is interesting to speculate how we would now regard international mediators if they had appeared in 1862 and settled the American Civil War in a compromise, guaranteeing the institution of slavery in the process."[31]

How would you begin to respond?

3

Culture, Relativism, and Human Rights

Introduction

Academic critiques of culture come from the right (the concept is not operationalizable, countable, or scalable enough), and the left (it is totalizing, essentializing, and tarred with a colonial genealogy). Outside the academy, in the altogether tougher neighborhoods where real politics is practiced, culture has attracted yet another set of critics, who worry less about problems with research methodology and hypothesis testing, and more about its implications for the moral fiber of youth and the body politic. Here, the specter of cultural relativism reigns, and culture (its postmodern critics notwithstanding) comes to stand for the nefarious deconstruction and de-essentializing of all that is essentially and necessarily true and absolute.

Parts of the left and the right come together in their hostility to culture when culture is invoked in discussions of human rights. Sometimes this coming together creates a curious sort of ethical schizophrenia, as it did for the first professional experts in culture, the anthropologists. Famously, in 1947, in its "Statement on Human Rights," the executive board of the American Anthropological Association (AAA), under the influence of Melville Herskovits, opposed the United Nation's (UN's) planned Universal Declaration of Human Rights under a doctrine of cultural relativism, asserting that the ethnographic record demonstrated the wide variety of different normative beliefs in societies and therefore no one monolithic listing could — or ought to — capture all of them.[1] In June of 1999, however, a declaration in strong support of human rights was voted by AAA's membership, emphatically rejecting and reversing the former position.[2]

Human rights engenders its own tensions with many in the conflict resolution or peacebuilding community, who sometimes see a rigid commitment on the part of human rights advocates to enforce individual rights by invoking public shame or threats of criminal prosecution against violators as a hindrance to getting them to come to negotiations and end direct, immediate violence.[3] This tension represents not so much an argument about culture or relativism as it does a confrontation between two principled Absolutes. Culture, on the other hand, problematizes Absolutes; but its relation to relativism is more complicated than is often presented in the seemingly endless debates about relativism and human rights. This chapter brings the sense of culture presented in Chapter 1 to bear on this debate.

How should we understand universal and relative claims with respect to human rights? To answer this question, we shall need to unpack different conceptions of culture, universalism and relativism, and human rights, including what it means to be "human." The point is not to try to sample all the world's cultures and discern their conceptions of human rights. My aim in this chapter, rather, is to show how the concept of culture has informed (and occasionally deformed) our approach to human rights, and to suggest ways to sharpen our understanding of the concept—in the sense of it presented in Chapter 1—so that it can be used to make our discussion of human rights—and, beyond discussion, their implementation—more productive.

In the Beginning: UN Philosophers, Human Rights, and Culture, 1947

Specialists in the study of culture, anthropologists, or others whose research or practice takes them to exotic, non-Western places, especially those who work in the area of aid and development, often complain that culture is never taken seriously enough by the economists, agronomists, engineers, or planners, working for the World Bank or similar international institutions, who design and implement vast programs of social change for others. A similar complaint is often heard when cultural specialists come into fleeting contact with the U.S. foreign policy establishment, for instance the State Department, in Washington. But in the area of human rights this was not always so.

At the very beginning of the human rights endeavor, in June 1947, while a newly formed United Nations committee was preparing first drafts of what would, in December 1948, become the Universal Declaration of Human Rights, a so-called philosophers' committee formed by UNESCO was busy analyzing the results of a questionnaire "asking for reflections on human rights from Chinese, Islamic, Hindu, and customary law perspectives, as well as from American, European, and socialist points of view" (Glendon 2001:73). Over seventy people responded, broadly corroborating the existence of human rights in their own cultural traditions, though many acknowledged the idea as being fairly recent and European in its articulation. Still, a few crucial reservations were noted at the time. Some Asian respondents, for example, including Mohandas Gandhi, emphasized that "duties" as well as "rights" mattered in their own traditions and should be featured strongly in whatever document was to emerge.

The work of the philosophers' committee was not without its flaws. Certainly it sampled only the elites of those various "nonwestern" cultures, many of whom had been extensively educated in the West, and the fact remains that of the original fifty-one member states of the United Nations, only three were from Africa and eight from Asia, and so the nonwestern perspective was distinctly a minority one in any case. Today the work of the philosophers' committee has been, if not forgotten, certainly repudiated by some who argue that for these and other reasons the Universal Declaration of Human Rights — and the entire idea of human rights — is culturally bound by and limited to the West. Still, it is important to mention the work of the committee to show that unlike in the areas of aid, development, or the foreign policy world of *machtpolitik*, "culture" has been a concern for human rights thinkers from the very beginning of international efforts to articulate it. Meanwhile, human rights and their attendant complexities, in one form or another, can be discerned in history long before any efforts to articulate them.

In the Kond Hills, India

Sometime in the 1830s in India, the British, still operating in the guise of the East India Company, pushed farther into what would become the Raj and learned of certain tribes in the Kond hills (in what is today the state of Orissa) who practiced human sacrifice *(meriah)* and female infanticide. "They were outraged," F. G. Bailey tells us, "at this affront to natural justice" (Bailey 2001:186). Despite the difficult terrain, the resistance of the tribes, and the depredations of endemic cerebral malaria, the Company found itself embroiled for the next two decades in what became known as the Meriah Wars, aimed, normatively at least, at eradicating these unnatural practices while bringing the entire area under "civil" administration. One of the Company's officers, a certain Captain Macpherson, thought that this was best accomplished through a sort of diplomacy, specifically by making the British into the de facto third party in mediating the many feuds and disputes that occurred among clans of the tribes, thus winning trust, gratitude, and influence among tribal leaders. He was replaced by General Campbell, Bailey writes, whose "method of bringing civilization was to hang the aged and infirm, who could not run fast enough, and to burn the crops and houses" (Bailey 2001:186).

Even though an articulated notion of "human rights" was undoubtedly missing from Macpherson and Campbell's vocabulary, in this fragment of imperial history can be found most, if not quite all, of the themes relevant for a discussion of culture and human rights. First, one encounters the powerful notion of "natural justice," more commonly framed as "natural law," which the British invoke to judge human sacrifice and female infanticide wholly immoral and absolutely unacceptable—no further explanations are needed. Second, there is the idea that natural law provides for the British a *warrant* to act, specifically, to invade the hills and force the tribesmen to halt the practices. (And let us recall that the British action was costly for them, not to mention for the objects of their action, and took almost twenty years to accomplish.) Third, there was the tribal resistance to British action, which occurred at least in part, Bailey tells us elsewhere, because such practices and rituals were bound up with tribal beliefs and cosmology and with the maintenance of their material well-being. Fourth, there was not, at least initially, a single or monolithic British plan for action. Neither "British imperial culture" nor, more narrowly, East India Company "corporate culture" specified a clear script or scheme. In fact, the two options were more or less contradictory. Macpherson tried persuasion; Campbell relied on force. (Of course, force prevailed in the end: *sic semper imperium.*)

Finally, there is an unsettling moral paradox buried not all that deeply in this story. The British acted on their understanding of an absolute morality and natural law, whereby human sacrifice and female infanticide were unconditionally wrong and ought to bear a universal opprobrium. How could one be relativistic in judging such matters? And yet, at the very heart of one response aimed at eradicating these "affronts to natural justice"—Campbell's—the actions of the British made their own morality seem relative in the extreme: It depended on hanging noncombatants and burning crops and houses.

Ethicists or moral philosophers sometimes explain this phenomenon by making the distinction between a consequentialist ethics, whereby good or moral ends can justify the morally questionable means by which they are achieved, and a rather more restrictive deontological ethics, wherein ends, no matter how good or moral in themselves, can never justify immoral means. For the purposes of this chapter, however, the lesson is different: It is that universalism and absolutism can never entirely escape the complexities of relativism in the real world where men and women act, in part because judgments—assertions—of universalism and absolutism are, in the end, at least for someone somewhere, inevitably relative.

Clearly we need to unpack further the notions of universalism and relativism. But first we have to get a better sense of what is meant by culture in all its different senses.

Culture as an Analytical and Political Concept

The first problem in defining culture is choosing which definition, among the literally hundreds that are available, to embrace. As noted in Chapter 1, culture is a concept that comes to us from the nineteenth century with several different senses (some of them mutually antagonistic) and a lot of political baggage (Avruch 1998:5–21). My own preference is for symbolic or cognitivist understandings of the idea: that culture provides for individuals cognitive and affective (emotional) frameworks, embodied in such representations as symbols, metaphors, schemas, or images, with which individuals perceive, interpret, and then act in their social worlds. A good portion of these frameworks has to do with interpreting the behavior and motives of others, both those socially nearby and those more distant. Other parts are concerned with framing existential aspects of one's world. These include the nature of social conflict (what are we fighting about and why?) and how to manage it. They include concepts of rights and duties owed oneself and others, of dignity, concepts of right and wrong, of sin and its opposite, of liability.

In the ideas of culture discussed in Chapter 1, there is the assumption that culture is an analytical or technical term in the social sciences, and moreover, there has been an intention on the part of anthropologists, sociologists, and political scientists to treat it this way.[4] Indeed, this is one reason why theoretical arguments about culture have continued apace and why newer conceptions replace older ones. But I noted earlier that culture comes to us from the nineteenth century with a number of different meanings, only one of them developed by anthropology. Some of these other meanings reflect intense nineteenth-century conflicts of ideology around issues of group identity and social class—conflicts that are with us still. Already mentioned was the sense of culture advocated by Matthew Arnold or, later, by T. S. Eliot. Here, culture is the possession of an enlightened few, "the best which has been thought and said in the world" (in Jenks 1993:21). It is a conservative and elitist concept, protective of English class divisions. More encompassing (and ultimately more dangerous) was the sense of culture developed by the German thinker Johann von Herder and his followers in the Romantic tradition (Herder 1968). Here, culture refers to the unique (and eternal) spirit, ethos, or genius of "*a* people." In its time, it was a counterrevolutionary idea, ranged against the revolution in thought and politics brought on by the French Enlightenment. More specifically, culture here supported an argument against the entire universalizing thrust of the Enlightenment, and in support of group—ethnic and nationalist—particularism, often expressed, as Michael Ignatieff (1994) put it, in the idiom of "blood and belonging." Here, culture is very close to notions of race. And in the Romantic tradition, in literature, music, art, and politics, the word took on tremendous feelings of emotion, passion, and group pride. It was in no way an analytical, technical term, subject to discussion or debate. Certainly if, say, Richard Wagner were to speak of "German culture," it is unlikely that he would have the contrast between high-context and low-context communicational styles in mind.

In fact, absent the passion and chauvinism, the Romantic's idea of culture was essentially the same as the early, inadequate ideas favored by many social scientists that used the term through the mid-twentieth century. The reason for this is that both meanings arose in the same German cultural matrix, though they eventually took on different characters. (The key figure for anthropology here is Franz Boas, educated in Germany, who emigrated to the United States and was central in establishing the study of culture as a scientific discipline in America from the early 1900s on.) In both understandings of the term, culture is presumed to be stable (resistant, at its core, to time and change), coherent, homogenous, and customary. It is *essentialized*. Possessing the force of custom (tradition), it determines (or, speaking politically, it *ought* to determine) virtually all the behavior of all individuals who carry it. It is *totalizing*. And in both senses, finally, culture points not to a universal identity for all people, but rather to uniqueness, to *difference*, and to particularisms of one sort or another, spiritual or racial (in Herder's world), or environmental or historical (in Boas's).

Cultural Analysis and Culturalism

This last point underlines the important ways in which the two senses of culture, despite their similar intellectual history, diverged. First, as befitting a scientific term, Boas and his followers drained the affect, the *Sturm und Drang*, from the idea and sought to make it analytical. We can't quite say, however, that Boas did away equally with all of its political content; but he did try to redirect it. Crucially, he decoupled "culture" from "race" and, he hoped, from mystical ideas of "blood." Membership in cultural groups (as in language communities) became contingencies, accidents of birth. Finally, although stressing the uniqueness of cultures with respect to one another, he sought to disentangle the whole notion of cultural difference from ideas of inferiority and superiority, from chauvinism or racism. Here, then, is the key difference between Boas and the Romantics. Both were reacting against universalism and in favor of some form of particularism. But they were not reacting against the same universalisms. For the Romantics, it was the universalism of the Enlightenment, embodied in the French Revolution and the Declaration of the Rights of Man and Citizen (1789), promising a new world of universal citizenship, equality, fraternity, and liberty. The Romantic counterthrust was for a world divided into cultural Self and Others, separated by language, custom, and eternal *geist*, or spirit. Boas, in contrast, was reacting to the nineteenth-century universalism of social evolutionists like Herbert Spencer or Sir James Frazier, who saw all of humankind ranged on a single evolutionary "ladder" from savagery, through barbarism, to civilization (i.e., the Church of England, Oxbridge-educated English gentleman). Against this evolutionist's universalism, characterized by ideas of primitive and civilized, inferior and superior, Boas proposed a world composed of equally genuine and valid, but different, human cultures.

For the Romantics and their intellectual and political heirs, culture is part of a larger ideology we can all "culturalism," that is, the use of culture to underwrite or legitimize ethnic, racial, or national differences—and their political consequences. For Boas (without denying his own liberal and antiracist political agenda) and the many anthropologists he trained, culture was first an analytical term, part of a larger project, aimed at the scientific understanding of difference, called "cultural analysis." As we saw in the preceding section, newer, less organic conceptions of culture have largely replaced the older ones proposed by Boas and other anthropologists; the latter are now seen as inadequate. Moreover, these newer understandings of the term have moved it even further away from its culturalist roots, and in this manner cultural analysis has become even more critical of culturalism.

Once again, these distinctions are, for the human rights movement, more than academic ones. The Romantic sense of culture, culturalism, opposing one form of universalism, has underwritten nationalism, both benign and malignant, as well as the ideology of ethnicity and, more recently and as a direct result of the human rights movement, "indigenism," or indigenous rights (see below). The Boasian sense, opposing another form of universalism entirely (but never the promise of the Enlightenment!), gave us cultural analysis. But it came also to underwrite something called relativism, a concept that has featured prominently in the debate on culture and human rights.

Relativism and Universalism

Few ideas thrown up by the social sciences have generated as much controversy as that of cultural relativism. In America, it has become a dependable anathema for conservatives, many of them inheritors of Matthew Arnold's sense of culture, but battling now in a political world where "multiculturalism" denies from the outset a single standard for judging "the best which has been thought and said." For liberal supporters of human rights, the same idea is viewed as a screen cynically or hypocritically held up by tyrants who abuse their people, to shield themselves from the disapprobation of the international community.

The idea of relativism became part of contemporary discussions of culture with the work of Franz Boas, but it was Boas's student, Melville Herskovits, who wrote most explicitly on it:

> Cultural relativism is in essence an approach to the question of the nature and role of values in culture .... [Its] principle ... is as follows: Judgments are based on experience, and experience is interpreted by each individual in terms of his own enculturation. (Herskovits 1964:49)

Herskovits's definition was influential in that it took the meaning of relativism directly to the level of values and judgments about it, rooting it in the life experience of individuals (which varies from culture to culture) and questioning the existence of any absolute moral standards that are separate from their cultural (and historical) context. Indeed, it is this meaning of relativism, opposed to the possibility of an absolute morality, that has been invoked in debates about the universality of human rights and formed the basis of the American Anthropological Association's 1947 Statement on Human Rights in opposition to the Universal Declaration.

Some more recent discussions of relativism have pointed to three different senses of the term (e.g., Hatch 1983; Spiro 1986; Black and Avruch 1999). The first sense may be called "descriptive relativism," referring to the empirical fact of cultural variability in customs, beliefs, values, and so on. The *existence* of such variability is literally undeniable, part of what anthropologists call the ethnographic record (and historians, the historical record). Consider, as an example, food taboos or proscriptions. Hindus believe beef to be unclean; Muslims and Orthodox Jews, pork. Consider ideas about the afterlife: Christians, Muslims, and Jews believe in a single life to be lived; Buddhists and Hindus, in a round of rebirths and reincarnation.

The *fact* of cultural variability, of difference, may seem self-evident, but it is not, for our first impulse is often to see everyone else, as Clifford Geertz once put it, as "less well got up editions of ourselves" (Geertz 1983:16) Descriptive relativism is the acknowledgment of differences rooted in culture or, as Herskovits wrote, in the process by which individuals acquire their culture, enculturation. For those who seek to learn about other cultures, descriptive relativism is also indispensable as a methodological guide. How can one hope to learn about or understand another culture if one does not, as a first principle, open oneself up to the possibilities of difference? One must be prepared to set aside ingrained ideas of what is appropriate, good, or true back home. As a methodological principle, descriptive relativism calls "for the suspension of judgments in the service of understanding" (Black and Avruch 1999:26).

The second sort of relativism is that propounded by Herskovits, called variously moral, ethical, or normative relativism. In its weak form, it is merely the extension of descriptive relativism to the area of values, morals, or ethics: the recognition that moral systems may vary with culture. But the notion, especially when subjected to excoriation, is never understood in its weak form. Instead, the strong form of moral relativism is taken to mean the recognition of difference combined with a requirement to *tolerate* or even *approve of* such difference. Alternatively, one can say that the strong form of moral relativism carries with it a proscription against criticizing (or interfering with) a moral system different from one's own. In other words, in its strong form relativism gets linked to tolerance, and—in an even more stringent extension—tolerance forbids action or critique (aimed at changing the other moral system). It is precisely the ban against action or critique that has led some critics of relativism (including those who recommend exorcism!) to accuse it of leading to "moral nihilism." And so far as human rights are concerned, it is the presumed ban against action or critique that is invoked by some who have denied the legitimacy of human rights instruments or regimes that have, so they argue, originated "in the West."

It is certainly the case that Boas and some of his followers linked the value of tolerance to the doctrine of relativism. For Boas, at the end of the nineteenth century and the first part of the twentieth, it was clearly part and parcel of his own politics, a move to counter the sometimes lethal intolerance espoused by racists and anti-Semites—Boas actively spoke and worked against lynching in the southern United States—or the gathering clouds (throughout the 1930s) of fascism and Nazism in Europe (Lewis 1993). But if we think even for a moment about the political roots of Boas's linkage of relativism to tolerance, we see that what drives it, far from moral nihilism, is a profound moral commitment to action and critique. This is one of the several paradoxes or contradictions at the heart of this understanding of relativism, namely, that demanding unconditional tolerance implies an absolute intolerance toward the intolerant. Furthermore, insofar as one recommends the *value* of tolerance in a world where all values are culturally relative, then one has to admit to the possibility of cultures wherein forms of intolerance are valued that then are (given moral relativism), of course, beyond critique or reformatory action. Finally, as the philosopher David Bidney noted long ago, by transmuting the fact of cultural difference (descriptive relativism) into the necessity for (strong) moral relativism, relativists commit the "positivistic fallacy," deriving an "ought" from an "is" (Bidney 1944; also Renteln 1990; Hatch 1997).

Before moving to consider the effects of these paradoxes or internal contradictions on the argument of relativism and human rights, I want to mention briefly the third form of relativism, called by Spiro (1986) "epistemological relativism." In some ways, it is, philosophically speaking, the strongest form that assertions about relativism can take. It holds that enculturation determines all reality. In its extreme form, epistemological relativism denies the existence of the really real, an absolute reality over and above all the variant cultural constructions of it. In the context of human rights, I summarily dismiss the extreme form wherein the really real ceases to exist, by pointing to the experience of thousands of human rights workers in the field: Examining and documenting the effects of fire, acid, truncheons, or electricity on the human body, every body, everywhere, they confront reality and make the denial of the really real existentially and morally quite simply insupportable. Affirming the really real implies accepting some sort of fundamental "external standpoint"—perhaps the key assumption of human rights discourse. I take up the implication of assuming (or denying) these standpoints in greater depth in Chapter 9.

The key is to keep in mind what moral relativism really does teach us: that values, morals, norms, and ethical standards do in fact differ from culture to culture and that the differences may be significant. The doctrine of moral relativism cautions us to be aware that our own values and ethical standards are not necessarily universal or absolute. In this way, it is a defense against moral tunnel vision or ethnocentric ignorance. But in no way does moral or ethical relativism necessarily commit us to avoid judging or tolerating all other ethical systems. What it does, quite explicitly, is to force us to focus attention on the nature of our own ethical or moral system—to be less smug about it, or, more positively, to make us articulate clearly the grounds for our intolerance toward others' practices as well as the grounds for any possible interference in them.

The doctrine of moral relativism argues against moral universals or absolutes, perhaps even against a universal human nature. But it holds no brief against political action or judgments of the "superiority" of our own morality. It is not the case, to twist around the French aphorism, that to understand all is to forgive everything. Such comprehensive understanding may lead us to the very opposite of forgiveness. The implications for human rights *activism* should be clear. Here is the philosopher Richard Rorty on the reason why human rights advocates feel that they must reject moral relativism:

> [S]uch relativism seems to them incompatible with the fact that our human rights culture, the culture with which *we* in this democracy identify *ourselves*, is morally superior to other cultures. *I quite agree that ours is morally superior,* but I do not think this superiority counts in favor of the existence of a universal human nature. (Rorty 1993:116, emphasis added)

Rorty, a relativist, at least in the eyes of others, freely admits to his own judgment valuing democracy and human rights as "morally superior."[5] What he denies is that he requires a transcultural, or metaphysical, doctrine of universal human nature to do so. Why do advocates of human rights seem to need such a *warrant* in order to justify themselves? Notice that we have moved from making relativism the problem for human rights to making universals problematic. We need to unpack the idea of universals and then return to the question of why their existence seems so crucial to theorists and activists seeking to advance the cause of human rights throughout the world.

The Problem of Universals

If, in anthropology, the social science most enduringly concerned with understanding culture, the idea of cultural relativism had such supporters as Boas, Herskovits, or Ruth Benedict, it is also the case that there were, early on, severe critics of the idea, and distinguished proponents of its seeming opposite: cultural universals. Clark Wissler, George P. Murdock, and Clyde Kluckhohn, to name three, all argued for the existence of traits, complexes, or patterns of behavior present (depending on the theorist) in all individuals, all societies, all cultures, or all languages—"provided that the trait or complex is not obviously anatomical or too remote from the higher mental functions" (Brown 1991:42). Today, the presumption of human universals, transcending cultural variation, strongly characterizes such academic fields as evolutionary psychology or Chomskyan linguistics. For many advocates of human rights, the existence of such universals is also presumed to be important for the establishment of a transculturally legitimate and effective human rights regime. But linguists, psychologists, and human rights advocates are not always talking about the same sort of "universals."

The search for human universals typically begins in the evolutionarily derived, psychobiologically composed set of human characteristics that laymen (or philosophers) call human nature. These are somehow innate or intrinsic, and thus precultural. They constitute the constants against (or within) which cultural variability takes place. It is not difficult—for me, at least—to agree that there exists some sort of psychobiological human nature under which all humankind is united. (Here I declare one of my several Archimedean cruxes.) But this leaves most of the interesting or vexing questions about humankind (and almost all those that have to do with human rights) still unanswered. For example: Are these psychobiologically innate universals the only sort there are, or even the most important ones? How is invariant human nature modified by culture—can one, in fact, ever imagine a complete, functioning, social individual who is unmodified by culture (who lacks enculturation, in Herskovits's words)? Why do we think that universals are so much more important in determining social life than culturally derived traits, complexes, or patterns are? How can we get from the assertion of universals based on cognitive structures or neural architecture, which may well underlie linguistic functioning and a "universal grammar," to an assertion concerning a universal morality? And finally, what exactly do we *know* if we can assert the existence of such universals as, say, family, marriage, or religion? To declare religion as universal and then to define it as, say humankind's "most fundamental orientation to reality" or to the "sacred," is to tell us very little about the different realities constituted and lived in by believers in Hinduism, Christianity, Islam, or Aztecan or traditional African religious systems. Like the devil, the sacred is in the details, and it is in those details (not in abstractions or "least common denominators") that individuals live their lives and make sense of their worlds. We *speak* English, Arabic, Hopi, or Bantu—all, as they say, mutually unintelligible. No one *speaks* a universal grammar.

Some of these questions can be approached by first making a distinction between human universals and what some have called human "absolutes." Following Herskovits, absolutes (such as those derived from evolutionary human nature) are fixed and invariant, changeless from individual to individual, culture to culture, epoch to epoch. Universals "are those least common denominators to be extracted from the range of variation that all phenomena of the natural or cultural world manifest" (Renteln 1990:81). Leaving aside the notion of least common denominators for the moment, this distinction opens up a range of so-called universals that are, in fact, experientially, culturally, or historically variable and contingent. One can argue, for example, that because of shared human experience with the sight of blood, the color red is nearly universally taken as a sign of danger. Or that because of the universally shared experience of growing up in some sort of family, certain behavioral dynamics emergent from family life will be nearly universally shared. (This begs the question of the considerable variation in types of "family" found cross-culturally.) One can also argue that capitalism is today virtually universal in its scope and its ability to affect the lives of people in all societies in the world. Yet one may trace capitalism's development (from within "the West") historically, from the late sixteenth century onward—one can see it, that is, as an emergent and contingent universal. It is certainly a stretch to assert that capitalism is somehow encoded in the human genome or locatable in particular ganglia in the cerebral cortex.

Much like the idea of relativism discussed earlier, universalism, which appears at first glance to be a straightforward and monolithic concept rooted in something called human nature, fractures into different types under closer examination. The most important fracture is that between the idea of invariant and fixed absolutes and other sorts of universals that are potentially emergent and contingent. In their own way, such universals are also relative in the sense, for instance, that capitalism is relative to specific historical epochs and societies, *even as it undergoes movement toward universalization.* The contingent (relative) nature of such universals is what renders less supportable the usual dichotomous conception of cultural universals and relativity as being unalterably mutually opposed. It also has important implications for the understanding of human rights—both their designation and implementation—considered cross-culturally.

How to Understand Human Rights

In distinguishing universals from absolutes, Herskovits wrote of the need to search for least common denominators, mostly constituted by human nature, which form the shared core or essence of all cultures everywhere. In fact, the search for such undergirding human commonalities in the area of morality has deeply influenced much writing, especially theorizing, on human rights and culture. In the main, these common denominators have been simply asserted, for instance, in Kant's categorical imperatives or Rawls's "veil of ignorance," the idea that when all culture and social identity is removed from individuals, a primordial conception of justice will emerge (Rawls 1971).

In the social sciences, some have tried empirically to ascertain, or count, these least common denominators. A. D. Renteln's work is most germane to human rights (Renteln 1990). After empirical investigation of the ethnographic record, she discovered one moral principle common (she says) to all societies: "retribution tied to proportionality," the *lex talionis,* or eye for an eye, of the Old Testament. Surely this principle can be as troublesome for advancing human rights as it is productive, for what constitutes "proportional"? Consider the principle in terms of Article 5 of the Universal Declaration: "No one shall be subjected to torture or to cruel, inhuman or degrading treatment or punishment." What counts as "cruel, inhuman, or degrading punishment?" And how do we tell the difference in a world where it is widely held by some in some places that amputation is proportional to theft, and by others in other places that persons defined by the

United Nations as "children" may be put to death by the state for certain crimes? Or that capital punishment generally is not cruel and unusual? As for counting them at all, the anthropologist Donald Brown (a proponent of the existence of human universals) cautions:

> The first and most obvious point about the demonstration of universals is that it is never done by exhaustive enumeration, showing that a phenomenon exists and existed in each known individual, society, culture, or language. There are too many known people to make this feasible, and there are too many shortcomings in the descriptions of "known" peoples. Thus all statements of universality are hypotheses or arguments based on various kinds of evidence. (Brown 1991:51)

Given one empiricism that leaves us with *lex talionis* as a basis for human rights, and another that reduces all universals to research hypotheses, it is not surprising that those universals of the first sort, where a priori assertions are made about what, minimally speaking, universal human rights *must* be, have been far more influential than empirical investigations of human rights cross-culturally. Perhaps the best way to understand how such a priori assertions do their work is to consider two or three possible and different verbs that can be used to talk about how we come to and designate human rights.

If we believe that human rights (or some essential subset of them) are intrinsic to humans—just *there*, as "the rights that one has simply because one is a human being" (Donnelly 1989:12)—then we might wish to explain why their formal articulation has occurred so late in human history and, arguably, originated in a particular human culture or civilization: the "West." On the assumption that human rights antedated their articulation, then the right verb to use is something on the order of *discovered*, or, in the analogy of minerals or gems buried in the earth but awaiting the miners, *excavated* or *uncovered*. In this case the question "Why so long?" is perhaps answerable by saying, "We were looking in the wrong place," or "We had to wait for a mining technology to develop to the point where we were able to excavate."

It is the second reason that some human rights advocates turn to when they invoke some variant of the natural law explanation for the existence of human rights (they were always there, waiting to be discovered and articulated) and combine it implicitly with an argument not for technological, but for moral advancement, progress, or development, or the march of civilization through history (from savagery to civilization), in order to explain why it is hard to find human rights expressed in the time of Attila the Hun, but not so in that of Thomas Jefferson. But the first response (we'd been looking in the wrong place for a long time) has its advocates as well. Here, the verb of choice for finding the right place and uncovering that which was already there is closer to *revealed* than *excavated*. And such revelations, about human rights, duties, dignity, and much more, are often brought by some special agent acting prophetically on behalf of a higher authority. The revelations, that is, come part and parcel with some local version of that human universal, religion.

To conceive of human rights as preexistent and then discovered is probably to refer them to natural law. To think about them as immanent and revealed is probably to refer to some sacred text, tradition, or theology. The verbs (and their referents) have more in common than not. Both natural law and theology, for example, ultimately prescribe universalist arguments about the way the world is (including morality) that seek to deny the legitimacy of relativism and difference by transcending culture. (Crucially, they also usually contain warrants for action in the world.) But culture is not so much transcended in such systems of belief as it is effaced or rendered invisible. Later on, when spokespersons for some religious traditions invoke them and seek to reject human rights as being Western, Christian, or individualist, culture is made visible again, though now enlisted in its culturalist guise to provide a basis for rejection.

First, the effacement. Recall the British in the Kond Hills in the 1830s. Bailey tells us that it was the "affronts to natural justice" (the violation of natural law) presented by human sacrifice and female infanticide that so incensed the British and moved them to act against the tribes. Yet how can we disentangle their judgments or their subsequent actions from the cultures of mercantilism and imperialism, of the white man's burden and militarism, that framed two decades of muscular "pacification" in the Hills (and most of the rest of India)?

An even clearer example of effacing culture can be seen in that great document of natural law (and human rights), the American Declaration of Independence. Famously, Jefferson writes, "We hold these truths to be self-evident, that all men are created equal, that they are endowed by their Creator with certain unalienable Rights, that among these are Life, Liberty, and the pursuit of Happiness." What better example of uncovering that which is preexistent than by declaring its "self-evident" nature? Yet at the time these words were written, the thirteen colonies held more than half a million persons of African descent, all but about 1 percent of them as chattel. The "truths" may be self-evident, but the definition of "all men"—*of what it is to be fully human, in fact*—seems contingent (culturally constituted and relative) in the extreme.

Where natural law effaces culture, sacred texts and theology do the same. The Prophet Mohammed rejects human sacrifice as abominable before God in the Koran, but slavery remains. Lord Krishna instructs Arjuna in the meaning of dignity, the righteous life, and duty (*dharma*) in the Bhagavad Gita, but caste remains (indeed, is revalorized). The universal morality in these (and all other) sacred texts and theologies seeks to efface culture and reject relativism because they are founded upon the revelation of (transcultural) absolutes. But, as is "self-evident" from looking around the world and at much of the conflict in it, there is no universal agreement in this matter; the precise nature of the absolutes is not agreed on universally, though many theologies promise a day to come when it will be.

Until that day comes, we should remember what the doctrine of moral relativism, as discussed earlier, has to teach us: that standards of ethics or morality do indeed differ from culture to culture or epoch to epoch, sometimes significantly so; and that verbs that point us toward discovering preexistent and immanent human rights, or having them revealed to us, cannot in the end erase the effects of cultural difference or the accompanying complexity of relativity. *Your* natural law and sacred theology may not be *mine*, and the way that you go about enforcing or propagating them may, in any case, appear to me immoral in the extreme.

Most of the thinking (especially from jurists or other legal scholars) on human rights has concerned itself, almost obsessively, with the nature of the rights themselves. From the perspective of cross-cultural analysis, however, an equally vexing question is directed toward the instability of the qualifier *human*. It seems foolish to spend time and effort convincing a world to accept a universal definition, or list, of rights when what is so often at stake is the prior refusal of some to grant to others their full humanity. The drafters of the American Declaration of Independence who supported slavery believed that Africans, who could be owned as movable property, were not fully human. The notions of *dharma* (duty) and *varna* (caste) in Brahminical Hinduism in the Bhagavad Gita conceive of different species of inherently unequal beings.[6] Study after study of genocide and ethnic violence points to the inevitable dehumanization of the Other as a precursor and pretext for the worst human rights violations imaginable (Staub 1989). In all these cases, we should be careful to ensure that our interlocutors can agree first on extending a common humanity to all, before we move on to designating specific rights.

Earlier, I wrote that such verbs as *discovered* or *uncovered* would lead to us to think of human rights in certain ways. But other verbs are possible. The alternative to seeing human rights as preexistent or immanent is to view them as *created* or *constructed*. Such verbs locate human rights within history, not transcendental to it, and as arising from within particular social and cultural contexts. Such verbs also allow for human agency in the articulation of rights, including new ones, and, crucially, in social activism aimed at their propagation.

At first glance, to see rights as situated within culture and history seems to weaken them, first by allowing for the relativists' argument that because they may not have arisen from "our" history, they do not apply to "our" culture, and second by removing the metaphysical warrants for action provided by natural law or sacred beliefs and values. My own belief is that these concerns are exaggerated and, moreover, are based on the inadequate conceptions of culture—and recourse to culturalism—discussed earlier. Nevertheless, such concerns have affected the way scholars and others have approached the issue of human rights cross-culturally, with a mixture of apology, defensiveness, or, in reaction, chauvinism. Thus, the great majority of theoretical work that focuses on human rights cross-culturally has concerned itself with the task of finding least common denominators—commonalities, analogues, or counterparts—to admittedly Western conceptions of human rights, within the world's other major religions or ethical systems. Sometimes such analogues are found to exist;[7] other times their existence is doubted.[8] Occasionally, they are proclaimed not only to exist in other traditions, but to do so in even historically earlier or purer forms than in the West, as in the Islamic Declaration of Human Rights. (*You in the West have no standing in instructing us: We preceded you in this.*)

What these works all share is the conviction that human rights, as found in the West, must also be immanent or preexistent in other cultures for such rights to enjoy legitimacy. If this were so, then it also means that should rights not be found, relativists could argue *a priori* for their nonlegitimacy in those cultures. But in both cases, the conception of culture used is inadequate in the senses I discussed earlier: It assumes culture's utter coherence, homogeneity, and stability; its totalizing effects on the behavior of individuals; and its essentialized, hermetic imperviousness to environment and change. This is the culturalism of romantic nationalism, enlisted now in the discourse of subalternism, anticolonial struggle, or in defense of sovereignty, and put in the service of an anti–human rights discourse.

To see rights, rather, as created or constructed is also to see them in line with the revised conception of culture that argues for its emergence and continuing invention in social worlds characterized by political and economic contestation and human agency. It is a conception of culture that is epistemologically hostile to absolutes—and in that sense "relativistic"—*but not to potential, constructed universals.* It is a conception of culture that denies the coherent holism of any cultural tradition in favor of more open, fragmentary, and contested traditions. Finally, it is a conception of culture that holds that no one "culture" speaks with a single and uncontested voice, nor can any one individual or entity, including the state, speak in one voice on behalf of the culture. This is the lesson on human rights that we get when we move away from the writing of theorists and go into the field, with cultural analysts on the one hand and human rights workers and activists on the other.

Human Rights in Practice, and the End of "Cultural Relativism"

If one is interested, it is possible to find surveys that review human rights by region, culture, or civilization (e.g., Renteln 1990; Messer 1993). But the further one moves from these macro levels, the closer one gets to rights on the ground—in a particular village or ward of a city; a particular mosque, temple, or pulpit; or from the perspective of a particular women's NGO or journalist—the more varied and polyphonic people's talk about rights becomes. This is the sense we get from two collections containing work on human rights from mainly local, cross-cultural perspectives (e.g., Wilson 1997; Cowan, Dembour, and Wilson 2001). At the beginning of this chapter, I demurred from sampling the world's cultures for their positions on human rights. A lack of space is not the only reason for this. More importantly, it is that any culture's position on human rights will depend on who, exactly, is given the privilege of articulating the position (and on the resources that agent has for disseminating and impressing it). An important work of the early 1990s that sought to capture as fully as possible Arab "voices on the human rights debate" demonstrated more than anything what a variety of voices there were to be captured and how diverse (and sometimes contradictory) were the conceptions of human rights within a Middle Eastern, mostly Islamic context at that time (Dwyer 1991).

Close to the ground (where most human rights workers are, as well) one sees human rights being actively constructed in the course of localized, ongoing political action: taking testimony; writing letters; organizing marches, demonstrations, and accompaniments (Bobbitt and Lutz 2009). Wilson has argued that human rights are created as narratives of their violation (or vindication) and are told and retold, and more boldly that "the category of 'human rights violation' does not exist independently of its representation in human rights reports" (Wilson 1997:134). This is where the human rights worker, often famously impatient with the work of scholars and academics on these matters, gets to turn practice into theory, thereby remaking theory. And human rights are not just created via narratives or stories, but also by way of the many institutions, associations, and organizations that local activists have put together, funded, and staffed to get the work done in whatever currency or language is native to the area. In many of these cases, a rhetorical distance from Western human rights practice (and practitioners) is critical to their success.

Whatever its original cultural or historical provenance, the discourse on human rights has become a universal one—even if only in discourse in opposition to it. It is easy to question the sincerity of regimes or states (or the individuals who speak for them) that oppose human rights on grounds of cultural relativism. Capitalism, originating in the West, finds an amenable enough home in some Asian Confucian cultures (like that of Singapore), whereas Marxist-Leninism (also of the West) found, at least for a time, a home in another (China's). But what is more telling for the future of human rights in the end is the plethora of human rights activists and groups *indigenous* to these and other non-Western cultures who reject the presumption that the leaders or party spokespersons speak for *them*.

The further we move from culturalist accounts of human rights toward empirical cultural analytical ones, the less homogenous or integrated do the particular accounts appear. The closer we get to voices in the field, the more polyvocal, contested, even contradictory the descriptions of human rights become. In fact, aside from the apologists, propagandists, or theologians, there is no single representation of what human rights are in any single cultural tradition. And this is potentially a very good thing for human rights. For if moral relativism teaches us that moral systems do differ significantly one from another, and that that of the Christian, democratic West is only one among many, then there are also other lessons to be learned: that cultures are open-ended and not hermetically sealed off; that change is possible (regardless of where the impetus for change originates); and that as the global discourse on human rights gets localized, what is relative is likely to become universalized.

Conclusions: Culturalism Once Again

In a world of human rights where paradoxes abound, I should close by noting that in the so-called third generation of human rights (the first being political and civil ones; the second, social and economic), that of indigenous rights or "cultural rights," culturalism returns (as if it ever left!), but this time on the side of human rights. Despite the reservations of many human rights advocates who see indigenous or cultural rights as endangering the all-important focus on the individual as the locus of rights (Donnelly 1989), the movement for protecting and enhancing such rights has grown tremendously since the late 1960s. (The key NGOs here include the International Working Group for Indigenous Affairs, based in Scandinavia; Cultural Survival, based in the United States; and Survival International, based in the United Kingdom.) In seeking to extend human rights protection to all members of a society based on their collective cultural identity, the movement for indigenous rights embraces what some have called a "strategic essentialism" with respect to culture (Hodgson 2002). The closer one gets to politics on the ground, the more complicated (and occasionally abusive to particular individuals) such essentialism can appear.[9] I will take up the question of who gets to represent culture, and the potential costs to individuals (and third-party conflict resolution outsiders), in Chapter 5. In any event, it does not appear that this (pro–human rights) use of culturalism in the service of indigenous rights will go away; and in the end, it is perhaps only further testimony to the protean appeal (and epistemological-political complexity) of culture in all its forms. Meanwhile, the problem of relativism is never really done with, and I return to it in the context of interests, third-party interventions, and power, in Chapter 9.

4

Constructing Identity

Introduction

For scholars of the postmodernist persuasion, the great insight into identity—ethnicity, nationalism, culture, history, or most everything else that is social, for that matter—is that it is socially constructed: not given, but rather made, and thus potentially unstable, inconstant, and negotiable. Taken to an epistemological extreme, usually by certain Continental theorists (or anti-theorists), this position exercises different sorts of foundationalists, truth-correspondence theorists, and conservatives, and has generated tremendous turmoil in the teapot of the academy. But what makes this insight worth pursuing (and it is, at least in the long run, essentially correct) is that it so sharply flies in the face of what most ethnic "actors," the players, themselves believe. For they are convinced beyond doubt that their group—its "culture," its customs, traditions, language, its religious beliefs and practices—stretches back in an unbroken chain to some primordial antiquity. This tension between the observers of ethnicity and the players, so to speak, has been remarked on by many: "Traditions," wrote Hobsbawm (1983:1), "which appear or claim to be old are often quite recent in origin and sometimes invented." Referring to nationalism (ethnicity with claims to a sovereign state), Anderson (1983:5) noted the "objective modernity of nations to the historian's eye versus their subjective antiquity in the eyes of the nationalists." But the notion of invention only takes us partway in understanding how ethnicity is constructed. Eller (1999) points out that the prime raw material for constructing ethnicity is usually the past—history as transparently conceived by the ethnics themselves, though usually not so transparent to outsiders or members of other ethnic groups. Such collective constructions of the past in turn demand the many arts of memory: of remembering *and* forgetting—and above all of interpretation.

Let me give two examples close to home. Many Americans (and perhaps especially African Americans) even today view the December festival called *Kwanza* as an ancient (if generic) African celebration as old as Christianity and Christmas. In a generation or two, after exposure to multicultural K–12 education, almost all Americans will believe this. In fact, *Kwanza* is quite new. It was invented (out of African cultural materials, certainly) in 1966 by Maulana Ron Karenga, an African-American academic and black nationalist who was quite explicitly politically motivated to create in America an *African* cultural counterweight to Christian Christmas and Jewish Hanukkah. But Hanukkah, in fact, is an earlier variation on the same theme. It is a traditionally minor Jewish festival that over time was blown up in importance in the United States to serve American Jews as a cultural counterweight—to shield their culturally vulnerable children from an unstoppable combination of mythos, spirituality, and consumerism—from the powerful allure of Christmas.

Taking the long, or longitudinal, view to the insight of the constructed nature of ethnicity is properly the province of the historian. But the historical, or diachronic, view is not the only way to get a look at ethnicity's constructedness. My own insight came—appropriately for a cultural anthropologist— synchronically, in the course of ethnographic fieldwork, interacting with that epitome of postmodern encounters, the Other.

At the Hotel Splendid

I was twenty-five years old, sitting anxiously in a room at the Hotel Splendid in Rabat, waiting for the Ministry of Interior to grant permission that would allow me to reside for a year or so in a Moroccan village and do my doctoral fieldwork. It was a bad time to seek this permission, worse than usual, according to old Moroccanist hands. In Spain, Generalissimo Franco was sick and dying, and Moroccan newspapers were already reflecting the government's line that a new era was dawning in the struggle against colonialism, that the future of Spanish Sahara lay in its "reintegration" into Morocco. The noises from Spain were that after Franco this old remaining bit of the Empire would, indeed, be jettisoned. But the noises from the colony itself, from its indigenous *saharouis*, were quite different. Talk there was of independence from both Spain and Morocco. The *saharouis* claimed that they were never part of Morocco's Maghrebian empire. This was the beginning of a movement, soon to be called the Polisario, that would engage Morocco in a draining insurgency war for decades. But, in fact, in those days—commencing in September of 1975— Morocco's main worry was not the Polisario guerrillas, but rather Algeria's (and to a lesser extent, Mauritania's) potential interest in the Spanish Sahara. It was war with Algeria that frightened Morocco the most and put the country, its ministries and armed forces, in a state of high alert. In November, King Hassan II sent hundreds of thousands of Moroccans down south in what was called *la Marche Verte*, "a green march of peace," to claim the territory for the Kingdom by virtue of their physical presence in it, well before Spanish troops even left. All transportation in the country was mobilized to move the marchers southward; all other work in the ministries stopped.

So I sat in Rabat, waiting out my three-month tourist visa and hoping daily for word from the Ministry. From down the hall every afternoon came the pungent smell of a *tajine* being cooked (illicitly) in a room, and one day Mohammed, the cook, invited me in to share some. Mohammed was, to my American eyes, a young black man about my age. He was excited to hear I was an American and told me he was in Rabat trying to get a passport so that he could leave Morocco and go to France or, better yet, America. (Couldn't I help him—didn't I have a job for him? Perhaps my father did?) Increasingly worried about my own prospects for job and career should doctoral fieldwork collapse completely, I reflected on this: he, a Moroccan national, in the capital, trying to wring the bureaucracy in order to get out; me, a foreigner, trying to wring it in order to be allowed in. One day I asked him why he wanted to leave. "Ah," he said, "I come from the south, and things there are bad and they are going to get worse. The worst thing is the Africans," he added. "The who?" I said, taken aback. "The Africans," he said, "*les noirs.* They are lazy and deceitful and not to be trusted. God help us if they ever get any power." I looked at him, confused. *Les noirs*? What did he think he was? I said: "I'm sorry, I'm confused; aren't you too African?" His eyes flashed angrily. "*Non! Je suis Arabe!* My father is a sheikh, I am a prince and a sherif, a descendant of the Prophet. I am no more African than you are."

At twenty-five, this was my first direct contact with ethnicity's essentially postmodern sensibility. True, I had come from multiethnic and polyglot Brooklyn, and bethought myself a big-city sophisticate in racial matters and what we today call "diversity." But despite this and my (self-proclaimed) advanced training in the social sciences and all-but-doctoral status as an anthropologist, in fact, I was culture-bound and cognitively trapped in my own ethnic and racial categories and calculus, and had never been confronted by another's. I was also a little angry, given something Mohammed had said with great self-righteousness the day before. So I said to him, not aiming to enhance the ethnographer's rapport, "But you know, Mohammed, in America you would be thought of as a black man." It was as if I had slapped him. He reared and said, "No! You are lying. I am as white as you are." And then, forsaking the *tajine* and further contact (I knew), I rudely put my arm next to his and said with mock mildness, "We are the same color?" Mohammed looked down at our arms and spit, "Yes, we are. But do you know why mine looks darker?" And before I could say a word, he said, "Because unlike you, you rich and spoiled American bastard, I have had to work outdoors in the sun all of my life, and not in an office. If I had your life and your money in America, and you mine in the south, you would be black and I would be white."

"Well," I said as I gathered my wits, a thoroughly ungrateful guest as well as a hopeless fieldworker. "That may be. But if ever you make it to America, Mohammed, to Los Angeles or Chicago or Houston, and you are stopped by the police one night in your car, you would do best to remember, for your own safety that, like it or not, you are a black man." Twenty years later, watching the awful video of Rodney King's beating for the nth time, Mohammed's face and that entire afternoon at the Hotel Splendid came back to me with a frightening clarity. Today, I realize also that I was then instinctively a good enough native informant of American culture to have recognized the mordant contingencies of what some call "driving while black." That day in Rabat, looking at me aghast, gathering his wits now, I thought, Mohammed repeated to me what he had said the day before, that which had gotten me angry in the first place. "Yes," he had said, after denigrating once again the Africans who stole from his father, *les noirs* whose laziness was surpassed only by their deceitfulness—"Yes," he'd said, "America is a great country except for one great problem." "What is that?" I'd asked. "But of course," he'd said, "but of course you know; everybody does: it is *le racisme.*"

Identity, Ethnicity, and Culture

This encounter was revelatory for me in 1975 (which, indeed, is why one does fieldwork in foreign places—or teaches undergraduates about them); but nowadays it seems passé. Now there are many accounts that ring familiarly of this: of the chagrin—to reverse figure and ground—that some African Americans feel on being classified, by their African brothers and sisters, as "Europeans" in many parts of Mother Africa (e.g., in Lee 1984); or the unhappiness of American-Jewish immigrants to Israel (who often traded an American materially good life for a less good one, but one that "maximized" their Jewishness) on being called "Anglo-Saxons" by other Israelis (Avruch 1981); or how the "subjective" perception of skin color seems to vary by "objective" social class in parts of Brazil (the higher you go, the lighter you are; Skidmore 1974). The next time I ran into the Moroccan paradigm was on the other side of the African/Arab/Muslim world, in the Sudan, where "black" (to the eye of our paradigmatic Los Angeles patrolman) northern (Muslim, Arabophone) Sudanese know themselves to be Arabs, and thus utterly different from the African (i.e., black) southern (Christian, non-Arabophone) Sudanese, with whom they have struggled in a bloody civil war for many decades now.

One of the effects of looking at ethnicity as socially constructed was to change our orientation from regarding it as a thing completed (Narroll 1964)—a unit-vessel filled with cultural content (which is how the ethnic actors themselves continue to view it).[1] We came to focus less on the assumed "primordiality" of the cultural content of ethnicity, and more on the processes of the production of this cultural content (Fox 1990). This revision has largely replaced an older concern in the ethnicity literature, a concern expressed by the Parsonian distinction between expressive and instrumental modalities. Both modalities sought after the uses of ethnicity, but use-values were differently construed. The expressivists saw the actors' concerns with ethnicity as self-evident ends in themselves or, if not quite self-evident, perhaps as means toward identity integration or authenticity. This naturally led them to focus on the cultural content of ethnicity, especially as it dovetailed with religion. The instrumentalists, in contrast, saw actors' use of ethnicity as a strategy for the mobilization of resources and personnel. Like Barth (1969), these scholars were mostly not interested in ethnicity at all, but in ethnic groups. Ethnic groups organized actors around leadership to compete for scarce resources against other groups. What mattered most were the boundary-maintaining mechanisms that separated one group from another, not the rubbery cultural content—tradition, custom, cult, kinship: ethnicity—inside the boundaries. In a consummate elucidation of this view, Abner Cohen (1969) demonstrated how changeable this cultural content really was. He traced how, in postcolonial Nigeria, the Hausa of Sabo, in order to protect their monopoly of the north–south cattle and cola nut trade from other groups, transformed the basis of their group solidarity from "tribal" Hausa (the colonial locution) to "religious" Tijaniyya-Muslim (acceptable in a postcolonial political environment that proscribed open appeals to tribalism). Today, of course, in the midst of worsening Muslim-Christian violence exacerbating regional conflicts, many Nigerians rue this turn in the postindependence era to confessional identity.

Now fast-forward to a modern classic of the constructivist view of ethnicity, Richard Handler's *Nationalism and the Politics of Culture in Quebec* (1988). Contructivists like Handler were less enamored of the "vulgar" for-profit market-model tone of Barthian instrumentalism and came to concentrate on cultural identity as *subjectivity,* in terms of power and hegemony: Gramscian concerns (Gramsci 1985). Handler demonstrates how, over the course of several decades, Quebecois nationalists sought self-consciously to construct a satisfying version of Quebecois culture. Some of the cultural raw material available to them, that which naturally set them off from the Anglophone majority—the French language, the Roman Catholic church, and indigenous rural village Quebec mores and folkways—were all, in one way or another, ultimately unsatisfactory to the intellectuals and elites who were the self-appointed culture producers. As to language (with French language here standing metonymically for French culture as well), a perception of France as the "neglectful mother," combined with a sense of inferiority to metropolitan (i.e, Parisian) French— abetted by the typical ungraciousness of the metropolis's speech community to all other variants (Marseilles or Nancy, much less Montreal or Quebec City)—rendered this suboptimal. As for the Church, the bulwark of francophone Canadian identity and solidarity through the nineteenth century, it struck many liberal or leftist intellectuals by the late–middle twentieth century as theocratic, rigid, and reactionary. As to authentic, indigenous village culture, demographically Quebec was an increasingly urban society by the 1970s; the village as prototypically Quebecois was already a thing of the past. And besides, rural Quebecois, the genuine Quebecois "folk" romanticism aside, were in the end villagers with wooden shoes and fiddle dances, folkish or *rustre* after all. So the intellectuals were caught in a bind: How to construct a satisfying culture when one rejects the "real" culture that is lying around? In the radical 1960s, one solution was to follow Fanon (1986) and declare Quebecois culture a "culture born of oppression," a culture thus shared with other victims of colonial oppression, like the Algerians. (The colonial oppressors were anglophone Canadians. However, comparing the conduct of anglophone Canadians to the French in Algeria, or the nature of the Quebecois struggle to the bloody viciousness of the Algerian one, turned out to have limited marketability on either side.) But if the intellectuals bickered and faltered, the politicians knew exactly what to do. First, gaining provincial power under the Parti Quebecois in the 1976 elections, one of the things they did was to empower a Ministry of Culture, charged with bureaucratically *creating* a culture for the ministry's *fonctionnaires* to administer. Gaining further power, as the 1980s and 1990s went on, the party spearheaded a move to separate from Canada. Ultimately, they (re)turned to the French language to make their points. Within Quebec, they and the revivified culture makers enacted a series of anti-English language and educational laws that have seemed unacceptably repressive to liberal champions of individual rights, as well as very frightening to the so-called *allophones*—the nonnative French or English speakers: new immigrants in increasing numbers, and aboriginal, First Nation peoples. Separatists later charged that it was these people (especially new immigrants in Montreal) that provided the very thin margin of votes that defeated the sovereignty referendum in 1995.

Works such as Handler's show some of the complications in connecting culture to ethnicity. They are not isomorphic concepts, either conceptually (deployed by the analyst) or practically, as used by ethnic actors, politicians, and entrepreneurs (see Chapter 5). *Objectively* speaking, it can take a very little bit of cultural content—cultural *difference*—to mark off one ethnic group from another; and, as Cohen's Nigerian work demonstrated decades ago, the choice of that content (from fictive kinship to religion, from language to dress) can be labile in the extreme. Ethnicity utilizes bits of culture that have been objectified by political actors, projected publicly, and then resourcefully deployed by actors for political purposes (Avruch 1998:29–31). "People who live their culture unproblematically tend not to be ethnic in the proper sense of the word," Eller remarks (1999:11), and he goes on to argue that ethnic groups in conflict are not fighting *about* culture, but *with* culture. Indeed, this is one reason (among several, as discussed in Chapter 6) why one must treat the "clash of civilizations" approach to new world order ethnic or national conflict with some skepticism (e.g., Huntington 1996).

Works such as Handler's can also be refracted through the lens that the older perspective for understanding ethnicity provides. One thing that comes into focus is power. Holding Barth and Cohen, on the one hand, and Handler, on the other, in the same frame, it would appear that the instrumentalists' view of ethnicity in effect presaged that of the postmodern constructivists, at least with respect to the transformable nature of ethnicity's cultural content. This is so because both regard ethnicity, whether viewed as resource or discourse, as a way that parties organize in order to contest with one another for power. Both see ethnicity as necessarily implying social conflict. The Barthian instrumentalist is likely to see all this as groups occupying some socioecological "niche" and in conflict for the resources of the niche. The postmodernist is likely to see groups as social congeries in more or less frangible states, competing for the fruits of hegemony, control over the dominant discourse of the society. The constructivist dismisses Barth's instrumentality for its ethnocentric "market model" of ethnic conflict. Seeking rather to reintegrate expressivist concerns with identity with instrumentalist ones of profit, the constructivist argues for the "constituting effect on individuals" of ethnic conflict (Fox 1990:6). From the contest flows identity. But does not the concern with power remain central to both views? Does it matter whether the vocabulary is hegemony or market share? Curriculum or cola nuts? As Gramsci reminds us, why fight to control the discourse if not to control the resources (with Foucault adding that the discourse *is* the resource)?

Looked at from the perspective of power, there is perhaps little—or less than one thought—to differentiate the postmodern from the instrumentalist view of ethnicity. Power seems to remain the obdurate social primitive in all manner of ethnic and identity calculi. But there is another variable, hinted at in Handler's analysis, that perhaps serves better to distinguish ethnicity and ethnic conflict in our period of new world disorder, and that is the intervention of state or supra-state bureaucracies in the matter of ethnic identity construction. There is a new super-ethnic category in the making, one that transcends the traditional particularist confines of blood, cult, and shared history, but is yet crucial for their articulation. I refer to the category of displaced persons, both internally displaced and as international refugees, created, on the one hand, as a fallout of the contests of states—this being an old process—and on the other, and rather more recently, by the new world order of United Nations and nongovernmental organizations (NGOs), in developing concert with the militaries of yet other states, and all in the context of new, twenty-first-century political-cum-bureaucratic briefs like conflict resolution, peacekeeping, and humanitarian assistance.

Ethnic Conflict after World War II

In his prescient analysis of ethnicity first published in 1975—just about the time the term itself was making its way into the social scientist's lexicon—Harold Isaacs (who himself preferred the term *basic group identity*, which never caught on) pointed to the forces that, since 1945, made ethnic conflict an inevitably increasing part of the world's political order.[2] The main impetus came from the collapse of power systems that had hitherto held together disparate clusters of people; the collapse acting as a sort of political centrifuge that broke the clusters apart and sent them flying off in different directions. One result is what is today called transnational or globalized institutions or personnel. Isaacs mentioned four sorts of power systems that disintegrated in the post-1945 world. He called them postcolonial, postimperial, postrevolutionary, and postillusionary.

Postcolonial. In Africa, for example, most of the national boundaries were drawn by Europeans in Berlin in 1882. The retreating Europeans—some of the final backwash was what I ran into in Morocco in 1975—left behind them African nationalist movements that cross-cut older tribal/ethnic identities, just as the boundaries of the new African states sundered some ethnic groups and bound together others. Biafra, the Ogaden War, the Polisario, conflict in the Horn and the Great Lakes, all come out as unfinished business in the wake of European colonialism.

Postimperial. Some time after the last European troops left and the Colonial Office disbanded, the "periphery" returned the favor of colonialism in some measure and came as immigrants or refugees to the old colonial centers: North Africans in France, Moluccans in Holland, Indians and Pakistanis in the United Kingdom. This movement was connected to broader labor flows, for example, the phenomenon of the guest laborer that also brought Turks to Germany and Sicilians to Scandinavia, a not quite postimperial manifestation. As their numbers grew and certain of their institutions and practices, especially those connected to Islam, became more visible, these migrants engendered ethnic and racial conflict in Northern and Western European democratic states—the very sort of conflict that in the past—*pace* Jan Myrdal—the Europeans could confidently ascribe to the United States, alone.

Postrevolutionary. In this, in 1975, Isaacs seemed most dismissable (and most prescient), as he claimed to discern fragility within the Soviet Union and China, the "revolutionary" states of the twentieth century. Russian power, he asserted, had been unable "to keep the added nationalities of its extended empire under effective control," and pointed further to but a "limited suzerainty over eastern and southeastern Europe." He even noted the efforts of an "aging Tito" to keep Yugoslavia from "exploding again into its Serbian, Croatian, Montenegrin, Bosnian, and other assorted parts" (Isaacs 1975:18). History has proved Isaacs right on the Soviet Union and Eastern Europe. Many will continue to dismiss him regarding China; but looking at the struggle of national minorities there, of Tibetan or Uyghur internationally recognized movements of protest, at the vast changes in Han society wrought by the movement from a sort of communism to hypernationalist capitalism, at often violent protests in the west and south over industrial safety and poisoned food and Party corruption, at Chinese dissident blogs and the Internet—and thinking of Tiananmen Square as unfinished business—Isaacs may be close to right in the long run.

Postillusionary. And here, finally, Isaacs turned his eye on the United States—the "illusion" he referred to was that of white supremacy—and the progressive weakening of American apartheid since Truman integrated the Army, Eisenhower sent troops to Little Rock, and Johnson pushed forward the Civil Rights legislation of 1964. Following this came black power, black nationalism, the white ethnic revivals of the late 1960s and 1970s and, of course, the American presidential election of 2008. Although noting the many barriers that stood against them in 1945 that appear to have fallen in the intervening three decades, Jews, Isaacs wrote in 1975, were "not likely to make it to the

White House any time soon" (1975:21). On African-American chances, he was completely silent.

For all his prescience, Isaacs could not see a fifth post-1945 (specifically, a post-1989, end-of-the-Cold War) dynamic: the degree and vehemence with which ethnic conflict in the postcolonial world could never stay isolated in the periphery. Partly as a precipitate of postimperial forces that physically brought the lately decolonized to the centers, partly through the rise of political Islam, and partly through a post-9/11 regime of renewed military intervention by the West, ethnic clashes in the unstable periphery have involved the old European colonial/imperial centers and the United States. Disturbances in Algeria sent yet more Algerians fleeing to France, which exacerbates interethnic tensions there. Indonesian repression sent Ambionese to Holland. Second- and third-generation youth, speaking the language of the metropole, feel trapped in banlieu and emerge as angry ethnic minorities. Today, refugees from Iraq, Afghanistan, the Horn of Africa, and so on, seek safety and are reduced to commodities in the political economy of human trafficking. To all this is added the dynamics of transethnic religious identity. Especially in conjunction with jihadist ideology, the disturbances in the periphery play out in acts of terrorism in the cities of the old centers. Even if they wanted to, the old imperial centers find it difficult to disengage from their peripheries, as the formerly colonized now arrive not just as labor migrants but also as political refugees, bringing the conflicts in their countries of origin with them. One response to this has been to declare immigration crises and tighten increasingly restrictive immigration laws: to keep the refugees out or, in the case of some Muslims, to find ways to expel them more quickly. In some cases, as in recent rioting in France, the problem looks to be ethnic/racial/class in nature. In other places—France as well, but generally throughout Western Europe where their population grows—it takes the form of Islamophobia. Whether parsed as race or religion (two of Isaacs's core components in his elucidation of "basic group identity"), it has been linked again and again to the rising electoral success of ultranationalist and racist or protofascist parties throughout western and central Europe.

In the period before 9/11, throughout the 1990s, most of the misery occurred in the ever present and "coming anarchy" (Kaplan 2001) of the periphery alone, and there was a widespread (if intermittent) sympathy among many citizens in the West for the suffering in Africa, Asia, or, closer to the center, in the Balkans. In that time, the sympathy was evoked when things got really bad—when the warlords and the civil war disrupted the harvest and famine came; when the ethnic cleansing produced mass graves and the new world order of concentration camps—and were all carried, thanks to CNN and satellite communications, on the television screens of citizens throughout Europe and North America. Especially, the children appeared. In that period, the governments of Western Europe and North America were pressed by some of their own citizens to intervene and help. At the same time, security analysts argued that the best way to help but keep them out (think Haitian boatpeople landing on Miami's beaches) was to address the problems "out there" in the first place. Thus was born the era of large-scale humanitarian assistance along with new bureaucracies, new international organizations (IO and NGO), and a new role for the center: an expansion of the old "peacekeeping operations" paradigm into that of multi-actor "complex humanitarian emergencies," under the United Nations or some regional (North Atlantic Treaty Organization [NATO], Organization of African Unity [OAU], Economic Community of West African States [ECOWAS], etc.) consortium. The old peacekeeping paradigm was first expanded under Boutros-Ghali's *Agenda for Peace* (1992). Military operations got blended with humanitarian assistance and an emerging rhetoric of conflict resolution as "peacebuilding" (e.g., Durch 1993; Charters 1994; Rubinstein 2008). It proved to be a fragile sort of paradigm from the very beginning, as Somalia first demonstrated (Clarke and Herbst 1997). From the beginning, as well, it had critics who called this reengagement by the center neocolonialism. But that was hardly the whole story, if only because many of the so-called neocolonialists seemed, even then, on the whole more Conrad than Kipling; they seem deeply conflicted and unenthusiastic about the task.

After 9/11 and terrorist acts in Madrid and London; after Iraq and Afghanistan, with the growing articulation of the conflict in terms of the West versus Islam (see Chapter 6); and identities increasingly denatured of ethnicity and nationalism and recast in the altogether more manichean casings of religion, what sympathy there was evaporated, and what has remained is only the fact of the refugee.

Refugee Camps and the New Ethnicity

In one sense, the refugee is as old as a neolithic clash between any two groups, in which one group vanquishes the other, destroys or occupies its habitation, and thus compels the other to flee to some new place. These refugees melded themselves into existing settlements or started new ones or perished somewhere between the two. This sort of refugee is as old as history. But the modern sense of refugee entails the state system and refers to the human precipitate of the conflict dynamics of states—interstate warfare, intrastate conflict and repression, state collapse. There are no longer any land bridges to cross over to empty continents. The territories to which these refugees flee are no longer the virgin forests of the neolithic; they are usually territories that are in the domain of some other state, and more often than not, already occupied by citizens of that state. Refugees may come as individuals or as family units to their place of refuge, and some are even admitted under special provisions of the refuge state's immigration law (the so-called political refugee), though post-9/11 fears of importing terrorists have weakened these provisions. Added to the more vigilant exclusion of refugees from Western states is the fact that state collapse means that refugees often flee en masse and must be dealt with en masse—and kept *away*. The setting to accomplish this is the refugee camp, administered by a congeries of new bureaucracies—governmental and nongovernmental, public and private, sometimes military—but most often and paradigmatically by the United Nations High Commissioner for Refugees (UNHCR). These camps became part of larger third-party operations organized under the rubrics of peacekeeping, humanitarian assistance, and conflict resolution/peacebuilding that took place in the aftermath of collapsed states, some natural disasters, or military incursions (by the West) that caused states to collapse in the first place.

Some of these camps are relatively temporary in duration, and some span generations, becoming more or less permanent *societies*. In either case, what are some of the implications for conflict of these new sociopolitical forms? There are at least three.

First, these forms are the hitherto neglected manifestations of ethnic conflict in the postindustrial world, the newest, post–Cold War extensions of what Isaacs called postcolonial and postimperial disturbances, and what today are likely to be precipitates of globalized economic catastrophe and "wars of the third kind" (Rice 1988). Although played out most often in the former periphery, these forms represent ways in which the centers get—willy-nilly and not always with great enthusiasm—reengaged in their collapsing affairs. Before 9/11 and the invasions of Iraq and Afghanistan brought "old-fashioned" military arms and operations back to prominence, in the 1990s the newest forms of military engagement with ethnic conflicts outside the centers came in the form of "peacekeeping" operations in "complex humanitarian emergencies," in which militaries were invited to reinvent themselves. In those days, the newest areas of the military crafts were called, in the United States, Operations Other Than War (OOTW). After the United States smashed Iraq to topple Saddam but had no conception of what was to follow (Secretary Powell was quite correct in his antique store analogy: the United States broke it, the United States bought it), the humble arts of OOTW (after the main combat phase ended) turned into the emergent Pentagon doctrine of "stability and reconstruction."

Second, the refugee camps themselves are veritable hothouses for the forced growth and nurturance of identities, ethnic, nationalist, or religious. Probably the paradigmatic case is that of the Palestinians—also one of the first refugee groups to have been administered by the United Nations, under the United Nations Relief Works Agency for Palestinians Refugees (UNRWA), established in 1948 as part of the first Arab-Israeli armistice. For many years, Palestinian camps scattered in Gaza, the West Bank, and Lebanon provided the fighters for the most militant PLO factions, such as Fatah, as well its ideological elite. (Financial resources came from elsewhere.) Schools—crucial elements in ethnogenesis—turned out the fiercest anti-Zionists and the most committed Palestinian nationalists. Increasingly, schools combined with other institutions under Islamist influences that provided social services, like Hamas, thus marrying Palestinian nationalism to Islamism, even as Hamas bloodily fought to defeat Fatah in Gaza. The Palestinian state may well be the first state in history whose underlying governance structures were partially built on the formative framework of the refugee camp—as Israel itself was partially built on the concentration camp.

Although paradigmatic, Palestinians are hardly the only example of this. Work by Liisa Malkki (1995) on Hutu refugees from Burundi in Tanzania in the 1980s contrasts those living in organized camps with those who chose to live among Tanzanians in the nearby city. She points that the "camp Hutus," by creating and fostering a compelling "mythico-history" (as Malkki calls it) of their relations with the Tutsi and their victimization, maintained a strong sense of "pure" Hutu identity, while the city dwellers sought to assimilate, even to intermarry, with Tanzanians. The camp Hutus strongly stressed their eventual return to Burundi (and, alas, their planned revenge on the Tutsis), whereas the city Hutus did not. Moreover, the camp Hutus directed some of their greatest hostility against their city-dwelling coethnics, whom they regarded as traitors and cowards.

If ethnicity is a constructed affair, then one of the prime sites of its construction is the refugee camp.[3] Moreover, considering the range of political goals that ethnic groups can aspire to, the camp is especially important for constructing the sort of ethnicity that feeds overtly nationalistic movements, those claiming the existence of a unique *nation* entitled to sovereign control over a territory: a *state* (see Smith 1991; Connor 1994).

Third, "refugee," as created by international law and practice, is a constructed category and, as my comparison of Palestinian and Hutu indicates, it can be read as a sort of super-ethnicity, for some persons, another kind of basic group identity. Such an identity can become a site for constituting a social group that is closely bounded and ecologically situated, with a shared history (oppression, persecution, ethnic/religious identity), a shared present (famine, isolation, uncertainty, the "wards" of United Nations and NGOs and reluctant host refuge states), and shared visions of the future (a state of their own, a return to a homeland, revenge taken on their oppressors). What is also shared, increasingly, is their formative exposure to the "culture" of the "international community"—the militaries, IOs and NGOs—that certifies refugee status and creates, supports, and administers the camps.

Finally, to return at last to the issue of culture, one might ask what is the "cultural content" of the category *refugee*. Surely, the Palestinian and the Hutu and the Sierra Leonean do not share the same culture? Of course not: at least not the way culture was traditionally bestowed on traditional conceptions of groups. But they do share culture (about which we still know too little). It is the culture shared by all those unfortunate enough to be the human precipitate of the struggle or collapse of states. And it is a cultural content shared by dint of the shared cultures of the governing institutions and bureaucracies (UN, NGOs, private voluntary organizations [PVOs], International Committee of the Red Cross [ICRC], USAID, Oxford Committee for Famine Relief (OXFAM), etc., about which we also still know too little)—as well as the various aid industries (see Hancock 1989; Maren 1997)—that conjoin to create and sustain them and each other.

5

Type I and Type II Errors in Culturally Sensitive Conflict Resolution Practice

Introduction

Continuing the theme of identity construction, this chapter deals with conceptions of ethnicity and multiculturalism. But I turn now to practice, seeking to address the nexus between culture and conflict resolution theory and practice, to contribute to the work of practitioners when they function as third-party interveners in intercultural and interethnic conflicts and disputes. I propose two conceptions of *culture*: a technical, "experience-distant" sense of the term, crucial for conflict analysis (and also for education and training), and an affectively laden, often politicized, "experience-near" sense of the term, at the root of so much intergroup conflict and thus implacably implicated in effective and ethical intercultural practice. Although I present this distinction in an authoritative, mostly straightforward way in this chapter, it is a controversial distinction for some practitioners, an issue I take up at greater length in Chapter 9.

The Cultural Turn in Conflict Resolution and ADR

Depending on which part of the field one considers central to it, the origins of conflict resolution as a distinct field of theory and *theory-connected* practice date back to the middle 1950s, to Kenneth Boulding, the group around him at the University of Michigan, and the founding of the *Journal of Conflict Resolution*; or the 1960s, to Johan Galtung and John Burton in Scandinavia and Britain, the *Journal of Peace Research*, established by Galtung in 1964, and the first "controlled communication" (problem-solving) workshop, organized by Burton in 1965. The origins of alternative dispute resolution (ADR), coming from schools of law and legal practitioners with a reformist agenda for American jurisprudence (and supposedly overly litigious Americans), are dated by some to the Roscoe Pound Conference, Perspectives on Justice in the Future, held in St. Paul, Minnesota, in 1976 (Nader 1993).

As noted in Chapter 1, however one wants to specify origins, what is striking about virtually all of the early work in conflict resolution and ADR is how little attention theory paid to the concept of culture, and how practice, inspired by theory (or vice versa—see Avruch 1998:78–80), seemingly ignored the importance of cultural differences among parties (including third parties) as relevant to the sources or outcomes of a conflict or dispute. In some cases, there seemed to be active resistance to incorporating culture to theory and practice (Burton 1987); in other cases, just a benign neglect brought on by the presumed universality of rational choice theory and economistic behaviorism as templates for panhuman cognition and social relations (Raiffa 1982). Certainly that protean classic of our field, *Getting to Yes*, in its first edition mentioned culture not at all (Fisher and Ury 1981), and in its second edition, presumably responding to some criticism of this, lumped culture alongside gender and personality as things to be aware of, without, however, affecting the basic tenets of principled negotiation (Fisher, Ury, and Patton 1991).

In the case of ADR, there is some mild irony in its initial neglect of culture, because some of the early reformers read in the anthropology of law (e.g., Gibbs 1963), and believed that a viable template for American legal reform—namely, ADR—could be found in the more "therapeutic" nature of dispute resolution in certain "tribal societies" (Danzig 1973). Although the recourse to what can be called ethnographic romanticism was never without its critics, both on conceptual (Felstiner 1974) and political (Galanter 1974; Abel 1982; Nader 1991) grounds, the practice of ADR itself developed initially in an environment almost free of cultural sensitivity (and ignorant of class consciousness) (Harrington and Merry 1988; Avruch and Black 1996).[1]

By the 1980s, beginning perhaps with P. H. Gulliver's groundbreaking work on negotiation (Gulliver 1979), an appreciation of culture began to inform conflict resolution and ADR practice. Some of this came from anthropologists and ethnographers entering the field and engaging with some early major theorists (Avruch and Black 1987, 1991) or arguing with lawyers on the defects of "disputing without culture" (Merry 1987). Some came from practitioners with significant cross-cultural experience, many of these working from within so-called peace churches (Lederach 1991; Augsburger 1992). Another important input came from scholars in intercultural communication (Gudykunst, Stewart, and Ting-Toomey 1985), often building on the work of E. T. Hall (1976) or Harry Triandis (1972), or from researchers in organizational behavior (Hofstede 1980).

By the 1990s, one of the founders of the field had added the notion of "cultural violence" to his earlier and seminal insights on structural violence (Galtung 1990). More to the point, the problem of culture in conflict analysis and conflict resolution had generated several edited collections (Avruch, Black, and Scimecca 1991; Fry and Björkqvist 1997) and anthologies (Chew 2001), including discrete sections in works devoted to ADR from legal and commercial perspectives (Trachte-Huber and Huber 1996). Today, in the web-based distance learning curriculum put out by the peace studies and conflict resolution program at the University of Bradford (U.K.), what Avruch and Black called "the culture question" in 1991 is addressed directly and explicitly as one crucial issue, among several others, that should be tackled by any peace studies or conflict resolution pedagogue, theorist, or practitioner.[2] It is the case, in fact, that nowadays any self-respecting curriculum in ADR or conflict resolution without at least a module devoted to culture would be considered deficient; this was decidedly not the case in 1981. Other scholar-practitioners see the culture question—sometimes parsed as the "politics of difference"—as central to the field (Brigg 2008). In any case, culture, it appears, has arrived, and if the struggle to integrate it into a mature conflict resolution and ADR practice is not yet fully won, surely the ensign symbolizing the Party of Culture is recognized on the field (and in the field) by all sides.

But how precisely is "culture" conceived in this Party? Without attending to all of the nuances that have differentiated scores of definitions of culture from one another over the years, it is fair to say that for most who have made the cultural turn in conflict resolution or ADR practice, culture has been conceived generally in terms of

- Constituting different norms, values, and beliefs for socially appropriate ways to process conflicts and disputes, including their management or resolution—what Avruch and Black (1991) called indigenous "ethno-conflict theories" and "ethnopraxes."
- Affecting significant perceptual orientations toward time, risk or uncertainty, affect (in self and others), hierarchy, power, or authority.
- Comprising different cognitive representations or discursive frames such as schemas, maps, scripts, or images, bound up in such metalinguistic forms as symbols or metaphors.

Although the first conception (norms, values, and beliefs) refers to the broad way in which culture provides *context* for conflict and disputing (Caplan 1995), the second two, highlighting perceptual and cognitive features, orient us to thinking about how culture affects a crucial component of conflict or dispute resolution, that is, effective *communication* among the disputants or parties, including potential third parties. This is why so many culturally sensitive approaches to conflict resolution or ADR practice (including intercultural negotiation or mediation) appropriately invoke ideas of communicational competence, extended to cultural competence, and direct our attention to different cultural styles or to other paralinguistic features (such as body language) of intercultural encounters or disputes (Hall 1976; Weaver 1994; Cupach and Canary 1997). Whatever else they may be, therefore, conflict or ADR professionals should be specialists in managing communicational process; this is an insight with deep roots in our field (Burton 1969).

Culture: Experience-Distant and Experience-Near

All three conceptions, from norms and values through schemas and symbols, convey collectively an idea of culture that can be called "culture in the technical sense of the term," that is, culture as an analytical category, even, permitting the hyperbole, as a scientific category. This is the familiar sense of culture as a social scientific term, central to most anthropological writing since the 1930s but also, through Talcott Parsons, to much of sociology and (through figures such as Harry Triandis) psychology as well. But *culture* is also a term in our ordinary, natural language and everyday speech, a term with a complicated history and bearing much political baggage (Williams 1976, 1981; Jenks 1993; Kuper 1999). So while practitioners need to be specialists in understanding the "technical" sense of culture, they must also be aware of how disputants or other parties to a conflict might use and understand the term, especially when they find themselves working in multicultural social settings. Mostly, practitioners need to recognize the difference between the two usages. To do this, I make the distinction between "experience-near" (hereafter, *e/n*) and "experience-distant" (*e/d*) concepts.

The distinction comes from the anthropologist Clifford Geertz, who in turn lifted it from the psychoanalyst Heinz Kohut (therefore undoubtedly from the experience of clinical *practice*):

> An experience-near concept is, roughly, one that someone—a patient, a subject ... might himself naturally and effortlessly use to define what he or his fellows see, feel, think, imagine ... and which he would readily understand when similarly applied by others. An experience-distant concept is one that specialists of one sort or another ... employ to forward their scientific, philosophical, or practical aims. 'Love' is an experience-near concept, 'object cathexis' is an experience-distant one.
>
> Geertz is careful to warn us that the distinction is not necessarily a normative one, in the sense that one concept is to be preferred as such over the other. Confinement to experience-near concepts leaves an ethnographer awash

in immediacies, as well as entangled in the vernacular. Confinement to experience-distant ones leaves him stranded in abstractions and smothered in jargon (Geertz 1983:57).

Given the complicated connotations (the *polysemy*) of the word *culture*, it is obviously an idea that can function in both experience-near as well as experience-distant ways. Analysts and practitioners will want to deploy it in its technical sense, as an experience-distant concept especially useful for identifying communicational impedances in intercultural encounters. But the players, disputants or other parties to a conflict, may well appropriate the idea of culture for their own uses. It then becomes an experience-near concept, useful to parties in at least two distinct ways. First, using notions of culture may help parties make sense of their own and their opponents' behavior—as a sort of folk social psychology and therefore much as the specialist might use the term. Second—here the historical baggage the term carries enters the fray—the notion of culture also carries with it moral connotations (e.g., of tradition or authenticity) and thus is also available for use as an ideological or rhetorical resource for parties or contestants, in pursuit of their goals. This happens especially when culture is used in conflict around ethnic, religious, racial, or nationalist matters—conflicts around identity.

Although Geertz wants to downplay any normative distinctions between *e/n* and *e/d* usages, when it comes to *culture* and conflict resolution we should be more careful. It is a problem when this technical, experience-distant idea is taken over and used by the very parties and actors it is meant to explain. The problem is greater than one of simply confusing logical types or levels of analysis—or of appearing pretentious before your dinner guests by substituting in conversation "object cathexis" for "love." For culture, given the political baggage it sometimes carries, can be a powerful idea, and thus any confusion by practitioners or third parties of *e/n* for *e/d* can turn out to be potentially deleterious for conflict resolution and, with respect particularly to some of the weaker parties in a conflict, ethically precarious as well.[3]

In the early twentieth century a good deal of the work done by anthropologists (starting with Franz Boas and his American students) to establish a modern, scientific, objective, and technical (i.e., an *e/d*) concept of culture—the one we discussed earlier in terms of norms, symbols, and schemas—was aimed at decoupling culture from race (Stocking 1968) and ridding it of the more mystical elements of Romantic thought—culture purged of *Volksgeist* (the eternal spirit of a people). Boas and many of his students were in addition politically active in liberal, antiracist, and antifascist movements (Hyatt 1990; Lewis 2001). In this sense, then, there was a political and moral component built into the scientific and technical meaning of the term *culture* from the very beginning. It was meant both to describe differences between social groups, without consigning such differences to biology—race or heredity—and to assert the moral equivalence of all cultures. Some have argued that the victory of this liberal and relativist political understanding of scientific culture is to be found in the adoption of this sense of the concept in 1945 by the United Nations Educational, Scientific and Cultural Organization (UNESCO), reacting against the fresh horrors of Nazi and fascist racism and genocide (see Finkielkraut 1995, who nevertheless writes in a highly critical mode).

The relationship of culture and race was born in the nineteenth century, and much of the modernist thrust in anthropology, giving us our *e/d* understanding of *culture*, was meant to disentangle them.[4] It was also meant to drain the term of its Romantic (in the sense of blood and belonging spirituality) and highly subjective *e/n* connotations. Professional anthropologists were expected to write objectivist ethnographic monographs rather than *Bildungsroman*, highly subjective works of fiction. But a term so powerfully meaningful in everyday speech can at times resist experience-distancing by academic specialists or practitioners. Culture still carries *e/n* meanings and may be used for purposes that are antithetical to its *e/d* meanings. Because of this, the relationship of culture to race as well as its other (subjectivist and spiritual) *e/n* connotations have never been fully resolved, and therefore continue to have relevance for how "culturally sensitive" conflict resolution and ADR practitioners do their work in the twenty-first century. Now we are close to seeing why *culture* is so potentially treacherous a term for conflict resolution, and why (third-party) conflict resolution and ADR practitioners need to keep the difference between *e/n* and *e/d* senses of it clearly in mind—and not to confuse the two. This latter point is especially important because it is highly likely that the contestants or parties to the conflict will have completely fused the two senses together.

Culture, Ethnicity, and Identity

When the parties use culture in an *e/n* sense, it is almost always part of an assertion about collective social identity and group difference. "Identity" because, in *e/n* usage, some *selected* symbols, norms, beliefs, and so on, of culture—usually the more obvious ones relating to religious practice, language, dress, commensality, or dietary rules, and the like—are used to define a social collective, to make statements about "who *we* are" and about "difference," because such statements (about *we*) always imply a *they*. "Collective or communal identity," writes Steven Lukes, "always requires ... an 'other'; every affirmation of belonging includes an explicit or implicit exclusion clause" (Lukes 1993:37).

Since at least the late 1960s (Barth 1969), most social scientists have argued that when culture is enlisted in this way by members of social groups, it is culture in the guise of *ethnicity*, and the social groups constituted from it are *ethnic groups*. (In fact, ethnicity may be thought of as an *e/d* term for the *e/n* usage of culture.) When many intergroup conflicts, especially those around identity issues, are analyzed in terms of ethnicity rather than culture, it brings into sharp relief the fact that culture and ethnicity are hardly isomorphic. It takes very little cultural content (say, a specific religious belief or practice) to manufacture a great deal of ethnicity. To make ethnicity, small bits or traits of culture are objectified, and these objectified bits are then projected—often performed—onto public domains, such as festivals, rituals, remembrance days, or marches. Ethnic groups are constituted out of linkages among members based upon ties of shared culture: language and religion, as well as putative ties of kinship or history. But the actual cultural content matters less than its ability to differentiate one group from another: "*We* march today, *they* do not." Ethnicity is about difference that is socially or politically significant; ethnic groups are defined by the boundaries between them; culture is used to constitute and maintain the boundaries (Ross 2007).

The research literature on the problematic relationship of culture (in the *e/d* sense) to often virulent ethnic conflict is impressive and growing (e.g., on "manufacturing ethnicity," see Roosens 1989; for detailed comparative case studies, see Eller 1999 and Ross 2007; on Northern Ireland, see Akenson 1991; on former Yugoslavia, Eriksen 2001; for the argument extending from ethnicity to nationalism, Gellner 1997). The point to these studies collectively is that the parties themselves will see their conflict in cultural terms: protecting tradition, preserving identity, keeping the faith; indeed, often in the starkest terms of cultural survival in a full-blown clash of civilizations.[5] Here, tied to identity and conceptions of authentic self for the parties engaged in the struggle, culture is a profoundly experience-near idea. To someone standing outside the conflict, impressed, say, by the cultural similarities between the Protestant and Catholic working class in Northern Ireland, or among Serbs, Croats, and Muslims in Sarajevo in the 1980s, it hardly makes sense to see the conflict in cultural terms. Eller has said it best: "When it comes to ethnic conflicts, such groups are not fighting *about* culture ... but fighting *with* culture" (1999:48, emphasis in original). The distinction between "fighting about" and "fighting with" is another (instrumental) way to approach *e/d* versus *e/n* conceptions of culture. Conflict analysts, third parties, and practitioners need to keep this distinction in mind, because it has potential consequences for all the parties in ethnic or identity conflicts, especially for weaker parties.

One reason why the distinction is consequential has to do with how ethnic identity is experienced phenomenologically by individuals, in Ignatieff's (1994) phrase, as "blood and belonging." As criteria of group membership, symbols and rites, even a shared past, may suffice to signal "belonging"; but "blood" entails something else. Blood implies ties of kinship and shared ancestry, of heredity and metaphysical biology. When belonging is linked with blood as criteria for group membership, then its expression as (*e/n*) culture takes on greater force. For now culture as tradition and customs—as heritage—becomes in addition culture as heredity and biology. In this way (in a return to nineteenth-century Romantic conceptions of the term that undo the Boasian antiracist sense of it), culture can become a cipher for race and, in certain sociopolitical settings, its functional equivalent.

Culture, Race, and Multiculturalism

In what sorts of sociopolitical settings can culture (e/n) become a stand-in for race? One answer, not surprisingly, is in overtly racist settings where, for some reason, outright biologism has become politically costly or embarrassing—a matter of public relations. Kuper (1999), for example, begins his critical discussion of the culture concept by noting how the term was used by many in the later years of Apartheid South Africa as a substitute for race and a sop to South African liberal sensibility. Balibar has described this "neoracism" as "racism without race":

> It is granted from the outset that races do not constitute isolable biological units and that in reality there are no 'human races.' It may also be admitted that the behaviour of individuals and their 'aptitudes' cannot be explained in terms of their blood or even their genes, but are the result of their belonging to histori- cal 'cultures'.... *Culture can also function like a nature....* (Balibar 1991:21-22, emphasis in original).

But overtly racist societies are not the only ones where culture can stand in for race. The substitution can occur with a great deal more subtlety in sociopolitical settings characterized by an explicit commitment to racism's ostensible antidote, *multiculturalism.*

Multiculturalism is one possible political response to societies characterized by recognized cultural (read: ethnic) diversity. It does not refer to the mere fact, the existence, of such diversity. Analytically, one can reserve the more neutral term *polyculturalism* for that. But polyculturalism as an analytical concept says nothing necessarily about the social context of diversity. It says nothing about the political implications of diversity, that is, that relations be- tween individuals and cultural/ethnic groups are necessarily characterized by socially recognized asymmetries of power or privilege, by forms of dominance and subordination. Of course, such a conception of a polycultural society is rather like the physicist's assumption of a perfect vacuum or a frictionless plane—or the economist's of a free market—fine for heuristics, but tricky to find in the real world.

In the real world, the fact of diversity is typically correlated with forms of inequality and stratification, and dominant groups can relate, both ideologi- cally and in terms of political praxis, to subordinate ones in a variety of ways. Apartheid, or some other form of caste-like social organization, is one such way. Another way is for the dominant group to insist on complete assimilation by others to its version of culture—not so likely, of course, if the dominant culture has been itself naturalized in a neoracist manner. Yet another way, the ideal for secular liberal democracy, is to recognize diversity but privatize or individualize it, rendering it irrelevant politically. Here is a *civil society* wherein civic group membership trumps ethnic affiliations in public spheres. Multiculturalism is a fourth possible response to diversity. Here the fact of diversity is both recognized and found virtuous; it is celebrated. A soft form of multiculturalism may be virtually indistinguishable from the liberal ideal noted above, perhaps with the addition of support for explicit government policies ensuring tolerance and protection of minorities or otherwise subordinate cultural groups. So-called hard or radical multiculturalism "goes further, conceiving of the nation [or society] as a confederation of ethnic groups with equal rights and construing ethnicity ['culture,' *e/n*] as the *preferred* basis of one's political identity" (Citrin, Wong, and Duff 2001:77, emphasis in original).

Both soft and hard multiculturalism give rise to a host of positions on social issues of importance in polycultural settings, for instance on immigration, affirmative action, or bilingual education, that put it in conflict with other possible responses, conservative or liberal, to these matters. But it is the hard form that has generated the most heated polemics, both in the United States (Schlesinger 1992) or Western Europe (Finkielkraut 1995). What are the implications of either form for conflict resolution practice?

The hard form is typically evident in more deeply rooted or protracted social conflicts around issues of identity, including racial, ethnic, and nationalist ones. But even if we set those perhaps more emphatic or dramatic conflicts aside, we find that conflict resolution third-party professionals—ADR specialists attached to courts or community centers, or ombudsmen working in universities, hospitals, corporations, or other institutions—will find themselves in polycultural settings wherein some version of at least soft multiculturalism (in the form of equal opportunity employer (EOE), affirmative action, or other legal or quasi-legal workplace regulations) predominates. Furthermore, conflict resolution and ADR professionals in the twenty-first century are now likely to be culturally sensitive, and surely wish to make their practice as responsive to culture as possible.

But to *which* culture ought they direct their sensitivity; to which do they owe response?

Experience-distant culture is a technical concept in the social sciences that refers to shared norms, beliefs, and values; public symbols and metaphors; schemas, images, and cognitive maps. Experience-near culture is a political idea found in polycultural settings. It refers to shared identities and demarcated group boundaries. Viewed by outside analysts, this version of culture is sometimes called ethnicity—even (under certain circumstances) race or nationalism. When *privileged* as a source of identity (social or political), this version of culture *is the culture in multiculturalism*.

For many sorts of academic analysts or theorists of culture, including the vast majority of those who have researched and written on intercultural communication, negotiation, mediation, or conflict resolution, experience-near culture no doubt is to experience-distant culture as military music is to music: a fundamental miscontrual, if not a polluting abomination. But practitioners of one kind or another, working as third parties in conflicts or disputes within polycultural settings informed by some form of multiculturalism—working in the proverbial real world, that is—do not possess most of the indulgences granted to pure research and ideal types. For practitioners will end up as inter-locutors with *parties* in intercultural disputes or conflicts who will often mean something very different by culture. For the political *actor* involved in a dispute in a multicultural setting—the ethnic politician, broker, or entrepreneur; the nationalist ideologue or cultural chauvinist; the immigrant or refugee rights activist—the distinction between *e/n* and *e/d* meanings of culture is almost certainly invisible and irrelevant. Worse, the distinction is potentially heretical or treasonous, particularly if asserted publicly by a dissenting member of the group, because merely by introducing *e/d* culture analytically in this situation, one essentially threatens to deconstruct or unmask the *e/n* variety.

What, then, is to be done? First, there is the question of what is to be done in the real world of conflict resolution or ADR practice; and then the more theoretical question of what is to be done with the culture concept itself.

Type I and Type II Errors in Intercultural Practice

Let us imagine that you, as a third party of one sort or another, are called to intervene in a dispute or conflict in an "intercultural setting": the parties appear to have come from different cultural backgrounds or communities. Having been trained or educated to take culture seriously, how do you factor it into your understanding of the conflict or dispute, and then into your process?

Your first task is (as in so much practice) essentially a diagnostic one. You must decide which sense of *culture* is mainly relevant here: the technical *e/d* sense, or the political *e/n* sense? Of course, the real world complicates matters immediately. Thus far *e/d* and *e/n* have been presented as mutually exclusive categories, in complementary distribution (when one is present, the other is absent). Semantically, this may be true. But the pragmatics of the thing—concerning the semantics as actualized by real persons in social intercourse—are different. Just because a psychoanalyst thinks in terms of object relations and object cathexis doesn't mean that she cannot experience the emotions of love. Moreover, especially as *e/n* conceptions of culture connect (in persons) with social identity and conceptions of self, it is the case that *e/n* culture may penetrate *e/d* culture in significant ways. This is why, for example, it makes sense analytically to speak of a social setting characterized by inequality and a highly racialized discourse of (*e/n*) cultural identities as a (*e/d*) *culture of racism*.

Right away, then, the real world conspires against simple binary thinking. Nevertheless, it is the case that so-called intercultural encounters will be differentially *e/d* or *e/n*, that one sense or the other may predominate, and that the job of the third party is to disentangle them. For heuristic purposes (that great elider of the real world of practice!), let us assume that they are more or less mutually exclusive, and that means that at least two sorts of diagnostic errors or mistakes are possible. As a third party, and thinking analytically of culture in the technical *e/d* meaning of the term, you may decide that there are *no* significant cultural differences among the parties and that therefore culture will have no significant impact on the processing of the dispute or resolution. Let us say that you are wrong: that cultural differences exist and they impact the contours of the dispute and the processes of resolution. If culture (*e/d*) is significant and you thought not, then you have made a Type I error. Culturally speaking, you have a tin ear.

Alternatively, let us say that you decide that there are significant cultural differences between the parties to the conflict or dispute and that therefore culture will have a significant impact on dispute processing and resolution. But let us say that you are wrong. You have mistaken expressions of cultural difference by the parties (or have imputed them yourself) as representing *e/d* culture when, in fact, they are manifestations of *e/n* culture. *You have mistaken ethnic differences for cultural ones.* The antagonists really all do "speak the same (cultural) language," in effect fighting *with* their culture, not *about* it. If culture (*e/d*) is not significant and you have decided that it is, then you have made a Type II error. Culturally speaking, you are hearing voices that aren't really there. These errors are summarized in Figure 1.

Type I errors undervalue culture, underestimating its significance in a conflict or dispute. A Type I error means that you are "culturally insensitive." Type II errors overvalue culture, overestimating its impact on a conflict or dispute. Since the general cultural turn in conflict resolution, there is a growing literature of the cautionary type warning against Type I errors, especially for intercultural negotiation. There has been much less said about Type II errors. One can begin by saying that Type II errors by third parties will probably occur under at least these two conditions:

- Where the conflict or dispute involves parties from self-evidently different identity groups, that is, the conflict is self-evidently interethnic or interracial

Figure 1. A Heuristic for Cultural Analysis and Conflict Resolution

Third-Party Intervenor Decision re: Cultural Impacts	Actual Extent of Cultural Impacts	
	Cultural Impacts "High" or "Strong"	Cultural Impacts "Low" or "Weak"
No Significant Cultural Impacts on Conflict or Dispute	Type I Error ("Tin Ear")	Appropriate Decision
Significant Cultural Impacts on Conflict or Dispute	Appropriate Decision	Type II Error ("Hearing Voices")

Note: *Culture* in this heuristic, in its *e/d* sense.

- In a social setting with an institutional bias or emphasis on multiculturalism as a legal prescription and/or a valued ideal

Now, our goal as practitioners is, of course, to avoid or minimize errors of all sorts, and generally to practice in efficient, equitable, productive, and ethical ways. We wish to avoid both sorts of mistakes. But speaking again heuristically, and with reference to efficiency, equity, ethics, and so on, which do you think is the worse error: underestimating culture's impacts or overestimating them?

Assuming that both sorts of errors will affect the efficiency of the intervention—affect the ease of communicational flow, perhaps—your practitioner common sense (as well as a liberal's tendency toward enhancing cultural sensitivity in the multicultural settings in which most of us do our work) might hold that in the end underestimating culture's impact may be the worse error of the two. What harm, after all, can a little oversensitivity to culture do?

Overvaluing Culture: Some Consequences of Type II Errors

The most obvious case for harm occurs in such settings as Apartheid South Africa where, as Kuper (1999) notes, culture was simply a crude stand-in for race. Racism operates according to a deficit model, where relations among cultural (i.e., ethnic, racial, or national) groups are hierarchical; diversity entails disparity; and cultural differences, from the perspective of the dominant group, become indices of deficiency—intellectual, moral, or human.

Multiculturalism, operating with a notion of relativism that valorizes all cultural groups, avoids this more obvious danger of racism. However, so long as ideological valorization of all is still accompanied by structural socioeconomic disparities among the groups, then the danger or harm is not so much avoided as driven underground, further from critical view.

This is the core of Howard Gadlin's (1994) critique of cultural approaches to conflict resolution in multicultural, multiracial societies where racism (as structural inequality and domination) is nevertheless an existential fact of social life. An experienced practitioner, Gadlin focuses on the United States and African-American–white conflicts in the workplace, often in university settings where the normative commitment to multiculturalism and nondiscrimination is quite strong. He points out that (since the cultural turn in conflict resolution studies and practice) "Cultural background is usually referred to as one of the contributing factors" to these interpersonal workplace conflicts (Gadlin 1994:36). He cites Kochman's (1981) study of contrasting African–American and white "cultural styles" in communication as evidence of this approach. His point is not so much to deny the existence of such styles (differential aggressivity, eye contact, and face-saving are three things he mentions; p. 37)—a point I shall return to later—but rather to think that one can abstract a notion of, say, African-American (or white) culture separate from the total context of black–white relations in a structurally racist society. Moreover, this context is what African Americans and white Americans *share*. Rather than thinking of culture, mechanically, as something that sets the groups apart and marks their difference, Gadlin argues that this context

> provides the framework within which cultural differences assume the significance that they do .... When intercultural conflict (conflict between members of different races in a racist society) occurs, it cannot be understood by looking only at the cultural differences between the conflicting groups because these differences, themselves, in part, constitute the very racism of which the conflict is one of many expressions. (Gadlin 1994:39)

An even more scathing attack on the misuse of culture comes from the Norwegian social anthropologist Unni Wikan, writing about the lives of immigrants and refugees (mainly from Muslim countries in the Middle East and South Asia) in Norway, and to some extent other Scandinavian and Western European countries (Wikan 2002). Her book is called *Generous Betrayal* (actually the title of a chapter in Finkielkraut 1995), her name for the "welfare colonialism" of liberal, even progressive, European states that sustains immigrants and refugees but insidiously so, at the cost of their ever attaining equality and independence. The main culprit, for her, is a slavish commitment to multiculturalism, to "preserving" and "respecting" the cultures of their immigrants—along with a fear (at least among public figures or intellectuals) of being labeled a racist for any action deemed disrespectful of culture. But whose culture is being preserved, at what costs—and who pays the price? Who are the principal victims of generous betrayal?

Wikan argues that the most marginalized and disempowered in the immigrant/refugee communities pay the price, particularly women and children. Involuntary arranged marriages, forcible repatriation to their (or their parents') countries of origin, beatings (and worse) for bringing "shame" or violations of family or clan "honor," or simply behaving too much like their Norwegian teenage classmates, have been egregiously ignored by Norwegian authorities (social and child welfare workers, the courts and police) reluctant to appear racist and disrespectful of culture. Once again, the question arises: Whose culture? Wikan notes that it is almost always men (elders, sages—patriarchs) from the immigrant groups who represent the groups to the authorities. When they seek to prevent the Norwegian authorities from interfering in their community's affairs, they speak passionately of "preserving their culture." Here, culture is a profoundly experience-near concept, representing faith, tradition, morality—identity. As political spokesmen for their communities, as ethnic politicians or brokers, they represent the community as having one voice—a perfectly shared culture, in effect. But this is not so. It is, Wikan recounts, a Bosnian male who asks an assembled group of politicians: "Why is it that if a Norwegian won't let his daughter marry an immigrant, it's called racism, but if an immigrant won't let his daughter marry a Norwegian, it's called culture?" (2002:45). In the end, nevertheless, it is the voices of her female interlocutors, the heart of the book, themselves members of these communities and victims of abuse (not all have survived), that are the most striking with respect to questioning a single and monolithic definition of culture. A Norwegian-Pakistani woman, Nasim Karim, survived a forced repatriation and marriage and severe beatings before she found asylum in a Norwegian embassy. Having returned to Norway and become an activist on behalf of immigrant and refugee women and children, she addressed the Norwegian Parliament: "When a man is subject to violence, it is called torture, but when a woman is subject to violence, it is called culture" (2002:107).

For Wikan, the question of who gets to define culture is ultimately a political one, meaning that it comes down to issues of power and privilege. The question of who pays for culture so defined is a moral one, indeed, a question of individual human rights. Here she cites the Indian anthropologist Veena Das: "Culture is a way of distributing pain unequally in populations." If this is the case, then Wikan concludes, "respect for 'the culture' is a flawed moral principle" (2002:28).

Reflecting on Gadlin and Wikan, it is clear that the simple and perhaps for practitioners commonsensical impulse to say that a little overattention to culture (our Type II error) can't hurt is problematic. This is so because overvaluing cultural impacts can be deleterious for the weaker, disempowered, or subordinate parties in the conflict or dispute. It can affect the equity of the intervention's outcome, its justice. But what must count here is, yet again, the sense or conception of culture that we mean. What is problematic is ignoring the difference between culture *e/n* and culture *e/d*, or mistaking one sort for the other. For practitioners at the point of diagnosing the cultural part of the dispute or conflict, it is the difference between pursuing *cultural analysis* and *culturalism*. Analysis aims to get at culture as an experience-distant idea—*and this includes plumbing the experience-near aspects of it*. In contrast, culturalism is a politico-moral stance, a statement about "identity politics mobilized at the level" of the ethnic group or nation-state (Appadurai 1996:15). Overvaluing culture (*e/n*), culturalism, can result in a practitioner's understanding of and approach to a dispute or conflict that proves harmful to some of the parties because it will

- Mask or efface underlying structural issues such as gender, class, ethnic discrimination, or racism, in favor of attention to individuating or communication-biased issues like communicational styles.
- Reify culture as an agent capable of action on its own terms.
- Essentialize culture towards a single and unified expression.
- Homogenize all group members toward invariant behavioral stereotypes.
- Risk replacing older, nineteenth-century notions of essentialized racial differences with twenty-first-century ideas of cultural ones—Balibar's (1991) "racism without race."

This final point is especially acute. We have gained nothing—on the contrary, promulgated much harm—if we embrace the cultural turn and end up replacing racism as a way of dealing with diversity with a culturalism enlisted for the same ends.

With this critique in mind, it is reasonable to ask, "Can or ought we preserve the concept of culture at all?" I think this question can be broken into two parts. The first part asks about the utility of the concept, its referents. This part I address below. The second question, more vexing, has to do with the way I have used culture in this chapter for the practice of conflict resolution. This I take up in Chapter 9.

Writing *for* Culture

Even as the importance of paying attention to culture has gained legitimacy in the conflict resolution and ADR community, the concept has come under acute criticism among scholars and theorists from fields ostensibly devoted to its study and elucidation: anthropology and cultural studies. Some have written explicitly "against culture" (Abu-Lughod 1991) or have advised doing away with the term completely (Kuper 1999). Brigg (2008:49) writes of the "constitutive incompleteness of culture as a way of knowing human difference." Yet even among the strongest critics of the notion, one finds ambivalence, reflecting the fact that if we do away with *culture,* we will just need to invent some other term to take its place. Immediately after voicing his critique, Brigg acknowledges the fundamental importance of culture. James Clifford writes, "Culture is a deeply compromised idea I cannot yet do without" (1988:10). Arjun Appadurai confesses, "I frequently find myself troubled by the word *culture* as a noun, but centrally attached to the adjectival form of the word, that is, *cultural*" (1996:12). Paralleling the distinction made here between experience-near and experience-distant, Appadurai borrows a distinction for the two senses of culture from structural linguistics ("marked/unmarked") and ends up simply assigning them numerals: "Culture 1 [i.e., "unmarked"—culture *e/d*], constituting a virtually open-ended archive of differences is consciously shaped into Culture 2 ["marked"—culture *e/n*], that subset of these differences that constitutes the diacritics of group identity" (Appadurai 1996:14).

The reluctance to lose culture entirely can be explained if we look carefully at the two works featured in this chapter that have been most substantively critical of it, Gadlin (1994) and Wikan (2002). Gadlin, even as he cautions us against over-deploying culture in our understanding of interracial conflicts in America, readily notes that stylistic elements important for interpersonal communication, such as aggressivity, eye contact, and face saving, "will be manifested differently in different groups, and expectations of the mediator will also differ for different groups. For that matter, noticeable differences emerge from one culture to the next in the preference given to group versus individual identity" (Gadlin 1994:37). These are hardly trivial matters if one is concerned with conflict or dispute resolution process or, more generally, communicational competence. More profoundly, the entire point of Gadlin's critique of cultural analysis is to further the conception of a "culture of racism" as fundamentally structuring black–white social relations in the United States. In the end, therefore, even as Gadlin criticizes culture, he falls back on relying crucially on the term for what it represents.

Unni Wikan, declares, on the one hand, that culture is a "flawed moral principle," and demonstrates with great passion the many ways that invoking its authority has served to foster the abuse of immigrant and refugee women and children in Scandinavia; but she later writes, "Can we then throw the 'culture' concept overboard? No, in my opinion .... But we can use the concept with sensitivity and care" (Wikan 2002:82). The concept of culture is not so easily jettisoned because, as one reads Wikan's book, it so obviously permeates the very core of her analysis and critique. How else can one describe (and deconstruct), as she does, such notions the immigrants or refugees bring with them as *honor, shame, clan* (solidarity), *patriarchy*—or ethnic identity and the liberal European state's "welfare colonialism," for that matter?

There have been more than a few candidates for culture's replacement, depending on the era, the theorist, or the idiom, including collective consciousness, discourse, episteme, habitus, worldview, mind-set, groupthink—even that old standby (itself not lacking much in the way of baggage from the last century or two), ideology. Like Appadurai, wishing to cling to the adjective if not the noun—or like Gadlin and Wikan, for that matter—I continue to believe the term is useful and, for what it represents for purposes of analysis and practice, is indispensable as well. In terms of the argument developed here, this means we need to keep the two senses of culture, the *e/d* and *e/n*, conceptually separate. We should not conflate or confuse the two, even as we may expect the parties in the conflict or dispute to do so routinely. Most crucially, we should not allow, in our analysis and practice, the *e/d* sense of the term to devolve entirely—or unchallenged—into the *e/n* sense of it, because in that way we admit the probability that culture will become, as so many have warned, simply a politically correct synonym for race (Balibar 1991; Gadlin 1994; Finkielkraut 1995; Wikan 2002). In the end, paraphrasing Appadurai, as culture *e/n* is "consciously shaped" out of the "archive," the raw material, of culture *e/d*, then—as theorists or as self-aware practitioners—we need a conception of culture "in the technical sense" in order to do our analytical, diagnostic, and interventionary work.

It is, however, precisely at this point that the second critical reservation about the culture concept is raised. This questions our very notions of analysis and diagnosis and, by implication, our warrant for interventionary work in the first place: our pretext. This I take up again in Chapter 9.

Part 2

Culture and Identity, Dilemmas of Power

6

Culture Theory, Culture Clash, and the Practice of Conflict Resolution

Introduction

In several chapters, I argue implicitly that in the emergent field of conflict resolution our accepted "practice" goes a long way to constitute our accepted "theory." I made this argument explicitly in *Culture and Conflict Resolution* (1998), referring to Fisher and Ury's seminal *Getting to Yes* (1981/1991) and the theory of interest-based principled negotiation. Skilled negotiators will distill years of practice experience into formalized theories of negotiation, in the manner of domain experts constituting expert systems. In conflict resolution, therefore, "where practice is situated, there theory is derived," and in our field for many years, "practice overwhelmingly has been culturally situated within a North American, male, white, and middle-class world" (Avruch 1998:78). This, indeed, was one of the several reasons for culture's neglect in the field; and it changed not only as scholars and researchers interested in culture began to participate in the field's development but also as the pool of practitioners diversified culturally (including gender) and began to question the relevance of accepted practice in other places—questioning the *consequences* of such practice has only recently been the case. Consequences become relevant as cultural others are made to conduct themselves (say, to negotiate or mediate) under a regime of practice not their own. In this case, the benefit goes to those who enjoy home court advantage.

But as is true in many fields, the relationship of practice to theory, or vice versa, is a dialectical one. One can start with practice and induce one's way to theory, or one can begin with theory—or in this case, with theories, about conflict and about culture—and deduce one's way to practice—though in either case it is perhaps Pierce's notion of *abduction* that makes better sense. In this chapter, I start with theory and the assumption that different theories of social conflict will prescribe different modalities of possible or desirable conflict resolution practice. Although many theories of conflict ignore the importance of culture, this chapter focuses critically on a theory of global conflict based on a particular conception of culture, Samuel Huntington's influential thesis on the "clash of civilizations."

Despite the (neo)realist dismissal of culture in favor of power as *the* important variable in understanding the relations of states in the international arena,[1] a particular take on culture did arise from applied social science conducted during the Second World War, a tradition of so-called national character studies, which conflated culture with nationality and linked the latter to individual personality traits (culture is nationality is personality writ large), relying largely on Freudian or developmental personality theories.[2] Occasionally, one could find national character work or conceptions cited even by arch realists (e.g., Morgenthau and Thompson 1985:151), but mostly this work fell out of favor in social science by the 1950s and was never of much influence in theorizing social conflict or conflict resolution (but see the following discussion of Patai). In any case, even as Peter Black and I bemoaned the neglect of culture in early conflict resolution theory and practice resulting from the dominance of state and power paradigms of realist or neorealist IR (Black and Avruch 1993), or criticized its effacement due to the universalizing biogenetics of basic human needs (Avruch and Black 1987) or rational choice theory (Avruch and Black 1990; and Chapter 7 in this volume), we also felt that the extant uses of culture, as in national character work, seemed theoretically thin and inadequate—and, in any case, of not much use or influence in broader conflict theory.

Culture Is Totalizing, Culture Is Primordial

The end of the Cold War, however, brought a revivified concept of culture onto the scene, mostly shorn of Freudian overtones, and challenging even the conceptual dominance of the state (though not of power) as the main actor in neorealist IR. Moreover, this view of culture was explicitly connected to explanations of social conflict and prescriptions for conflict management—if not resolution. And unlike national character theory, it has proved influential in American policy-making circles. This view of culture is best represented by Samuel Huntington's Clash of Civilization paradigm (Huntington 1993, 1996). The outline of this theory is widely and well known. It has predecessors in Toynbee and Spengler, both in the substance of his argument and the degree of pessimism in his predictions. A civilization, according to Huntington

(1993:24), "is the highest cultural grouping of people and the broadest level of cultural identity people have short of that which distinguishes humans from other species." Seven major civilizations are identified: Western, Confucian, Japanese, Islamic, Hindu, Slavic-Orthodox, and Latin American; "and possibly," as an eighth, African. From the very beginning, Huntington made it clear that he was not using the idea of "clash" metaphorically. He was proposing a strong theory—strong in the positivist's predictive sense—of social conflict. "The clash of civilizations will dominate global politics," he wrote in the earlier influential essay, which preceded the book and appeared in *Foreign Affairs*. "The fault lines between civilizations will be the battle lines of the future" (Huntington 1993:22).

The critical response to Huntington's thesis was almost as vigorous as the thesis itself and came from many quarters: anthropology (Gusterson 2005), area specialists (Bieber 1999), cultural studies (White 1994), conflict resolution (Rubenstein and Crocker 1994), and political science (Ajami 1993), to cite just a few examples. Among other things, critics cited the weakness of Huntington's definition of civilization or the misalignment of its scale (Japan, a single nation-state, as equivalent to more than 1 billion Muslims worldwide); his misreading of the evidence in recent history (many pointed to the more frequent—and deadly— occurrence of conflict within civilizations than between them); his maligning of Islam ("Islam's borders are bloody" [1996:256]); his simplification of global dynamics (as in the phrase "the West vs. the Rest"); and his ethnocentrism—his brief for the uniqueness and superiority of Western civilization.

Some critics spoke of Huntington's theory explicitly as a result of and a response to the end of the Cold War and the loss of the West's main ideological rival, the Soviet Union. In 1989–1990, the ideological battle between East and West appeared over and done with. But world peace or a new world order (under a beneficent *pax Americana*) did not materialize. Throughout the early and mid-1990s, deadly ethnic conflicts rended societies; states fell apart or into civil war; concentration camps reappeared in Europe, and genocide, in Africa. In the Middle East, existing conflicts remained as intractable as ever, and new ones soon emerged. The UN proved impotent in Bosnia and criminally negligent in Rwanda; and the United States proved a failed humanitarian and conflict resolutionist third party in Blackhawk-down Somalia. Pessimism seemed appropriate, and a new collection of adversaries, this one linguistic, racial, ethnic, national, or religious—civilizational or cultural—seemed to be the cause of it all. Huntington's clash of civilizations epitomized these post–Cold War times perfectly and provided policy makers (as we shall see) with a blueprint for (re)action.

Huntington's conception of civilization also epitomizes most of the inadequate conceptions of culture that I discussed in Chapter 1. For one thing, the vastness of scale of, say, Islamic civilization, had the effect of homogenizing important and obvious cultural-historical differences among societies as different as Morocco, Pakistan, and Indonesia. For another, the imputation of strong and long-lasting political alliances among states due to the natural "kin feeling" of shared civilization flew in the face of much evidence to the contrary. More Muslims died in the eight-year war between Iraq and Iran—estimates range up to 1.5 million—than in any modern encounter with the West. Shared Islam was insufficient to keep West and East Pakistan (Bangladesh) united. These civilizational units were portrayed as stable entities acting with a logic of their own, their vast and sociologically/ethnically/linguistically diverse populations acting as if they were undifferentiated (and somewhat robotic) masses. To this list, one can add the sense of timelessness, or ahistoricism.

In fact, the idea that these units somehow exist "out of time" and now face us, and one another, in guises virtually unchanged since their ancient beginnings—that they are *primordial*—is to be found in several conceptions of the place of culture in post–Cold War times. A good example is Robert Kaplan's work, and particularly his book *Balkan Ghosts* (1993), which presents the entire region to readers as "the last remnants of Europeans' tribal mentality ... locked into a past where ethnic loyalties and violence reign, a timeless place that is both a great producer and exporter of evil to the rest of Europe" (Bringa 2005:61). The resonances here are remarkable: not just timelessness and locked-in lack of change, but psychic evolution is invoked, an older stratum of European Mentality from which Belgians, French, and Germans presumably evolved that nevertheless survives deep in the brains of residents of the Balkans. Completing the picture of Dantesque primordial violence, there is export-quality Evil. And Kaplan's book *was* read. One of the readers of *Balkan Ghosts* in 1993 was President Clinton, and reading the account of ancient and intractable hatreds and feuds influenced him, it is said, from refraining to commit American forces to Bosnia in 1993 (Bringa 2005:61).[3]

Even older national character conceptions of culture found a new audience, Raphael Patai's *The Arab Mind*, first published in 1973. The book was featured in Edward Said's (1978) seminal attack on Orientalism. It was likewise dismissed by most area specialists or scholars of the Middle East—ethnographers in particular, who had the most lived experience on the ground. In their view, *The Arab Mind* is a throwback to dubious national character studies, one published two decades after that tradition's heyday.

But Patai's book, we are told, "continued to be read in diplomatic and military circles." It was reissued in 2001, with a new introduction by the director of Middle East Studies at the JFK Special Warfare Center and School at Fort Bragg, and was regularly taught there.[4] Seymour Hersh, in his May 5, 2004, article in *The New Yorker*, on the roots of the Abu Ghraib torture scandal, writes that he was told that *The Arab Mind*, with its analysis of Arab attitudes toward sexuality, shame, and humiliation, became "the bible of the neocons on Arab behavior." Its "findings" were apparently integrated into the interrogation routines—which we now know included sexual torture and humiliation—carried out at Abu Ghraib.[5]

I do not mean to imply that Patai, who died in 1996, ever intended his work to be used as an instruction manual for torturers, any more than Kaplan wanted his *Balkan Ghosts* somehow to be responsibly connected to the atrocities of Srebrenica.[6] Both books raise questions about the uses of social science knowledge by political and military actors—important questions that I do not, however, engage here.[7] Here, I want to underline the nature of the knowledge, specifically the representation of culture, that Huntington, Kaplan, and Patai's works all feature. In all these works *culture* is essentialized and totalized, reified and stripped of internal complexity or sociological diversity, removed from time (history) or projected backward into some unchanging (and usually dangerous or savage or unevolved) primordial past. And in all these cases, as well, the works proved themselves influential in certain political, policy-making, or intelligence-gathering circles—despite their dismissal by area specialists or scholars. "There is nothing so useful," Kurt Lewin (1951) famously remarked, "as a good theory." It is the various *uses* to which theory is put that concern me here: What understandings of social conflict, and which practices of conflict resolution, are entailed by this conception of culture?

Conflict Theory in a Totalized and Primordial World

The first thing to be said about Huntington's theory (elaborated in some ways by Kaplan's primordializing of history and Patai's homogenizing of mind) is that it *is*, fundamentally, a theory of social conflict. He does not intend the idea of "clash" metaphorically. Like realism and neorealism, it is also fundamentally a theory espousing the importance of power: "Culture," he writes, "follows power" (1996:310). Unlike the neorealists, however, who steered clear of issues of morality or values—except to bemoan leaders or states who foolishly invoked them, usually to the detriment of their country's national interests—Huntington engages morality and values as central to the dynamics of the clash. Specifically, he emphasizes the uniqueness of the "cultural core" of the West, including its "central component, Christianity," and what he comes to epitomize as "the American Creed … liberty, democracy, individualism, equality before the law, constitutionalism, private property" (1996:305).

The great dynamic of modern history, Huntington contends, is the interaction between modernization and Westernization. In the course of its own history, the West (epitomized eventually by its "core country," the United States) modernized and developed its unique Western "cultural core." But modernization does not imply, as once was assumed, Westernization. Japan successfully modernized without becoming Western. The rest of the world is modernizing in important ways—mostly technological and militarily— but remaining "traditional" in other ways, for instance in supporting non-democratic forms of governance, in favoring collectivism or communalism over individualism, with a concomitant mistrust of ideas of individual liberty and other neoliberal ideals. The military and technological modernization of the other civilizations, particularly Asian but increasingly Muslim as well, together with a West that "no longer has the economic or demographic dynamism required to impose its will on other societies" (1996:310) means that Western hegemony is decreasing, while Asian and Muslim ("Confucian and Islamic") civilizations are economically, demographically, and militarily on the rise. The groundwork for future and fateful civilizational clashes lies in a global arena characterized by power shifts and the uncertainties of changing hierarchies.

Interestingly, the first conflict or clash is not between civilizations but, so far as the West and the United States are concerned, *within* them. Here Huntington (1996:305) takes "multiculturalists" and other sorts of "liberals" to task for weakening the integrity of the American Creed by seeking to dilute it with a deadly mixture of political correctness, cultural relativism, and the unabashed welcoming of unassimilable immigrants (particularly Muslims in Western Europe and Hispanics in the United States). They also deny or denigrate the virtues of a common American culture while promoting "racial, ethnic, and other subnational cultural identities and groupings." Although Huntington's critique of the "multicultural" liberal left does not partake of the animus displayed by such conservative polemicists as Dinesh D'Souza (2007)—who, like the Reverend Falwell, also blames the liberal left for the 9/11 tragedy—it does point to the value conflicts that characterize current American political discourse.

Finally, if one takes Huntington's notion of civilizational conflict, and especially his depiction of a Western "cultural core" and "the American Creed" as, momentarily, ethnography and not "theory" (i.e., as a true *ethnotheory* of conflict)—a valid description of how certain neoconservative Western "natives" (a few of them more than a little politically influential) view the world—then attention to general conflict theory not surprisingly leads us to the idea of images and imaging, enemy images and mirror images in particular (Boulding 1956; White 1965; Kelman 1997:222–226). Edward Said (1978) wrote of the way the West "orientalized" the Other, referring mainly to Islamic societies and cultures and the sorts of depictional inadequacies of culture mentioned above. It is not surprising that symmetrical perceptual processes can be found in the form of "Occidentalism" (Carrier 1995; Buruma and Maragalit 2005). Occidentalism features the same homogenizing, totalizing, and essentializing view of culture and civilization as does its Western "mirror-imaging" counterpart. Together, Orientalism and Occidentalism form what Bruno Latour (1993) has called a "symmetrical anthropology." Moreover, if Occidentalism is as influential a worldview "out there" as "the West versus the Rest" is for guardians of the American Creed, then in effect it makes the clash of civilizations symmetrical—and also, crucially, a potentially self-fulfilling prophecy.[8]

These are the ways in which Huntington's understanding of culture, as a mega-concept called civilization, implies a theory of social (indeed, global) conflict. Theories of conflict also entail associated ethnotheories (native or folk theories) of conflict resolution, and associated (ethno)practices as well. What sorts of *conflict resolution* does the clash of civilizations imply?

Conflict Resolution in the Clash of Civilizations

Theories are practical, to echo Lewin, precisely because they can specify, pre-scribe, or justify modes of *practice*, action in the world. Take the postulates of neorealism as a theory of nation-state conflict. In an essentially amoral universe of autonomous states seeking rationally to maximize national in-terests through the arts of deploying power, it may not be useful to think of "conflict resolution" at all in the sense that many in the field do. Pruitt and Kim (2004:190–191) identify a continuum of problem-solving outcomes, from "conflict management," dealing mostly with procedures to deescalate conflict or prevent further escalation; to "conflict settlement," which goes beyond procedural matters to take up substantive ones dealing "with enough of the issues that parties are willing to give up their ... struggle"; to what they called "conflict resolution, an agreement in which most or all of the issues are cleared up." A similar continuum is offered by Ramsbotham and colleagues, who include an even more radical understanding of conflict resolution favored by a new generation of specialists, one that strives to go beyond mere resolution to what they call "conflict transformation," whereby the very relationships among the contesting parties are changed, and the "underlying tasks of struc-tural and cultural peacebuilding" are engaged (Ramsbotham et al. 2005:29). Thus, transformation of "conflictual relationships requires healing trauma, addressing the roots of the conflict, and pursuing justice" (Schirch 2006:78). These are strong requirements, indeed.

Now consider what conflict *resolution* looks like in a realist's world. Given the postulates of realist/neorealist conflict theory, it is easy to imagine a prac-tice built around the *management* of conflicts between states, and even their occasional *settlement* (though most settlements are rarely taken to be final and definitive). In an imagined world where real or perceived power imbalances have the potential to unsettle the status quo state system, stable balances of power, achieved through real alliances or such shared or recognized perceptions as the threat of Mutual Assured Destruction (or other forms of deterrence), are the surest means of managing potential conflicts. The idea of "contain-ment" of dangerous or threatening states also becomes a practical goal. On the other hand, *resolution* of conflicts, outside the state of affairs that might follow war and the unambiguous defeat and unconditional surrender of an enemy—Nazism or Japanese imperial militarism in 1945—or that follows regime change of other sorts, is more difficult to imagine as a practice flow-ing logically out of realism. Meanwhile, conflict *transformation*, concerned with reconciling relationships, trauma, healing, and justice, is unimaginable as a mode of practice (statecraft, diplomacy, warfighting) given the theory's postulates of amoral, maximizing, interest- and power-seeking states.[9]

What sorts of practice can be associated with Huntington's clash of civili-zations understanding of culture? Both Huntington and realists/neorealists make power fundamental to their thinking. But whereas morality and values are at best irrelevant to realism, they are central to Huntington's definition of a civilization's "cultural core." For realists, national interests are the unchanging center in a changing global environment: Achieving, conserving, *maximizing* them are the sine qua non of successful statecraft. Morality and values can only get in the way.[10] For Huntington, values (as in "tradition") are central and perduring. Satisfying or being true to them—which may also mean actively resisting the imposition of alien values or traditions—and to other "kin countries" who share them, are key civilizational goals.

In fact, Huntington's prescriptions for managing conflict are more nuanced than some of his harshest critics imply. In the earlier (1993) *Foreign Affairs* essay (as in the later and more elaborate 1996 book), he distinguishes shorter- from longer-term approaches. Both are oriented toward a longer-term historical view that features a decline in the West's power (economic and military strength) vis-à-vis the Rest (especially vis-à-vis a potential Confucian-Islamic alliance). Given this concern with power, the short-term approaches most closely resemble realist or neorealist ideas in practice: nurture alliances with countries within (Western) civilization, or encourage cooperation with those civilizations normatively—"genealogically"—closer to the West (e.g., Slavic-Orthodox ones). Some prescriptions look like classic conflict management cum preventive diplomacy: "prevent escalation of local inter-civilizational conflicts into major intercivilizational wars." A few might raise an eyebrow or two among the some residents of the Rest: "limit expansion of the military strength of Confucian and Islamic states." And some might appear to the Rest (and some of us in the West) as downright neocolonial and straightforwardly Machiavellian: "exploit differences and conflict among Confucian and Islamic states" (1993:49). As with realists, conflict management is possible and extolled; conflict settlement, rarer; and conflict resolution, not so likely.

The longer-term modalities of practice suggested by the Clash are more interesting, nuanced, and often overlooked by Huntington's critics. Civilizational differences based upon core values or traditions will not go away or, for that matter, change very much. (Here is where culture's "timelessness" counts strongly.) The West is modern and "Western." The Rest are unevenly modernizing (mostly in technology and military areas) and not much Western—Confucian and Islamic civilizations aggressively so. And the power of the West is in decline. Therefore the long-term prescription for managing (intercivilizational) conflict, though it will certainly require the West to maintain sufficient power to protect its interests, will also require *accommodation*. Huntington (1993:49) continues: "It will also, however, require the West to develop a profound understanding of the basic religious and philosophical assumptions underlying other civilizations and the ways in which people in those civilizations see their interests. It will require an effort to identify elements of commonality between Western and other civilizations."

In the elaboration of this argument in the book (1996) a few important changes from the 1993 essay are evident. First, in a list of conflict management and accommodative steps the West should follow, the straightforward Machiavellian tactic of encouraging or sowing division and conflict within rival civilizations is now nowhere to be found (1996:312). It is replaced by an opposite admonition, what Huntington calls the "abstention rule." This rule holds "that core states abstain from intervention in conflicts in other civilizations is the first requirement of peace in a multicivilizational, multipolar world" (1996:316). He would agree with realists who have argued that the neoconservative drive to export democracy through armed invasion and forceful regime change, as the United States is attempting to do in the Middle East, is misguided. But agreement in this regard stems from different sources. Realists might feel that such a use of American treasure and blood along with the intensification of anti-American attitudes and alliances that ensue are clearly not in our national interest. Huntington would more likely say that the "American creed" is quite simply unexportable—and any attempt to do so "is probably the single most dangerous source of instability and potential global conflict in a multicivilizational world" (1996:312). Many of Huntington's more liberal or progressive critics—or conservative supporters of the "West versus the Rest" thesis, for that matter—underestimate his strong opposition to an American Empire or imperial interventions, most especially in their hypermoralizing ("bring democracy, freedom and liberty to all!") manifestations (1996:310).

Yet, he is no simple isolationist, another possible reaction to a multicivilizational world that some conservative thinkers adopt. In his book, Huntington elaborates on the notion, raised in his essay, of searching for mutual understanding and "commonalities" among civilizations. In another curiously nuanced argument, he reiterates his condemnation of "multiculturalists" operating *within* the West (as noted above), whose celebration of non-Western values or traditions as examples to be appreciated by the West, or even for the West to emulate, has the effect of weakening Western identity and solidarity. But this is later balanced by the necessity to realize that, viewed as a whole, the global civilizational *system* is by definition "multicultural." That is the whole point of theorizing vast and perduring civilizational blocs that will not go away because of globalizing capitalism. (Indeed, such globalization, now viewed by some among the Rest as "penetration," is another reason to resent and resist the West—another source of conflict.) "In a multicivilizational world," he writes, "the constructive course is to renounce universalism, accept diversity, and seek commonalities" (1996:318). Huntington here is not a Cold Warrior prescribing a conflict management policy based upon *containment* of the Other, à la George Kennan's "long telegram" and the Truman Doctrine; nor is he an isolationist suggesting a fortress mentality and retreat from the global system of civilizations. Searching for commonalities implies an engagement with the Rest (though "keep your powder dry").

Although he does not call for it precisely in such terms, one way to understand Huntington's search for commonalities is by invoking the idea of dialogue. The former president of Iran, Mohammed Khatami, reacting explicitly to Huntington's clash of civilizations, offered the idea of a "dialogue of civilizations," in a speech before the United Nations. For its part, the United Nations voted in November of 1998 to make 2001 the Year of Dialogue among

Civilizations. It also did so explicitly in reaction to Huntington's formulation: in voting for a year devoted to dialogue, the "assembly rejected the notion of a 'Clash of Civilization' which is based on the notion that inter-civilizational understanding is impossible. The General Assembly expressed its firm determination to facilitate just such a dialogue ... through an active exchange of ideas, visions and aspirations."[11] And 2001 did witness a major UNESCO conference on dialogue held in Japan, and a number of workshops organized by the United Nations University (in Tokyo) on dialogue in science, ethics, education, and the media. According to the UN's website, all occurred before or during the summer of 2001. All occurred before September 11.

Some would argue that given the events of 9/11 and the Global War on Terror—to many the bloody embodiment of Huntington's Clash—such dialogue is called for now more than ever. Certainly, at the local and community levels, dialogue has been used to bring together ethnically and religiously diverse members of a multicultural Northern Virginia community to address some of the fears, uncertainties, and prejudices that have arisen in the post-9/11 world (Cheldelin 2006). Dialogue has been used in other parts of the United States, sometimes framed as "public conversations," to explore many of these same issues.[12] Dialogue has established itself among some conflict resolution practitioners as a technique or tool different from negotiation, mediation, ADR, problem-solving workshops, and so on. It is especially suited for conflicts involving deeply held values or contentious issues of morality—abortion, capital punishment, gay rights—and even in some land use and development disputes (Maiese 2003).

Nevertheless, there are problems with envisioning dialogue as the full antidote to civilizational clash. First, dialogue presupposes the agency of individuals. At the level of civilizations clashing, agency is rare. Instead, one gets the sense of demographically huge, culturally monolithic blocs, or creeds or core values, colliding. It is hard to sustain a place for mutually engaged and agentic individuals within the terms of Huntington's mega-formulation. Second, there is the problem, pointed out by critics but also recognized by many who advocate dialogue, presented by power imbalances among participants. It is hard to imagine such imbalances not intruding on "civilizational dialogue," because power asymmetry is intrinsic to the structure of the international system of states as well as central to the conflict dynamic of Huntington's theory of civilizations. Latin America and Africa (to speak momentarily in Huntington's coagulating voice) certainly would not feel they enter a dialogue with North Americans as equals. Islam and China both feel the iron grip of imperial and colonial history degradingly around their throats. It would be difficult, in any case, to keep power or histories of oppression outside of the dialogue room.

Finally, there is the question of what dialogues accomplish—a question raised mainly by its critics. In the end, dialogue is about talk and exchange of ideas, mutual learning and the sharing of understanding, the gaining of trust and the creation of empathy. This is no small thing, but it seems some distance from conceptions of conflict resolution or transformation that imply *changing*

existing structures of disparities and inequities, resource extraction or distribution, capital and human flows. Such structures comprise the "systems of
inequality," as the critics from a conflict resolution perspective of Huntington's
search for commonalities have said, "that make social life around the globe
a struggle for individual and group survival—systems that feed the illusion
that either one civilization or another must be dominant" (Rubenstein and
Crocker 1994:128). The challenge for dialogue is to confront power. (To be
fair, I think this remains the challenge for all of conflict resolution, taken up
in Chapter 9.) The challenge for dialogue, if cultural conflict is conceived in
mega-civilizational terms, is how a practice focused on individual voices (on
talk) can effect systemic—indeed, *global* systemic—change.

Conflict Theory and Practice within the Clash of Civilizations

Although the critique of dialogue is substantial, nevertheless the search for
commonalities is not to be dismissed. After all, the shared understanding of
common *interests*—the desire to avoid mutually assured destruction—func-
tioned as a partial conflict management device during the Cold War. Given the
limitations of intercultural dialogue when culture is conceived as civilization,
the theory of conflict that precipitates from the clash of civilizations resembles
in the end nothing so much as realism, and thus the conflict resolution practices resemble realism's as well: contain, deter, and discomfit your enemies;
maintain hegemony if possible, and if not, balance power through alliances
at all events. Along with realism, Huntington disdains U.S. foreign interventions with moralizing rationales, such as spreading democracy and freedom.
If anything, he goes further than many realists by calling such intervention
"the single most dangerous source of instability and potential global conflict"
in the world today (1996:312). Thus, the line that supposedly helped keep
the United States out of efforts to prevent a fragmenting Yugoslavia (with its
"ancient tribal hatreds") from complete dissolution in the early 1990s—"we
don't have a dog in that fight"—summarizes a large part of both realist and
Huntington's foreign policy prescriptions.[13] In this sense, the more hardheaded
and Machiavellian prescriptions outlined in Huntington's 1993 essay may be
closer to "practical truth" than the search for commonalities in his 1996 book.
The practices suggested by both realism theorists and Huntington resemble
conflict *management* at best. Resolution, on the other hand, is doubtful, and
transformation is a chimera. The key difference is that realism presumes a
world with rational actors seeking to maximize recognized utilities. In the
clash of civilizations, rationality is replaced by assuming the predominance
among actors—at least those in the Rest, if not the West—of the nonrational
calculi of premodern (fundamentalist or primordial) religious belief and blood
and belonging ethnic nationalism.

In all this, what is noteworthy to conflict theorists—if also disheartening—is
how sturdily Huntington's "inadequate ideas" about culture (Avruch 1998)

have withstood the critiques of so many accomplished scholars from across the social sciences. These scholars have attacked the theory from any number of possible points, including its empirical—historical and evidentiary—base. To maliciously paraphrase Lewin, "There's nothing so practical as a bad theory." It almost does not seem to matter whether Huntington's theory of culture is social scientifically valid or not: Ethnic conflict, conditioned on complex and interacting factors of economy and politics, shifting social identities or self-interested leadership and ethnic entrepreneurs, is now reduced to ancient tribal hatreds. Some homogenous, suprahistorical, and geographical entity called "the Arab Mind" is now taught to aspiring diplomats and in military colleges. In all these cases, the *players* have adopted these ideas—both in the West and, judging by jihadists and others, in some significant parts of the Rest as well. These ideas have become part of an overarching ethnotheory of conflict, with associated ethnopraxes, in Avruch and Black's (1991) original sense of the terms. In the "clash of civilizations" view of things, Orientalism has gone far beyond the literary and artistic productions that were the focus of much of Said's (1978) original critique; and in its symmetrical anthropology, Occidentalism has gone far beyond resistance to Coca-Cola and Disney.

We are once again back to the impacted and protean nature of the idea of culture itself. What do the ivory-tower experts know, anyway—historians, anthropologists, social scientists, or area scholars of all kinds? To think of cultures, as the "clash of civilization" model of the world does, as stable, homogenous, undifferentiated, enduring, essential, and totalizing entities is a masterwork of cognitive simplification, of perceptual miserliness in the face of a very complex world. In this view, culture is not an analytical concept at all, but a heuristic or schema by which men and women, some of them influential and with immense power (or weaponry) at their disposal, reason their way through the world. This understanding of culture has other uses in the world. It is also a very powerful discourse and politically motivating ideology. On the one hand, it directs us (as it did Toynbee and Spengler: good Hegelians) to see cultures in idealist terms as stable "norms and values," and away from seeing culture in terms of materialist issues, connected to social change, as resource and capital flows—and away from perceiving inequality and empire. On the other hand, it makes conflict between and among cultures appear primordial and inevitable. Certainly it appears that way to many people worldwide today. Why should this be so?

Especially since the tragedy of 9/11 and the tragedies that have followed in its wake, one could argue that Huntington got something profoundly right: the tendency for global conflict in the post–Cold War era to be understood by many in the discourse of civilizational clash and for contending parties on all sides, in fact, to mobilize around this idea. One might say that Huntington's original analysis in 1993 was prescient. But the many evidentiary problems with the theory pointed out by numerous critics, particularly as evident in the empirical and historical record, belie the validity of the theory and suggest another interpretation of its apparent prescience. For if the theory of civilizational clash is an ethnotheory, a heuristic for understanding global conflict, then, as heuristics do, it will guide the behavior, actions, and reactions of all the parties who use it to reason their way through complex (and threatening) events. If it is *the* heuristic utilized by the elite—political leaders and their ministers and secretaries of defense, media and pundits, religious leaders and others who mold public opinion—then their decisions and actions, capable of producing real effects in the world, will be shaped by its prescriptions. And finally, if this heuristic is effectively symmetrical in its distribution, so that the images among contending parties in different civilizations are mirror images, then a theory of civilizational clash will produce responses, political and military actions, appropriate to the theory. Such policies and responses will produce a particular state of global affairs and international relations. Rather than pre-dicting the state of the world and global conflict, the clash of civilizations helps to bring it about.

"Civilizations" in Conflict? An Alternative Approach to Culture and Conflict Resolution

An alternative to thinking of the world as beset by inevitable conflict between unchanging and monolithic civilizations has to begin with a reassessment of culture—in effect, to decouple the notion of culture from the mega-concept called civilization. It also demands a far more nuanced theory of culture, one that is more attentive to history and ethnography—to social change and the power of locality—and far less imperious with respect to claims of causality.

The apparent monolithic character of any civilization, its homogeneity and coherence, as any historian will tell you, disappears as one examines more closely the dynamics of historical change—population movements, wars, revo-lutions, counterrevolutions, religious reforms, and syncretisms—that combine to bring social change about. Culture, as a far more localized and historically contingent concept, is a better way to "look inside" so-called civilizations. Of course, culture is also a concept constructed by scholars. But compared to civilization, culture has two main advantages. First, when attached to social groups it covers much, much less ground—demographically, geographically, and historically—than does civilization; and second, partly because of its sen-sitivity to more localized settings, it is far more sensitive to social dynamics, including socially based variation (as within subcultures) and historical change.

But for conflict resolution theory and practice, the concept of culture re-quired to improve upon Huntington is not one that merely reduces the scope of what civilization refers to, achieving simply a reduction in scale. For it is possible to have a downscaled version of civilization called culture and still reproduce civilization's main conceptual inadequacies: ideas of homogeneity and historically enduring stability—an essentialized and reified entity capable of action. What we need is a different conceptualization of culture entirely (e.g., Avruch 1998, 2003a, 2003b, 2004). Such a concept of culture is focused closely on the understandings of the world by historically *situated* individuals, and the images, encodements, schemas, and symbols—passed down from generations past (tradition or custom) or formulated by individuals or their contemporaries in the crucible of immediate lived experience and exigency (Avruch 1998:16–21)—with which they make meaning, reason, feel, and act.[14]

Compared to civilization, such a nuanced theory of culture has several advantages for advancing a coherent notion of conflict resolution. *First*, ideas of social transformation and change are intrinsic to the definition. Ideas of timelessness and century-spanning stability cannot be sustained in a definition of culture that requires it to be responsive and adaptive to its environment, and constituted by the cumulative social practice of situated individuals. *Second*, situated individuals, even within a culturally constituted social grouping, are not all identical. Culture is sociologically and psychologically distributed among group members, and thus it is inconceivable to think of individual actors as social robots, all subscribing to the same creed, value sets, or morality, all moving along the same behavioral assembly lines. *Third*, culture conceived in this way—with socially diverse individuals in potentially changing social systems, who may in fact be bearers of multiple cultural identities—means we can think of it as something different from simply a label, a way of naming certain ethnic, religious, or national groups. Rather than referring to mostly static and monolithic social entities, like civilizations, this conception of culture orients us to see complexity and dynamism as inherent social qualities. Put differently, we see culture as contingent, emergent, contestable, and contested. Thus, we can see the social, political, and moral conflicts that are "inside" cultures, and we are less apt to accept uncritically any one public version of it—from political platform to fatwa—as authoritatively or eternally representative or true. *Fourth*, this way of understanding culture helps us to think of it as providing the social and cognitive contexts for behavior but drains it of the necessity also to be causal. This means we ought no longer to think of culture—cultural *differences*, to be precise—as the main causes of social conflict. Culture does not cause conflict. It is, however, the lens through which the causes of conflict are ultimately refracted (Avruch and Black 1993; Avruch 1998). The main causes themselves are more likely to be sought and understood in the systems of inequality, global and local, to which Rubenstein and Crocker (1994) and so many others have referred.

Fifth, and finally, understanding culture in this way rather than as a megaconcept called civilization allows us to reengage the most conflict resolution-friendly response to global conflict that Huntington did in fact propose—a "profound understanding" of other cultures, accommodation to difference, and a search for commonalities. Whatever its limitations, as noted earlier, the promise and hope of dialogue and similar intercultural encounters ought not to be jettisoned too quickly. And by locating culture with historically (and thus politically, religiously, and economically) situated individuals, it is possible to conceive a more realistic sense of dialogue—or any other conflict resolution technique, like problem-solving workshops—in the search for commonalities.

By basing the definition of culture on the notion of shared understandings—cognitions, schemas, symbols—by members *within* social groups, it makes the search for commonalities, or shared understanding, *across* social groups or cultural divides more sensible.

Such an approach even helps us to reframe the apparent timelessness of culture. The past may be relevant to parties in the present not because culture is changeless or primordial, but because the past exists in and informs the present—helping to shape and change it—as one more schema available to actors striving to make sense of their world. Perhaps, as Huntington suggests, we should begin by striving for understanding the others. In his first major address to the American people after 9/11, President Bush declared, "This crusade, this war on terrorism, is gonna take awhile."[15] A few days later, in his State of the Union Address, the president—apparently in an impromptu aside—again used the word *crusade* to describe the coming campaign and (what some now call) the Global War on Terror. The response in the Arab and Muslim world was immediate and—given *their* historical consciousness (images, encodements, schemas, and symbols)—understandably hostile. They understood what *crusade* implied. A serious engagement with culture would mean that an American president understood this—at least this—too.

7

Negotiating Beyond
Interests

The Poverty of Buyer and Seller

Introduction: Negotiation and Conflict Resolution

It is widely understood today that negotiation covers a large territory, both conceptually and behaviorally. At one extreme is the very broad sense of the term as conceived by Anselm Strauss (1978), whereby all of ongoing social life is negotiated by actors *qua* interlocutors, and therefore the social order is fundamentally a negotiated order. At the other extreme, negotiation commonly describes highly specific social arenas or behavioral interactions, some fairly common, as in business, legal, or organizational settings; and others more dramatic, as in the case of hostage or crisis negotiations, like that of the Branch Davidians, referred to in Chapter 1 (Docherty 2001; Rogan, Hammer and Van Zandt 1997). The last example connects negotiation directly to the concerns of conflict resolution. Indeed, negotiation is fundamental to conflict resolution, yet its precise relationship to the field, in theory or practice, is yet to be fully articulated. In this chapter, I try to fit negotiation into the wider configuration of the field and its practical goals by problematizing its dominant heuristic, the *buyer-seller* model and its underlying conceptual framework, rational choice theory.

Given the centrality of negotiation to conflict resolution's concerns, it is tempting perhaps to see the two terms as virtually overlapping, to conceive of conflict resolution as negotiation *tout court*. The immensely influential work of Roger Fisher and his many associates at Harvard's Program on Negotiation can sometimes give this impression, even if its several publications and its flagship journal, *Negotiation Journal*, have always welcomed contributions that ranged beyond negotiation itself, on mediation, say, or ombudsmanship or general conflict resolution theory. But as the field developed, both as a subject to be researched, theorized, and taught and as a field of practice, it soon became apparent that however fundamental negotiation is, it cannot constitute the entire *field* (as a set of practices) or *discipline* (as an academic and teachable domain). This became even more true as for many in the field, conflict resolution came to include conflict transformation, drew closer to peace studies, and broadened its purview from the "getting to yes" of getting parties "to the table" and agreements signed, to encompass a wide and growing range of post-settlement concerns commonly called *peacebuilding* that are connected to development, human rights, reconciliation, and so on. On the practice side of things, this means that negotiation skills are but one component of a large set of skills that conflict resolution practitioners must possess. On the discipline side, this has meant that academic courses or practical training on negotiation had to be oriented differently from those taught in schools of business, management, or law; this is less a matter of differing negotiation skill sets than of the conception of the process itself.[1] The two requirements are related in that practice and pedagogy reflect the centrality of *third-party processes* to conflict resolution, beginning with mediation.

Third-Party Intervention

Imagine a range of "classic" conflict resolution processes set out on a continuum, as in Figure 2. On the far left are processes of addressing a conflict that are unilateral in nature, reflecting decisions made by each party separately, such as avoidance, exit, yielding, or contention: all are varieties of self-help. To the right of self-help is the large terrain of negotiation. Recognizing some degree of mutual interdependence, or possessed of mixed motives as to the desired nature of the outcome, the parties enter into some form of strategic joint interaction, such as bargaining—some form of conversation, broadly conceived. Although, of course, many negotiations involve multiple parties, the paradigmatic form is two party, bilateral in nature, and much of negotiation theory and training is built upon the two-party model (and recognizes how much adding extra parties complicates the whole endeavor). To the right of negotiation lies the even larger terrain of third-party processes. Here, the major distinction involves third-party processes where the third-party facilitates the parties' interaction—ideally their participation is voluntary—and (classically) does not possess the power to stipulate a decision or outcome. We say the parties "own their agreement." The prototypical form of this process is *mediation*. To the right of mediation lies a range of third-party processes in which the parties forego some amount of voluntariness of participation and lose some or much of their power to determine an outcome and "own" it. In *arbitration,* the parties may choose to come to arbitration and often choose the arbitrator (within limits) and agree to abide by its decision; the extent to which such agreement is enforceable is a matter of contractual or legal considerations. In *adjudication,* the third party has the power to summon the parties to the process (perhaps by sending out the sheriff to collect them); their participation is not, in theory, at all voluntary, and in some cases the "full weight of the law" (the state) and its sanctions stand behind the decision of the third party/judge. There have developed various blended or intermediate forms—for example, *med-arb* (mediation followed by arbitration)—whose efficacy generates debate in the field.

If one considers the entire spectrum of possible ways for parties to address conflict, what is striking is that the field of conflict resolution traditionally has concentrated almost entirely on two main forms: negotiation and ways to facilitate negotiation, that is, some form of mediation.[2] This is certainly the thrust of the ADR movement (see Chapter 2). In fact, one can say that the field has really concentrated on only one of these forms: varieties of third-party intervention, including mediation. This is because if the parties themselves are able to negotiate their differences, then they can resolve the conflict without outside intervention. The field of conflict resolution *begins,* in a sense, with the assumption that the parties have failed to negotiate an agreement, failed even to imagine negotiation of any sort, or have negotiated one that is so far below the optimal outcome possible that it almost guarantees the recurrence of conflict. In this case, the role of the third party is to bring the contending parties together and help them, through using such skills as interest analysis, agenda setting, reframing, active listening, and problem solving—the entire range of skills taught mediators in certification programs all over the world, in fact—to negotiate more efficiently and successfully. The *sine qua non* of this is the integrative agreement that, in addition to being most "fair" to all

Figure 2. Conflict Resolution Processes

DECISION POWER WITH PARTIES			DECISION POWER WITH OTHERS	
UNILATERAL	**BILATERAL**	**TRILATERAL**		
Self-Help	Negotiation	Mediation	Arbitration	Adjudication
Avoid	Bargain/Distributive	Facilitative	Med-Arb	Without Litigation
Yield	Interest-Based /Integrative	Evaluative	Nonbinding	With Litigation
Exit	(Mixed Motive)	Transformative	Binding	
Contend		Narrative	Final Offer	
		Insight		
		Med-Arb		

parties (read: "profitable," indicating the least amount of "value" left "on the table"—the so-called win–win), is also therefore the most likely to lead to a self-sustaining agreement (Fisher and Ury 1981 [1991]; Hopmann 1995).[3]

To say that third-party involvement begins when negotiation fails is not to downplay the importance of negotiation to conflict resolution, but to put it in perspective. In one sense, of course, the third party is also always negotiating, in gaining access, getting parties "to the table," even in some forms of caucusing.[4] But this is negotiation as a means to perfecting mediation, whose outcome the parties themselves classically control. If one examines a standard text of facilitative mediation (e.g., Moore 1986), the chapter headings teach skills in mediation that almost exactly parallel the skills that a problem-solving, interest-based negotiator would need to learn: agenda setting, uncovering the parties' hidden interests, generating options for settlement, and so on.[5] In this sense, the conflict resolution specialist acting as a third party must be first also a negotiation specialist—perhaps a negotiation virtuoso in difficult cases—but puts this knowledge and those skills to work in order to be a better third party. One section in Moore's book calls this "turning the negotiation session over to the disputants" (1986:168). An important difference therefore emerges in how negotiation is conceived in conflict resolution curricula and those of law or business schools. In the latter cases, students are taught that negotiators act as agents who represent principals and negotiate on their behalf. In teaching negotiation in conflict resolution, in contrast, students learn that the prototypical third party, acting as a *neutral*, should not regard either party as the principal. Insofar as the third party is an agent at all, he or she is an agent on behalf of the integrity of the process (but see below). The principal–agent connection, so crucial to legal ethics and practice, is often construed differently in conflict resolution—as responsibility to the process itself.[6] This is usually framed as a commitment to third-party neutrality or impartiality. Presuming a clear definition of conflict of interests, neutrality is not an issue for attorneys negotiating on behalf of their clients, or any negotiator on behalf of his or her constituency or, of course, individuals on their own behalf. In some sense, the nature of responsibility is much clearer for these latter negotiators. For conflict resolution third parties who act as negotiators and emphasize neutrality or impartiality, it is responsibility to the integrity of the process rather than the parties that dominates. This overwhelming commitment to process, however, quickly leads conflict resolution into its own ethical dilemmas, as Laue and Cormick (1978) and Slim (2001), among others, have pointed out. This occurs, as noted in Chapter 9, in cases where power asymmetry is marked between the parties and whenever a concern with the social justice of the outcome—understood as different from a Pareto optimal solution—are considered important.[7]

For the remainder of this chapter, I want to consider negotiation and mediation in terms of the dominant metaphors or heuristics that have respectively guided research and practice. By far, negotiation has enjoyed the stronger (more dominating) heuristic, that of buyer-seller as undergirded by rational choice theory. Mediation, by contrast, appears a very fuzzy semantic domain, reflected in the multiplicity of forms that have developed in the field along with conflict resolution in general (see Herrman 2006). This is not surprising. If we consider that third-party conflict resolution begins when negotiation between the parties has broken down, then third-party work always deals with the hardest cases, including those that negotiation specialists might simply consider *nonnegotiable* and write off. But these are precisely the cases that test the limits of interest-based negotiation and perhaps of rational choice theory: these are the cases that deal with values, identity, and basic human needs.

Mediation in Practice: A Multiplicity of Forms

To begin to consider the multiplicity of forms that mediation can assume, take the nature of the mediator first. What does this sort of creature look like? How stable a role is it? Although the personal characteristics, skills, knowledge, and social backgrounds of mediators are expected to vary, the overall sense of what a mediator is seems to be taken for granted, an unexamined amalgam of the classic descriptions of the role and its tasks, right out of, for example, Folberg and Taylor (1984), Moore (1986), Beer and Stief (1997), or Wilmot and Hocker (2001). Prototypically, the mediator is neutral and impartial, an outsider to the dispute and unrelated to the parties, lacking the power and authority to stipulate decisions or settlements (or, indeed, enforce compliance with them). The paradigmatic mediation is conceived as a one-off session even if separated in two or more parts by some days. Functionally, the mediator mainly facilitates the process of negotiation between the parties, and any agreement arising from this negotiation must be one that the parties themselves own. For their part, the parties come to mediation voluntarily. There are other prototypical characteristics, but these will suffice for now.[8]

That we operate cognitively in terms of prototypes is not surprising and in fact is unavoidable. But what we must remember is that prototypes are *constructed* cognitive entities, and (1) they never describe a comprehensive picture of the phenomenal world they purport to depict (i.e., not all entities covered by the prototype resemble the prototype), and (2) prototypes can vary either with variations in the phenomenal world or in the cognitive communities inhabiting such worlds.

These points are based on the pioneering work on prototypical thinking by the cognitive psychologist Eleanor Rosch (1972, 1975, 1976). Within a given cognitive community (say, a culture), agreements on typicality will generally be high. For example, in the category of things called "birds," Rosch shows that high prototypicality for Americans resides in such birds as robin and sparrow, with low agreement on prototypicality for emu and penguin, and with crow and parrot falling somewhere in the middle. In other words, when one calls up a mental image of *a* bird, it is likely to be a robin and unlikely to be an emu—or a turkey, for that matter. This is not to say, of course, that complex cognition cannot recognize turkeys, owls, or flamingos as kinds of

birds, but that—for reasons of cognitive economy—we think in terms of prototypes, and such prototypes structure our thinking (and probably also our
learning). Rosch herself worked cross-culturally, and following her work,
cultural anthropologists and psychologists have demonstrated how prototypes
in fact may vary from culture to culture, for example, prototypes for "tree"
among American and Tzeltal children differ significantly (see Keller 1978; and
D'Andrade 1995:115–121).

Now let's return to our prototypical mediator and ask how such an implicit
and embedded construct can structure our thinking so that we take the very
category, as prototypicalized, for granted: "Mediators *are* neutrals as robins
are birds." Importantly, just as complex (or adult) cognition understands that
chickens are birds, too, so can complex cognition deal with the fact that not all
mediators are neutral. In fact, adverting to the outsider/neutral characteristic
mentioned previously, one of the first modifications urged on our prototypical
thinking about mediators came from practitioners with extensive cross-cultural
experience, who realized that in other cultures not outsider/neutrals, but rather
what they called insider/partials, were the rule—and thus the prototype. Lederach argued this based upon his Central American experience (Wehr and
Lederach 1991), and more recently work in some Middle Eastern societies
demonstrates the same phenomenon (Abu-Nimer 1996). Yet another critique
of mediator neutrality has political sources, already mentioned (the work of
Nader, e.g.); and today the entire notion of third-party neutrality as a key or
defining characteristic is subject to critical questioning, as in Bernard Mayer's
recent *Beyond Neutrality* (2004). Among other things, all this demonstrates
that in an emergent field of inquiry prototypes are subject to revision—on the
whole an encouraging finding.

But one need not go to cross-cultural work or political critique to find a
certain instability in the prototype of the mediator (Avruch 2006). In place of
mediator-as-facilitator, consider Bush and Folger's (1994) notion of the mediator as a restorer of damaged relationships; or Winslade and Monk's (2000)
idea of narrative mediation. Winslade and Monk portray the prototypical
mediator as storyteller or even, alongside the parties, a collaborative cocreator
of stories (see also Cobb 2004). Other metaphors for mediation are possible.
Neil Katz (2006) borrows Bolman and Deal's (2003) four frames or metaphors
for organizations and their leaders, finding them relevant to different sorts of
mediators as well.

The four frames Katz discusses are the *structural* frame (where metaphorically the organization is a well-oiled machine and the leader is an architect or
analyst); the *human resources* frame (the organization is an extended family
and the leader is a facilitator or servant); the *political* frame (the organization
is a jungle and the leader is an advocate or a negotiator for the parties); and
the *symbolic* frame (the organization is theater or temple, and the leader is
playwright, poet, or prophet). Building upon Katz's own interesting discussion
of these frames and metaphors, I suggest they correspond neatly to four major
understandings of mediation current today. The structural frame is perhaps

closest to our prototype, the standard model mediator, focusing on problem solving, revealing interests beneath positions, and extending to dispute systems or process design and architecture (cf. Moore 1986; Ury, Brett, and Goldberg 1988). The human resource frame, with its relational and family metaphors, seems to me to echo the concerns of transformational mediation (Bush and Folger 1994). The political frame, concerned with power and justice, brings to mind the rather activist, politically engaged and "trouble-making" third-party work of such Quakers as Adam Curle (1986) or C. H. Yarrow (1972), or even some of Lawrence Susskind's third-party work in the public policy arena (Susskind and Cruikshank 1987). Finally, the symbolic frame, with its playwright/poet/prophet roles, brings us back to the mediator as master narrator or storyteller, to Winslade and Monk.

What, then, is a mediator? Certainly, the semantic distance separating facilitator, manager, therapist, advocate, poet, and prophet would seem to undermine our confidence in a secure and stable prototype. Part of the problem in conceptualizing the mediator role has to do with our primary conceptualization of mediation. Bercovitch echoed many definitions of mediation when he wrote, "Mediation is, at least structurally, the continuation of negotiation by other means" (1997:127). But negotiation, relying upon the core heuristic of the market and buyer-seller (see below) is a particularly robust idea, even cross-culturally so, whereas any third-party intervention seems far more conditional and contingent by comparison. This is demonstrated even in Bercovitch's own work on international mediation—perhaps accounting for his adding a subclausal qualification to his definition: "at least structurally." From the beginning, the idea that mediation was simply "facilitated negotiation" seemed less than fully sustainable. In the same article in which Bercovitch begins with the simplest of definitions, he goes on to cite work by Carnevale (1986), Kressel (1972), Stuhlberg (1987), and Touval and Zartman (1985), all of which offer more or less expansive typologies of mediators (roles and tasks), and complexify the idea. The more we mediate, and the more we study and analyze its practice, the more uncomfortable does the basic definition (and its prototype) appear. Instead, we have come to recognize that the addition of a third party—any third party—to a dispute or negotiation seems to transform some of its key parameters and dynamics. A single robin in a cage has somehow become a full and many specied aviary, and not one that is so well confined.

What does mediation, or the mediator, look like if we admit its multifarious manifestations and forms and the instability of its prototype? We have several typologies of mediator *roles* from which to choose. Well-known varieties include interest-based mediation, transformative, or narrative. I want to call attention here to a typology of third-party roles presented by Christopher Mitchell in 1993 and then, influenced by notions of contingency (phase-structure) introduced by Fisher and Keashly (1991) and refined in a later publication (see Mitchell 1993, 2003). Unlike many mediation models that come from interpersonal, domestic, commercial, or lower-court-affiliated settings, where the third party intervenes in a two-party negotiation, Mitchell's typology comes from his comparative study of peace processes in complex deep-rooted conflicts, often identity based. Nevertheless, the different roles might better express or capture what all sorts of mediators do, or *ought* to do (Mayer 2004). Note that Mitchell's fourteen mediator tasks and roles are divided into three different stages, or phases, of intervention.

Perhaps with the exception of the "implementer" role (able to impose sanctions on noncompliant parties, looking more like a classical arbitrator), the number and diversity of these roles collectively argue against a single prototype for "the mediator," unless, of course, one methodologically restricts the definition of *mediator* to only one or two of the possible fourteen roles, probably around "facilitator." This would indeed preserve the prototype, but at the cost of losing a great deal of information about what "mediator-like"

Figure 3. Core Mediator Roles and Tasks in Conflict Resolution

Intermediary Role	Tasks and Functions
Prenegotiation	
Explorer	Determines adversaries' readiness for contacts; sketches range of possible solutions.
Reassurer	Reassures adversaries that other is not wholly bent on "victory".
Decoupler	Assists external patrons to withdraw from core conflict. Enlists patrons in other positive tasks.
Unifier	Repairs intraparty cleavages and encourages consensus on interests, core values, and concessions.
Enskiller	Develops skills and competencies needed to enable adversaries to reach a durable solution.
Convener	Initiates process of talks, provides venue, and legitimizes contacts and meetings.
During Talks/Negotiations	
Facilitator	Fulfills functions within meetings to enable a fruitful exchange of versions, aims, and visions.
Envisioner	Provides new data, ideas, theories, and options for adversaries to adapt. Creates fresh thinking.
Enhancer	Provides additional resources to assist in search for positive-sum solution.
Guarantor	Provides insurance against talks breaking down, and offers to guarantee any durable solution.
Legitimizer	Adds prestige and legitimacy to any agreed-upon solution.
Post-Agreement	
Verifier	Reassures adversaries that terms of agreement are being fulfilled.
Implementer	Imposes sanctions for nonperformance of agreement.
Reconciler	Assists in long-term actions to build new relationships among and within adversaries.

Source: Adapted from Mitchell (2003:84).

third parties actually do in the real world, in deep-rooted conflicts. Mitchell's listing allows us to see "the" mediator changing roles, functions, and form as the process unfolds. We can also think of this as the mediation changing the mediator, or as a successful and effective mediator as one who is receptive to role/task change throughout the process.

However, Mitchell points out that given the contradictory nature of some of these roles, for example, the "unifier," working within a party to reduce cleavages, or the "enskiller," working on behalf of a single party, it is unlikely that they would be acceptable to the other side later on in the process; they would be seen as highly partial and not neutral, for example. In other words, the same individual (or even organization) cannot play all the roles as the process unfolds. (Think of how the Quaker American Friends Service Committee [AFSC] worked for many years to build skills in the Palestinian community in order that the Palestinians may one day productively engage the Israelis as symmetrical partners in peace negotiations. The AFSC has entirely and irrevocably lost the confidence of the Israelis to act as neutrals in any way—although the whole point of Friends' activism is, in their view, ultimately in the service of peace.) The implication of this notion that the same third party cannot mediate throughout the process is that no single and unique actor called *mediator* is possible for all conditions and contexts in a conflict or dispute. (I return to this in Chapter 9.) Once again, we can certainly preserve the "purity" of the mediator role (or the cognitive acuity of our prototype) by limiting it to the impartial and disempowered facilitation of the negotiating parties. But this would lose sight of what, working with parties in complex and deep-rooted conflicts, third-party interveners actually *do.*

The extreme lability of the third-party role makes that of the negotiator seem stable and predictable by comparison. This is so partly because the agent-principal dynamic, though at times situationally complicated, so long as conflicts of interest are adequately defined, presents no *fundamental* ethical dilemmas for negotiators, whereas it can be a minefield for third parties, particularly as power asymmetry among the parties and concerns for justice as part of the outcome are involved. It is also the case because the reigning heuristic for negotiation, even in its advanced problem-solving and interest-based form, is that of the buyer-seller, and the presumptive underlying cognitive model is rational choice: Both are very robust. Yet there has been active research in negotiation theory and practice, and in the words of some, an attempt to progress beyond a "first generation" of negotiation theory and practice to a second one that can perhaps move beyond interests.

A Canon for Negotiation

Beginning in 2003, as part of the Broad Field Project in conflict resolution directed by Christopher Honeyman in collaboration with Professor Andrea Schneider of the Marquette University Law School, an effort was made to elucidate a universal (or near universal) and interdisciplinary "canon of negotiation."[9] Briefly, the six topics Honeyman and Schneider list as part of the extant common core canon are (1) the idea of personal style or strategy in negotiation, including adversarial versus interest-based and problem-solving styles; (2) communication skills; (3) integrative versus distributive negotiation; (4) ideas of ZOPA (zone of potential agreement), reservation price, and BATNA (best alternative to a negotiated agreement); (5) use of brainstorming and other option-creating techniques in problem solving; and (6) the importance of preparation to efficient and productive negotiation. More specifically, the point was to go beyond the existing "common core of negotiation" — topics or concepts readily agreed to be part of any negotiation curriculum, training module, or (indeed) theory — and see whether, thirty years after Fisher and Ury's *Getting to Yes* and Raiffa's *The Art and Science of Negotiation* (and forty-six years after Walton and McKersie's *A Behavioral Theory of Labor Negotiations*),[10] the influx of new disciplines and the expanded sensibilities of conflict resolution as it relates to negotiation, have made any new topics or concepts centrally part of a more comprehensive common core. The results of this effort, reported in the special issue of the *Marquette Law Review*, indicate that such an expanded canon is indeed suggested by interdisciplinary research, and with the involvement of practitioners of wide background and negotiation experience. Among the twenty-five essays emerging from the special symposium, ones that discuss the role of emotions, culture, apology, narrative and metaphor theory, power, and identity stand out as especially good candidates for inclusion in an expanded and canonical common core.

This is especially true if negotiation theory and practice are ever to be fully relevant to conflicts involving divergences of values as well as interest, and deep markers of positionality such as gender, culture, and identity. My goal in the remainder of this chapter is to argue why and in what ways the negotiation theory and practice of the canonical "first generation" are not at present wholly relevant to these sorts of conflicts — in fact, in what ways their irrelevance is intentional and self-inflicted. I then suggest that a new heuristic, built from the start around the problematic of values-based conflict, can help us begin to expand the range of relevance of negotiation theory and practice.

The First-Generation Heuristic: Rational Choice and the Buyer-Seller

An examination of the six topics listed by Honeyman and Schneider as part of the already accepted canon of negotiation — for example, positions versus interests, the notion of negotiation efficiency (as in Pareto optimal solutions) or problem solving — reveals its basis in the larger theory of rational choice (or rational decision making) and the key heuristic of the buyer-seller encounter. The two, theory and the heuristic, are, of course, inextricably entangled in neoclassical economics: rational choice as its conceptual foundation and the buyer-seller transaction as its paradigmatic praxis. Many of the metaphors in negotiation theory and practice reflect this, for instance, claiming or creating value (*not* "values!"), leaving value ("money") on the table, maximizing one's surplus, and so on. Both classic and contemporary texts on negotiation presume throughout their analyses and prescriptions some sort of buyer-seller interaction as the fundamental practice,[11] as did most first-generation work by experimentalists[12]; but ranging further afield, even a classic of applied diplomacy defines diplomatic negotiation as "essentially a mercantile art.... [T]he foundation of good diplomacy is the same as the foundation of good business."[13]

No one can deny the rigor, parsimony, and productiveness of the rational choice paradigm even if, as one commentator notes, the model is not without flaws, "not least through the real world's bloody-minded obstinacy in simply not conforming to theory" (Evans 2004:110). The apparent, frequent disconnect between actors' behavior as predicted by the paradigm and their actual behavior has long been noted by scholars, both those working within the paradigm and those critics outside it. Perhaps the explanation for the disconnect that is most friendly to the theory involves information. Rational choice requires actors to possess rigorously valid and reliable information about many variables in order to arrive at a decision. In the real world, such information is very often partial or imperfect, and hence, expectedly, decisions are far from optimally rational (Simon 1982).

However, how friendly to the overall paradigm the information defense is depends on where the main sources of imperfection are held to lie. If they are in sense external to the actor, in the situation or the environment—in the nature of the world—then the defense of rational choice is robust. It's the booming, buzzing world that's to blame, not the decision-making actor. But if we presume instead that the information deficits are to be found mainly as a result of something "in" the actors' own *regular* cognizing processes—for instance, in a range of fairly frequent and "standard" cognitive distortions—then the basic presumption of the cognizing actor as a *rational* decision maker becomes a shakier one. Such distortions can result from structural limitations in the capacity of the cognitive apparatus to store, retrieve, or process information, or from a range of other distortion-causing mechanisms; many of these are supported by the apparent organismic requirement for "cognitive miserliness" (or risk aversion), resulting in such framing biases as attribution errors, just-world thinking, mirror imaging, illusory correlations, reactive devaluation, and so on. In fact, the negotiation literature is by now full of research, discussion, and analysis of such distortions as being part and parcel of regular cognitive processing.[14] More recently, that most important distinction in the theory of mind assumed by rational choice theory—a bifurcation, actually—between "cognition" on the one hand and "emotion" on the other has been questioned. Affect and cognition appear to interpenetrate one another all the time in our thinking.[15] And if our conception of thinking, of cognition, no longer allows the partitioning away of (messy, irrational) emotion, then how can we assume that rational choice theory predicts any actor's behavior any time? Simon

(1955) long ago identified these limitations under the rubrics of "satisficing" and "bounded rationality," an admission that our reasoning is probably best conceived as good enough for frontal cortex work. Negotiation theorists know about, and negotiation trainers certainly warn about common cognitive distortions, such as attribution errors or gain–loss risk anomalies. Perhaps the value of the theory as stipulating a set of practical, normative prescriptions remains undiminished: "When negotiating, this is how one ought to act to maximize utilities when and if …," and so on. But the value of rational choice theory for prediction (the sine qua non of imperious positivism), for describing how people actually reach decisions in the bloody-minded real world (and coincidentally for supporting its purported evolutionary roots in our psychological past), seems much diminished.[16]

These are some of the critiques that have emerged from within cognitive psychology itself, at the foundation of rational choice theorizing. I will not engage here the important problem of how one gets from the behavior of an individual rational actor to the behavior of the collective, a problem that has occupied some of the best minds in a variety of the social sciences. It is long recognized that rationality in the form of maximizing behavior at the individual level can result in irrationality (severely suboptimal system outcomes) at the level of the collective, the well-known tragedy of the commons;[17] or that it is impossible to reliably derive from aggregated individual preferences a preference set for the collective; or that some sociological analogue of the market's invisible hand will make things come out all right at the social or collective level.[18]

Other critics have come at rational choice not from the perspective of its (problematic) sociology, but from anthropology, for example, a cultural critique that questions the universality of utilities divorced from their encompassing contexts of meaning and valuation (Avruch 1998). Of course, the nature of utilities is not a problem at all in neoclassical economics because if one defines a utility as something—anything—desirable or valued, then one simply needs to identify what, in a given culture, is desired or valuable, and then look around to discover individuals striving to maximize it left and right. The adequacy of this conception of utility for understanding other cultures has long been questioned (Sahlins 1978), but the questions become harder if one imagines trying to transact (say, negotiate) *across* different "utility universes." For even if we assume that a behavioral theory of utility maximizing holds across all cultures, if we admit that the nature of utilities varies cross-culturally, then, to imagine intercultural rational transactions we would also have to assume that culturally specific utilities are everywhere essentially fungible.[19]

The fungiblity of utilities is (if we adopt the discourse of neoclassical economics, at least) one issue at the heart of a theory of intercultural negotiation—or intercultural transactions of any sort, for that matter. But for now I want to hold cultural variability constant, as it were, and redirect the discussion of *utility* to the related notion of *interest*, central to contemporary and canonical negotiation theory and practice.

In what one might call the first Copernican revolution of negotiation theory and practice, the idea was advanced that if individuals could be shown that most unproductive and inefficient negotiation involves arguments around surface demands or positions, then the act of having parties move beyond positions to analyze their underlying interests would free them to engage in a whole range of creative problem-solving activities. Put more formally, one could in many (though certainly not all) situations move from distributive (fixed-pie, zero-sum) bargaining toward problem solving and integrative (expanded-pie, positive-sum) solutions, toward the famous win–win agreement.[20] The question that some within our field have asked is whether anything capable of motivating behavior or social action lay beneath interests. This is the crucial question if one wants to assess the relevance of negotiation for conflicts around issues involving ideology, identity, or values. How one answers it determines how one assesses the adequacy of the existing canon of negotiation, or the need for its expansion.

Basic Human Needs and the Critique of Interest-Based Negotiation

To imagine motivators' underlying interests is to adopt an essentially stratigraphic or archaeological view of the person as social actor (Avruch and Black 1990). As elaborated by Warfield (1993:186), this yields a layered model of conflict (or social transactions generally), one that puts positions on the top layer, at the surface. Beneath these lie interests. Positions, often phrased as demands in a negotiation, may be consciously strategic or political, or may stem from emotionally occluded—as by anger—or inadequately analyzed interests. Interests refer (as in Fisher and Ury) to utilities-connected desires or wants. At these two top levels, one is operating within the bounds of the rational choice paradigm, and interest-based negotiation theory and practice suffice. However, beneath interests lie values, resulting from social learning and enculturation. At this level, Warfield says a "nonrational choice paradigm" applies. At the bottom, ontologically and foundationally, there lie basic human needs; here a biogenetic paradigm is called for.[21]

It is from the deepest level of biogenetics, of basic human needs, that John Burton (1990) distinguished *conflict* from *dispute* and mounted his critique of interest-based negotiation (or any third-party facilitation, such as meditation or ADR, which are merely extensions of it) as a response to what he called deeprooted conflicts. Social conflicts resulting from the suppression of individuals' basic human needs are not negotiable (or mediatable). Only the satisfaction of the needs can resolve the conflict. The sort of problem solving called for in these cases involves the formal analysis by the parties, aided by a panel of experts in basic human needs theory (but not necessarily in the substance of the conflict!), of how the needs of the parties are being suppressed and of ways the parties may achieve mutual satisfaction of them.[22]

Now, although Burton's conception of conflict resolution was certainly a critique of interest-based negotiation, he did not so much desire to expand the canon of negotiation as replace it entirely as a technique for resolving deep-rooted conflicts. This is because basic human needs trumped mere interests, and therefore an entirely different practice or technology of conflict resolution (the analytical problem-solving workshop) was called for. Burton sidestepped what I earlier referred to as the problem of the fungibility of utilities (or the closely related notion of interests) by postulating the primary, ontological power of basic human needs. But because he argued that these needs were indeed ontological—the same everywhere and universally shared—they were by definition also transcultural, and the whole problem of transactions across what I have called utility universes never arises. Unlike interests, one doesn't have to devise integrative-solution sorts of trade-offs or other manipulations (bridging, logrolling, alternative compensations, etc.) between different species of needs, because (1) one in any case cannot: all the needs imperiously require satisfaction eventually; and (2) every individual has the same set of them. Thus, Burton would certainly agree that the essential heuristic of rational choice and interest-based negotiation, the *buyer-seller,* is grossly inappropriate for fashioning a resolution to deep-rooted conflicts; but this is because basic human needs, being *given*—literally *inalienable*—can never be bought, traded, or sold. Insofar as we need a new heuristic here, it would be, as Warfield suggests, something in line with a biogenetic paradigm. In one way, the notion of rationality can remain, if differently conceived and located. The microsociological rationality of the calculating, maximizing individual of neoclassical economics is somehow to be replaced by the perduring evolutionary rationality of the adaptive, inclusive-fitness-seeking genome. There is here, of course, little room for culture as constituting significant difference (as in motives) if we leave all to biogenetics (as interests are now genomic and evolutionarily conceived; Ross 1997).

Values-Based Conflicts, Interests, Rights, and Power

Sandwiched between the presumed universal comparability of utilities, opening the way for creative problem solving at the level of interests, and the bedrock universality of basic human needs lies the layer Warfield (1993) calls values. Inculcated in individuals through socialization and enculturation, values in his scheme cover a wide range of notions, including such ideas as beliefs or morality. Values are also connected to identity, insofar as the self is experienced as a morally valanced subjectivity. In any case, instead of being linked, through the notion of utility, to what is useful, desired, or preferred, values are linked (through a different calculus?) to what is deemed good and true or, in the case of identity, perhaps *authentic* as well. In this way, values are also linked to motives. Warfield argues that at this level some sort of nonrational choice paradigm is the appropriate one for understanding social transactions—conflict or its resolution, for example. At the least, values-based conflicts may resist the sort of rational, problem-solving negotiation practices that often and demonstrably work well to address conflicts involving competing interests. In the past, many such values-based conflicts have been labeled as intractable, especially if they involve basic incompatibilies between the parties at the deepest levels of worldview, or perceived threats to personal or group identity (Kriesberg, Northrup, and Thorson 1989). In any case, if a negotiation canon is to be expanded at all, it would be at the point of addressing values and particularly identity-based conflicts.[23]

A first step is the formulation of a different heuristic for orienting oneself to these sorts of conflicts, different, that is, from the *buyer-seller* metaphor that is central to interest-based negotiation theory, research, and practice. Kahneman, Slovic, and Tversky (1982) and Lakoff and Johnson (1980), among others, were pioneers in pointing to the ways in which heuristics play an important role in decision making and how they figure as metaphors in cognition and perception generally. The metaphor/heuristic of *buyer-seller* is hardly in itself value-neutral in this regard. Consider, for example, how it orients us to the notion of "trust" in negotiation. Discussing the (canonical) concept of reservation point—essentially the quantification of one's BATNA—Leigh Thompson assesses the wisdom of one party revealing her reservation point to the other, in part thereby demonstrating "good faith and trust" in the other party. Thompson writes, prescriptively: Negotiation is not an issue of trust; it is an issue of strategy. "The purpose of negotiation is to maximize your surplus, so why create a conflict of interest with the other party by 'trusting' them with your reservation point?" (Thompson 2009:53). Given the underlying and orienting heuristic, this seems a perfectly reasonable, indeed rational way to structure a buyer-seller relationship and approach negotiation within one.[24] But if one is negotiating with another in the context of a values-based conflict, ought the matter of trust be dismissed so emphatically? If one thinks not, then what sort of heuristic can move us away from thinking of negotiation in a "maximize your surplus," buyer-seller modality?

Before suggesting such a heuristic, it is worthwhile briefly to examine how rational choice and interest-based negotiation theorists have themselves addressed values-based conflicts. The two main ways pull in rather different directions.

First, one can simply deny that any significantly different sorts of motivators underlie interests. This is the tack taken by Dean Pruitt and Sung Hee Kim, who see "interests underlying interests," although they do agree that interests cluster into "hierarchical trees," the deepest or most basic level of which consist of such Burtonian basic human needs as identity, security, justice, and self-esteem. However, they do not agree with needs theorists "about the need to draw a sharp distinction between interest-based conflicts and needs-based" ones (Pruitt and Kim 2004:199–200). Negotiation of what we would call values-based conflicts in this view consists of the parties moving up or down their respective interest trees until they reach mutually bridgeable ones. This, indeed, is how Thompson understands the problem. In a discussion of the difficulties in negotiating differences when what she calls culturally determined "sacred values" are on the table, she first avers that treating such values with the usual techniques of interest-based negotiation, like logrolling or other trade-offs, would likely be considered "unacceptable and reprehensible." Thus, negotiation, as she understands it, simply shuts down. Or maybe not. A paragraph later she writes: "Truly sacred values cannot exist because we make value trade-off every day, meaning that 'everyone has their price.' ... The critical issue is not how much it takes to compensate someone for a sacred issue but, instead, what factors allow trade-offs to occur on sacred issues" (Thompson 2009:281). She then reminds us that a party's labeling some issue as sacred may even be a tactical negotiation ploy, and to be on the lookout for these "pseudo-sacred" values. Thompson introduces the sacred only to discredit it.

The second tack—skeptical that all values are merely deeper held interests and agnostic on the assertion that everyone can be bought and sold—is very different. Agreeing that values-based conflicts are rarely if ever amenable to interest-based negotiations, these analysts suggest that two other modes of settlement or resolution may be called for, one based upon power; the other, upon rights (Ury, Brett, and Goldberg 1988). Both power and rights may be deployed in the framework of a negotiation, although such negotiations rarely present the same opportunities, as do interest-based ones, for creative or pie-expanding problem solving (Lytle, Brett, and Shapiro 1999). Power implies coercion of one sort or another, whether deployed as threat or exercised in some sort of contest—the outer limits of negotiation? Rights refer to standards of legitimacy, justice, or fairness, whether formally codified in a contract or generally understood in some cultural context. (The context may vary in scope. One may speak of an organizational culture where salary is "rightfully" or "justifiably" tied to seniority, or of culture more broadly, where "justice before the law" is the right of all. Rights may be generally socially accepted, but they are often as not contested as well—in fact, at the core of the conflict—frequently looping us back to power.)

Here are our two camps: Those who believe all motivators, including values and basic human needs, can be collapsed into the category of interest and therefore open to negotiation and those who believe values and needs are not reducible to interests but may be subject to a discourse of rights or the deployment of power. In the former case, the existing negotiating canon is therefore probably sufficient; in the latter case, it is probably irrelevant. Moreover, once rights or power are invoked, the chances that outcomes will be regarded by all parties as integrative are greatly reduced. Instead, rights conflicts are most often settled through stipulative or adjudicatory processes of one sort or another, usually producing winners and losers (see Figure 2). The interests of individuals (the starting point of the rational choice, interest-based heuristic) are often supplanted here by the more distal and abstract interests of the corporation, society, or the state. Meanwhile, power-based negotiations may reduce merely to communication between the parties (metaphorical or not) about the terms of ceasefire or surrender—with correspondingly little scope for creative brainstorming or elaborate problem solving.[25] In addition, power-based settlements are notorious for their less than optimal sustainability, engendering as they do resentment and vengefulness—the seeds of the next round of conflict. But bringing power into the mix in any way tends to confound many approaches to mediation—see Chapter 9.

When faced with values-based conflicts, then, the choice with regard to negotiation at present seems to be between presuming that such conflicts are not qualitatively different from other sorts of interest-based conflicts, even if more ingenuity in moving up and down the hierarchical interest trees is called for; or presuming that the notion of interests no longer productively applies, and negotiation itself constricts to power plays or rights contests. For myself, I am doubtful that deeply held values or needs can be lumped with other sorts of interests, but I am reluctant to leave the field thus open only to power and rights. Might it be that what we need, precisely, is an expanded canon of negotiation? Some thinking in this direction has already occurred with respect to power—consider Kenneth Boulding's (1989) "three faces of power" (only one of which is coercive) as an important step in this direction; and several of the articles in the *Marquette Law Review* (Honeyman and Schneider 2004) and *The Negotiator's Fieldbook* (Schneider and Honeyman 2006), referred to earlier, carry Boulding's ideas forward and suggest that power considerations beyond coercion or force be assimilated and added to the negotiation canon, a theme I explore further in Chapter 9.[26]

And what about rights? If one thinks of such commonly conceived rights as fairness, equity, or justice, it seems as if we are very close to the domain of values as this is commonly conceived as well. Can we imagine an expanded canon of negotiation capable of addressing these sorts of conflicts? If so, I think we have to begin by conceptualizing a heuristic for negotiation different from that of *buyer-seller*. If Tversky and others are correct about the orienting role heuristics play in our thinking, then the purpose of a new heuristic is to orient us away from thinking of negotiation predominantly in terms of utility talk and rational choice, and toward a sense of it more open to conflicts around values, needs, and worldviews.

A Values Conflict

If one thinks about a deep values conflict in our contemporary society, then something like abortion or capital punishment is immediately suggested. But if we want a heuristic similar in type to *buyer-seller*, focused (microsociologically) on dyadic actors in a specified and delimited decision-making situation, consider the following scenario:

> A couple, each deeply religious but coming from very different religious traditions, has a child. Religion is extremely important to both of them, and although

each respects the tradition of the other, a decision must be made as to which tradition the child will be affiliated with and raised in. How do they go about negotiating this?

Perhaps the first thing to note about this—let us call it the *two-religions* heuristic—is that it does *not* present us with a case similar to the one described by Jayne Docherty (2001) and noted in Chapter 1. There, federal agents and Branch Davidians faced one another across the chasm of significantly different worldviews, implying different conceptions of morality and faith—of social reality generally. In this case, by contrast, each person shares one deeply held value: that religion is important for the ultimate, spiritual, soteriological well-being of their child. Where they differ is in valuing different religious traditions. In theory, at least, this is a much less intractable conflict than one based upon radically different worldviews. It also means that we should view conflicts sourced below the interest level archeologically, in strata descending from differences of values to differences in ontologies.

The second thing to be said is that how, by its limitations, the *two-religions* scenario highlights the robustness and appeal of *buyer-seller*. Even imagining how this scenario can generate something as precise as a heuristic is a task. For one thing, *buyer-seller* has wide, virtually universal applicability as an example of a decision-making situation. Buyers meet sellers in different sorts of markets all the time and everywhere, and although the nature of these markets is hardly the same, the essential roles are remarkably constant and recognizable.[27] In stark contrast, the *two-religions* heuristic is only *imaginable* in an essentially liberal society in which religion is culturally constituted as a matter of individual conscience, privatized and free of coercive pressures from larger social groups—at least larger than each of the couple's immediate family.[28] In many of the world's societies, today and historically, this scenario would make no sense. It is, compared to *buyer-seller*, narrowly historically and culturally contingent.

Accepting the cross-cultural constriction of the heuristic (not a small thing), how would rational choice, buyer-seller thinking apply? Simple solutions of the fair divisibility sort are immediately objectionable. Children (as the great arbitrator Solomon pointed out in a much-cited precedent) oughtn't be divided in half. A child can't reasonably be raised in one tradition in the months that end in thirty-one days, and in the other in the months that don't. Shall the couple agree to alternate traditions with each new child? Raise boys in one and girls in the other? Pick a third, alien religion to both of them? It's difficult to imagine the parties' maximizing mutual value if each believes that only his or her religious tradition will lead the child to full heavenly reward (or whatever soteriological goal is desired). Perhaps they should raise the child simultaneously in both traditions, leaving the ultimate decision up to the child when he or she reaches legal majority?[29]

It's also difficult to imagine a power process being applied to this decision without great damage to the relationship, and perhaps eventually to the child as well. If, however, power is conceived beyond the bonds of the dyadic relationship and generalized to society, then one can imagine a rational decision being made to raise the child in the tradition that is more closely identified with the power structure of the society, for the future advancement and benefit of the child. This, indeed, is why Moses Mendelsohnn was a great Jewish philosopher in the Austro-Hungarian empire in the eighteenth century, and his grandson, Felix, a great Christian composer in the nineteenth. But note that we have now clearly turned religion into an *interest*, amenable to utility talk. History is certainly replete with examples of this, what Leigh Thompson called pseudo-sacred values, where everyone or everything has its price. "Paris is worth a Mass," said Henri IV, famously, as the Protestant king converted to Catholicism, to take the city in 1594. Religion as interest is widely to be found in the politics, especially urban, of multiconfessional societies: The mayor is an "X," the city council president is a "Y,' different wards have their predetermined religious/ethnic representative, and so on.[30] But here religion is an ethnic-like label, not necessarily reflective of deep individual faith or identity. Everything I wrote about Type II errors in Chapter 5 applies here. In that case, under some circumstances values do get treated like interests and negotiated as one would negotiate interests. This happens in the U.S. Congress or parliaments or in democratic electoral politics generally—not to mention in labor-management relations—more often than not. But if we insist on preserving the genuine and deeply held values—the nonutilitarian nature of the couples' thinking (and *feeling*) as they make their decision—then choosing on the basis of secular, profane, and interest-based advantage should be offensive to both parties.

If power is to be applied only problematically in this situation, what of rights? In one sense, rights are inextricably embedded in the heuristic, as implied when I specified the kind of culture, society, or polity in which this scenario is even imaginable.[31] But if there exists no set of rights—objective, legitimate, widely recognized, and shared standards—available to help the parties make their choice (even if rights make their *choice* possible), then are we thrown back to power?

Finally, consider this scenario from the point of view of the respective religious *communities* of the two individuals, particularly the leadership. Presumably, they would have strongly opposed the marriage in the first place. The couple, in getting married, did not necessarily have to confront the dilemma of different faiths because neither was required to give up his or her own. The dilemma came with the birth of their child (as the elders knew it would). From the perspective of the communities, the couples' decision to privilege their own scared value of mutual love, and maximize their individual interests in fulfilling it through marriage, had to lead eventually to the danger of weakening the community with the birth of children through the loss of new members to the collectivity, because should such marriages spread, the community (particularly if a minority) would feel itself to be at risk of demographic collapse. We are back to the problem of moving from the rationality of individual interest-maximizing decisions to ultimate deleterious effects on a collectivity, the tragedy of the commons.

Negotiation Beyond Interests?

Earlier I referred to the call among some negotiation theorists and practitioners for a second generation or expanded canon of negotiation theory, research, and practice. What does the *two-religions* scenario demonstrate about the limitations of the older canon, based on rational choice and buyer-seller, in approaching these sorts of conflicts? It is not clear, *pace* Pruitt and Kim, how we can conceive of the religious values of *these* parties (they are not horse-trading or logrolling Congressional Democrats and Republicans, after all) in any productive way reducible to interests. Nor does it seem that identifying or acknowledging a deeply rooted basic human need around religious meaning, affiliation, belief, or spirituality, *pace* Burton—which both parties indeed share—points us toward decision or *solution*. I can see that based upon the older canon of negotiation, we might well call this conflict fully intractable and nonnegotiable. The potential zone of agreement appears to be nil. Examining the best alternative agreement for both parties, despairing of power- or rights-based solutions, the advice of a third party to this couple might then be to forego bringing children into their relationship entirely—or rethink the sustainability, if not the value, of the relationship. Hardly win–win.

But if new heuristics guide or orient our thinking about problems in new ways, then what might the *two-religions* scenario suggest in the way of alternative heuristics for deep value conflicts? For one thing, the list of topics for a new common core in an expanded canon of negotiation, suggested by many of the authors in the *Marquette Law Review* and *The Negotiator's Fieldbook*, includes subjects under apology, culture, emotions, ethics, identity, power (beyond coercion), narrative, and metaphor. If the older canon seems too restricted to imagine negotiating the *two-religions* conflict under it, it is equally difficult to imagine a negotiation—were one possible—that did not include recourse to some of the subjects listed above.

One important question raised here is under what circumstances does the interest-based paradigm work or fail when confronted by values-based conflicts: When are values reducible or irreducible to interests? I think we need a more nuanced—processual and dynamical—way of describing negotiations in values-based conflict. Wallace Warfield, for example, suggests that we shouldn't so much see interests and values in a hierarchical relationship where one trumps the other—my earlier game metaphor—as understand the ability of oppositional parties in negotiations of various dimensions to engage in what he describes as "rapid shifting" between "negotiable interests and so-called non-negotiable values." Reflecting on his own conflict resolution training and workshop practice in post-genocide Rwanda, Warfield says, "Thus Rwandans (Hutus and Tutsis) were able to negotiate around interests in a scenario that dealt with organizational conflict, because organizational structure and culture provided negotiators a bridge. Whereas, those same parties, when it came to fundamental issues of genocide and forgiveness, struggled to find a common ground." He suggests the need for heuristics and models that depict not static layers, but "shifting ... boundaries driven by situation and perhaps other characteristics."[32]

Building on Warfield, another solution to the challenge faced by the *two-religions* scenario is suggested by Robert Ricigliano. Referring to the scenario itself, and reflecting on conflict transformation work in the Democratic Republic of the Congo, Ricigliano notes that the buyer-seller heuristic conceives of negotiation as a transactional process, and that "needs and values, for the most part, cannot be satisfied at the transactional level alone" (Ricigliano 2006:56). But rather than accede to the limitations of the canon, he argues that two other dimensions of negotiation be considered in the case of value or identity conflicts: a temporal dimension that treats individual transactionally derived agreements over time as ways to potentially change the context—the structure and the nature of the relationship, for example, increasing *trust*—in which both parties operate. Transaction, time, and context are linked in that contextual change occurs slowly and only if the parties can remain in some sort of minimally mutually beneficial relationship, achieved through at least some successfully negotiated transactional outcomes, producing a "virtuous cycle" of conflict reduction. A fine example of this is provided by John Forester's account of how experienced mediators have approached public disputes involving conflicts of values—and histories of racism, mistrust, and hurts. He argues explicitly against promising the resolution of value conflicts, because "resolution" might well seem too facile or smell fishy to the parties—and may be unattainable. (Nevertheless, even though value conflicts may indeed be irreconcilable, at least initially we shouldn't assume this, thereby making it a self-fulfilling prophecy.) Instead, he writes, "focus on the specifics of practice rather than on the abstractions of worldviews" (Forester 2009:108). Elsewhere, and more colloquially, he speaks of the need for mediators and parties to "explore together how we can keep our disagreements about what 'God' requires of us, even as we might still come to agree about where the stop signs should go" (Forester 2009:75).

A third way, a more radical departure from the first two, is suggested by Jayne Docherty (2006), building upon Tom Burns's (1992) distinction between two different sorts of rationality found in social action, each specifying different models of human agency in decision making, normative orientation, and "the power to reshape social structures." Burns called one model rational choice theory (RCT) and the other, social game theory (SGT). Summarizing Burns, Docherty writes that RCT views the individual agent as "asocial" and oriented toward the self, "extracted" from larger social or cultural contexts. SGT sees the individual agent as socially constructed and located in encompassing webs of relationships, historical memory, and cultural frameworks. Normatively, RCT abjures norms, morals, and ethics as relevant to rational action—the morality of the free and unregulated market is the ideal. SGT views agents as "fundamentally moral creatures whose moral sentiments" factor into their social action. As for the power to change larger structures, RCT "presumes a type of agent who makes choices according to a single principle (maximization of utility) within a *given* situation." The agent does not deviate from the rules of the game or seek to transform them. By contrast, the SGT agent possesses creative or destructive capability, the capacity to restructure situations, rules, options, or preferences (Docherty 2006:13). As this chapter argued, although it is difficult to imagine an RCT theory of negotiation *alone* adequately addressing values and needs (cf. Forester 2009)—other than by finding ways to deny, unmask, or turn them into interests—it seems that a form of negotiation based upon an SGT conception of the social world has that potential. The problem is this: What would that *form* look like? Would it resemble negotiation at all as we know it?

Alternative Forms and the Role of Third Parties

Negotiation, as Strauss (1978) has argued, covers a large territory of social interaction, up to and including the entire social order. So the term seems protean and limitlessly elastic. Yet when we consider what social interactions around deeply held and contested values or moral sentiments involve, and abjuring recourse to invoking power and rights for solutions, we may have difficulty in thinking of negotiation in its interest-based and problem-solving modality as the right or best term. Conflict resolution—*conflict transformation* particularly—engaging deep-rooted or intractable conflicts, especially ones involving identity or suppressed basic human needs and with histories of violence, has struggled with this, and its practitioners have sought to imagine kinds of *conversations* (the basis, after all, of every negotiation) that can carry these concerns. Here the attraction is sometimes to Habermas (1981) and his notion of a discourse ethics that, in the ideal speech situation at least, can imagine interlocutors engaging in dialogue open to anything, factual or normative, of deep concern and free from coercion or other structural distortions. As noted in Chapter 6, many have adopted the idea and practice of dialogue as a key conflict transformation process, rooted (like negotiation) in intersubjective communication, but different in its goals and normative orientation—much closer, in fact, to the rationality of social game theory (SGT). In dialogue, consensus replaces agreement as a sign of success, and the attainment of *empathy* becomes a superordinant goal of what analytical problem solvers instrumentally call the information exchange phase of negotiation. This form of unfettered communication presumes, for Habermas, a universal human moral framework motivated by the desire of interlocutors to achieve mutual understanding. Firmly rooted in the Enlightenment, Habermas thus proclaims the domination of reason; he offers us, in effect, yet another version of rationality, different from the strategic rationality of buyer-seller and cost-benefit in its use of reason in the service of individual emancipation and democratic freedom. The ideal speech situation describes the paradigmatic form of citizen participation in such a democracy.

Yet Habermas's conception of the ideal speech situation has drawn its share of critics, most famously Gadamer (1993), who also believed in dialogue but mistrusted Habermas's universal methodology and doubted from the outset that interlocutors (or social theorists—the "third parties" in this philosophical exchange) could ever really free themselves from the distortions of their prejudices or traditions; from Foucault (1980) who doubted that power (including coercion) could ever be disengaged from the knowledge/consensus that dialogue aims to create; by critics concerned that differences in *culture* entail precisely the sort of dissimilar normative horizons or shared linguisticality that make efforts to reach consensual truth so difficult to achieve; and lastly, by postmodern thinkers who wish to dismiss the universalizing presumptions and accompanying theoretical "tyrannies" of modernity and the Enlightenment *tout court.*

Leaving aside dialogue, in conflict resolution these philosophical issues have been played out, not surprisingly, in the proliferation of forms of third-party engagements—responses to failed negotiations or abandoned conversations. If the standard model mediation closely followed the form and processes of interest-based negotiation itself—the aim of the intervention being precisely the facilitation of negotiation through improved analysis of interests and problem-solving technique—then the forms that followed (such as transformative, narrative, or insight) have to one degree or another abandoned the notion of negotiation with its goal of settlement or agreement. These latter forms all strive to free mediation from its logical anchor in negotiation. In doing so, all claim to address and remedy different shortcomings of standard model mediation and negotiation. (The standard model nevertheless remains the dominant and most widespread form, as it remains anchored to negotiation in being connected to mediator training/certification for court and legal proceedings.) In one way or another, all seek to undermine the dominating heuristic of negotiation as an interaction between a buyer and seller.

They all do this by disprivileging to a greater or lesser extent the hegemony of interests. In transformative mediation approaches, this is done by focusing on distorted relationships, rather than the presenting problem itself, and viewing conflict as essentially a symptom of a deeper "crisis in human interaction." Successful mediation (re)empowers a weak or unself-confident party while encouraging recognition of the needs of the other party. The emphasis is on realigning and balancing the relationship, allowing the parties to recognize the destructive aspects of their conflict, get past the crisis, and explore possible terms of resolution. Or not: They may leave the mediation without settlement (the goal of facilitative mediation), but with an improved relationship that augurs better things for the future (Bush and Folger 1994).

In narrative mediation, attention is directed to the socially constructed narratives—the stories by and through which people live their lives and interact with others. Some stories are conflictual, often because they inscribe dominant cultural hierarchies or relations of unequal power. The narrative mediator draws out these stories with the aim of first deconstructing them to unmask power and other conflictual or destructive elements and then, along with the parties, coauthoring new narratives that are incompatible with earlier agonistic accounts by highlighting threads of cooperation, understanding, or respect that may also exist in the relationship but have been discursively displaced by the dominant conflict narrative. Analysis and problem solving as techniques here give way to questioning and deconstruction, used to shine light on (and "deauthorize") one set of stories while encouraging the discursive shift to an alternative, nonconflictual set (Winslade and Monk 2000).

Neither transformative nor narrative mediation address values conflicts as such, though proponents of both approaches would doubtless maintain that they do a better job than interest-based facilitative mediators would. The newest formal entry into the mediator's aviary, however, is quite explicit on the matter of values, based as it is on the philosophical system of Bernard Lonergan, a Catholic social philosopher and theologian. Pointing to the notion of *insight* as a central feature of Lonergan's epistemology and theory of learning, they call their approach "insight mediation" and seek to differentiate it from earlier forms (Picard 2003; Picard and Melchin 2007).

Lonergan wrote that learning, or "coming to know," is composed of four stages: experience, understanding, judgment, and decision. Experience is the information-gathering stage but involves a comprehensive sense of information, to include feeling, imagining, and remembering, as well as seeing and hearing. Understanding is when the learner first approaches insight, which can be *direct* or *inverse*. Direct insight refers to a kind of "aha" moment of clarity into the nature of a problem and its solution. Inverse insight means the revelation that one has been wrong, following a dead end, and must search for a new solution. The judgment stage refers to how one verifies one's insights, direct or inverse. Decision refers to the action one takes as a result of the learning process (Picard 2003).

Picard and Melchin adapt Lonergan's theory to a form of mediation in which the third party seeks to bring the negotiating parties to mutual insight through a series of stages connected to Lonergan's model. The "linking" stage encompasses experience ("data gathering") and parts of understanding. "Delinking" focuses on the elucidation of inverse insights, a key task for parties who have been engaged in destructive conflict and ineffective negotiation. "Verification" corresponds to Lonergan's judgment phase; and "decision" represents the outcome of the mediation, actions undertaken by the parties.

Picard and Melchin note that many of the mediator skills found important in transformative and narrative mediation—listening and questioning carefully, awareness of power and other relational dynamics, attention to narratives—are important to insight mediators as well. But insight mediation is rather more structured than the other two in terms of the mediator's role, and less dismissive of presenting problems and the role of interests. Where insight mediation differs (again based on Lonergan's philosophy) is to see some interests as under-girded by commitments to values, and values connected to feelings (emotion). "Very often," Picard writes, "parties are not fully aware of their own values; nor are they aware of how the values have an impact on the conflict situation" (2003:481). The insight mediator must move the parties beyond the present-ing problem to "understand the deeper cares, concerns, values, interests and feelings that underlie the problem" (Picard and Melchin 2007:50). In this way, much as facilitative mediators seek deep analysis of interests, insight mediators turn to elucidating held values as their main goal. The crucial step forward is that insight mediators recognize that values held by one party can be seen as a threatening to the other party. "Insight mediation sees the conflict dynamic as fueled by threat in which one party feels that his or her concerns are threatened by the interests of the other party and by the other party's consequent lack of regard for his or her interests" (Picard and Melchin 2007:51).

The advantage of insight mediation, it seems to me, is that it coherently links the rather technical process and skill set of third-party intervention with a particular theory of social learning, as well as to the recent work in *threat narratives* as a source of conflict and escalating violence, undertaken by Daniel Rothbart and Karina Korostelina (2006). The latter concentrate not on indi-vidual (negotiation), but on group dynamics, seeing mutual threat narratives as a source of dangerous outgroup devaluation and ingroup glorification; in the extreme, this leads to demonizing or dehumanizing threatening outgroups and justifying the worst sort of genocidal violence perpetrated against them. The potential for the micro–macro connection in the understanding of conflict and techniques of resolution are what seems most promising here.

On the other hand, mediators of the other three approaches—facilitative, transformative, or narrative—might well argue that each of them also seeks to bring about the parties' achievement of insight in one way or another; Bur-ton might have argued that such insight was precisely the goal of his earliest problem-solving analytical workshops. Some narrative or transformational practitioners and theorists, as well, might object to the more structured na-ture of insight mediation, seeing a sort of rigidity of practice, and to the role the insight mediators explicitly claim as diagnosticians of the conflict, even while maintaining, as good mediators, that it is the parties who own it and its solution (Picard and Melchin 2007:51). Reacting to claims of diagnosis, those critics who believe that current conflict resolution practice is altogether too Western-centric, imperious, or concerned with the governance of others are likely to be heard from here. In the end, it is insight mediation's unequivocal concern with values, emotion, and threat that seem to me a step forward in formulating any new canon for a second-generation construction of nego-tiation. But what possible model of *negotiation* would this interventionary form correspond to? Perhaps the closest analogue to achieving insight as a road to resolution—Lonergan notwithstanding—comes from the conceptu-alization and role of insight in orthodox psychoanalysis. And here the role of the third-party psychoanalyst is clearly neither neutral nor disconnected from potentially fraught dynamics of power, tied up in pyschoanalytics with problems of transference.

Finally, almost all of the discussion around different mediation formats has tended to hold culture constant—to efface cultural difference as affecting the efficacy of each format. How much insight can a cultural outsider reasonably expect to provide? Honeyman, Goh, and Kelly offer some compelling case studies, from Aboriginal Australia and multiethnic Malaysia, to demonstrate (yet again!) how "culture plays such a subtle role that only an indigenous mediator is able to pick up the important nuances in order to create a successful mediation" (2004:498). They note that Western-trained mediators tend to be transactional and focused on interests and settlement, whereas indigenous-oriented mediators might well focus on relational issues. In mediation settings composed of Western-oriented disputants, such an approach may be appropriate, or at least understood as appropriate (even if ultimately unsuccessful in reaching a settlement). If such a transactional approach is used, say, by a white Australian mediator in a dispute involving at least one Aborigine, it might be seen as inappropriate—*illegitimate*—as yet another example of majoritarian efforts at "governance." But culture complicates power (and notions of appropriate governance) in other ways. For example, in considering mediation in Singapore, Ian Macduff has pointed out that the ideal Asian mediator is someone of relatively high status who actively participates and authoritatively directs the process—that a cultural Asian predilection for "high power distance" means accepting the legitimacy of social inequality, being committed to its maintenance. Moreover, disputants see the conflict in terms of powerful cognitive and affective categories of hierarchy, authority, and deference such that "not all participants will see issues at stake in the same interest-oriented terms; they will also see disputes as values-based" (Macduff 2009:118). When culture is not held constant, but allowed to vary, the discourse around interests becomes even more complicated, and perhaps much less assured. Instead of assimilating values to interests, the utility-minded solution (everything sacred is pseudo), interests get turned into values.

Conclusions: Negotiation Beyond Buyer-Seller?

This chapter began by exploring the central place of negotiation in conflict resolution, and inquiring into the nature of negotiation by way of its central heuristic, the buyer-seller. The focus on negotiation in its paradigmatic two-party form soon broadened to include the most common third-party intervention into failing or troubled negotiations, some form of mediation. Compared to the robustness of the buyer-seller heuristic, which lends to negotiation a special clarity and coherence, mediation appears to be a multifarious form that over the years has spawned different variants, all distancing themselves from the first-generation interest-based facilitative mediation, each distancing itself more or less from the very concern with interests or problem solving. Neil

Katz's (2006) conception of possible metaphors for grasping the mediator's role, from facilitator to manager, to therapist, advocate, poet, and prophet, as I wrote, seems to undermine our confidence in a secure and stable prototype. Christopher Mitchell (2003), working from cases of third parties trying to negotiate the end to violent conflict, sometimes in formal peace processes, pays close attention to the time-phased nature of interventions and presents us with a list of third-party roles that strains the requirements for impartiality, neutrality, or mediator powerlessness in favor of a conception that some have called "mediation with muscle."

That mediation presents us with a less stable prototype than does negotiation is not surprising. Mediation, along with any number of third-party interventions, takes place most often at the point at which negotiations have become stuck or broken down. There could be many reasons for this, from faulty communication between the parties to a lack of specific technical information needed for generating options, to a lack of trust. In all of these cases, mediators can play a positive facilitative role. But unless one agrees with Leigh Thompson that there are no really sacred values and everyone has her price, at least one set of reasons for negotiation failure must involve the inapplicability of applying the buyer-seller heuristic to the conflict at hand. Deep values or identity conflicts are the likely candidates here. In that case, resorting to a discourse of rights or power to bring about settlement is one option (Ury, Brett, and Goldberg 1988). Another is to find a kind of third-party intervention, a form of mediation, that can disengage from the hegemony of interest and engage with values and issues around identity and meaning. In their own way, transformational, narrative, and particularly insight mediation all make this claim.

It would be interesting to ask specialists in all three genres—I am not one—to take on the *two-religions* scenario and speculate on what their "resolution" might look like. I suspect none would confidently claim to offer a solution or a settlement. I expect all would claim to leave the two parties better off as a result of their intervention: wiser and more reconciled to whatever decision each has reached.

8

After Violence
TRCs and Reconstructing Identity

Introduction: From Conflict to "Post-Conflict" and Back

One of the hallmarks of the growth and development of the field of conflict resolution is how it has widened its purview and the range of what it considers legitimate concerns. In the early days, the researching and theorizing of negotiation (particularly from game theory) dominated, along with paranegotiation third-party processes built around mediation or ADR—or critiques of such processes, including Burton's work on such third-party nonmediatory techniques as interactive problem-solving workshops. Burton aside, the focus was on getting to settlement, getting agreements signed—on "getting to yes." If one were concerned with international conflicts, with interstate or even civil war or substate conflicts, the concern was with understanding and facilitating "the peace process," and the end state of this was the peace agreement. This rather constricted, goal- and technically oriented perspective was, indeed, part of what separated conflict resolution from the more expansive goals of peace studies in the same period, and formed part of the critique of conflict resolution by peace studies: that it was overly pragmatic, cold or heartless, blind to issues of structural violence, and unconcerned with social justice and the possibilities for positive peace. As I wrote in Chapter 2, reflecting on the institutional history of ICAR/S-CAR, there was in fact reluctance on the part of the founders of the master's program in conflict resolution in the early 1980s—the Reagan years—to have the word *peace* any where in the title of the program, the degree, or its first curricula.

As it developed, both as a discipline in the academy and as a field of practice, conflict resolution moved to engage in theorizing the steps that preceded or surrounded negotiation (e.g., Saunders 1996), but also with what followed the signing of the agreement, with what came to be called (erroneously) "post-conflict" concerns. At the same time, scholars of negotiation began to call for a "new canon" that moved beyond pure rational choice conceptions of the process to include emotions, apologies, and dialogue, among other so-called nonrational elements; as well, specialists in mediation left pure interest-based facilitation behind in a welter of new third-party forms. Through all this, conflict resolution was itself challenged by a conception of the field that put "transformation" at the forefront and sought to replace settlement goals with more radical empowerment or permanent relationship-altering ones.

Two other factors contributed to the growing diversity of topics legitimately included in conflict resolution curricula. First, new generations of students, often from conflict areas themselves, brought with them a broader conception of the goals of the field, one that has brought conflict resolution and peace studies closer in the new millennium. Second, the publication of Boutros-Ghali's *Agenda for Peace* in 1992, during a short-lived period of post–Cold War enthusiasm for what a revivified United Nations might accomplish, conceived of achieving peace or conflict resolution as a combination of preventive diplomacy and settlement making (*peacemaking*) mainly in the official diplomatic sense, but also by then informed with the possibilities of Track 2 efforts alongside traditional UN roles of *peacekeeping*.[1] The innovation lay in the third goal, post-conflict *peacebuilding*, which Boutros-Ghali defines as "action to identify and support structures which will tend to strengthen and solidify peace in order to avoid a relapse into conflict" (1992:21). Though this was hardly as strong an injunction as John Burton's wish for "true" conflict resolution to get to the root causes of serious social conflict (the suppression of basic human needs, in his case), it certainly widened the conception of the field beyond getting an agreement signed to post-conflict matters. In addition, it opened the way for conflict resolution to engage legitimately with a plethora of topics, today including, for example, human rights, human security, democratization, and sustainable development.[2]

One of the most intriguing topics, having to do with the restoration of the "rule of law" in a post-conflict society, is in the area of transitional justice.[3] Within this, in turn, notions of what constitutes justice itself have garnered interest, and here the truth commission (or the more ambitious truth and reconciliation commission) has taken center stage, particularly after the South African use of one in the post-Apartheid period.

In this chapter, following the expansion of conflict resolution beyond negotiation, mediation, and problem-solving workshops, and toward such ambitious goals as transformation and reconciliation, I want to consider some of the main features of truth and reconciliation commissions, their history and structure, and their characteristic concerns with respect to their central dilemmas: how they grapple with notions of truth, justice, liability, reconciliation, apology and forgiveness—reconciliation, in particular, being a topic of great concern in the field today—as well as how they address the need to support the "reconstruction" selves and identities in the wake of massive trauma and collective violence. A particular concern is how such commissions (or related tribunals) engender what I call the "one-to-many" dynamic: how to effect social reconciliation while focusing attention, via their testimony and storytelling, on the traumas and suffering of individual victims.

TRCs: History and Structure

Truth—or truth and reconciliation (the difference is not trivial)—commissions (TRCs) are, most generally, "bodies set up to investigate a past history of violations of human rights in a particular country—which can include violations by the military or other government forces or by armed opposition forces" (Hayner 1994:600). Since 1974, more than thirty truth commissions have been established, about ten each in Latin America (Bolivia, Argentina, Uruguay—twice, Chile, El Salvador, Ecuador, Guatemala, Peru, and Panama) and African countries (Uganda—twice, Zimbabwe, Chad, Rwanda, Burundi, South Africa, Nigeria, Sierra Leone, and Ghana). The remainder occurred in Nepal, Sri Lanka, Haiti, Yugoslavia, and East Timor.[4] The first such commission in the Arab world was established in Morocco in January 2004, by the new king, Mohammed VI. Called an "Equity and Reconciliation Commission," its final report was released in December 2005 (see also Slyomovics 2005). A Canadian commission, focused narrowly on addressing the past forced removal of First Nation children to boarding or "residential schools," the majority run by the Catholic Church, was announced in 2007 (see www .irsr-rqpi.gc.ca/TRC-eng.asp).

For the majority of analysts, a few things can be said to characterize all such commissions (Hayner 2002:14): They focus on the past (usually on violations committed under a previous regime), are temporary in duration and are expected to issue final reports, and are established and authorized by a state. In legal terms, truth commissions are to be distinguished from tribunals, or other more strictly judicial entities such as war crimes commissions, because they do not possess the formal power to prosecute or otherwise render justice—an important point to be discussed in the following pages (see Minow 1998). In a few cases, truth commissions operate alongside tribunals (East Timor and Sierra Leone) or parallel to other judicial processes (Rwanda).

Yet what characterizes these commissions is how they differ or are at best wide variations on a theme. Take their duration and the issuance of final reports: They typically complete their work within six months to two years. In a few cases, the commissions were disbanded before their work was completed and reports issued (Bolivia and Ecuador); in other cases, final reports were completed but never issued publicly (Zimbabwe, Uganda, Philippines) or were issued in severely censored versions (Haiti). By contrast, in South Africa's case the report, published in 1998, received extremely wide distribution, and the work of the commission itself was reported extensively by South African and international media. Argentina's report, issued in 1984, published under the title of *Nunca Más* ("Never Again"), was widely read in Spanish, translated into English (1986), and republished commercially in Britain and the United States.

Take their mandates and the basis of their investigative authority: Most have strictly delimited mandates, both as to duration and what counts as violation. In the Chilean commission's mandate, for example, only cases where victims actually *died* under torture were to be counted as human rights violations and investigated. This left many victims of torture and abuse who had nevertheless *survived* angry with the commission and alienated from its work.

Take the state-based nature of its authority: The majority of commissions were established by executive order (less frequently by legislatures) of the new post-conflict or post-abuse government. Nevertheless, in the case of El Salvador the United Nations established the commission, and it was headed by non-Salvadorans. In this case, it was felt that because the abuses had occurred during a civil war, none of the Salvadoran parties had clean hands. In a few cases, a nongovernmental organization (NGO) established the commission, as in Rwanda and earlier in South Africa by the African National Congress, to investigate its own abuses.

Such variations distinguish other aspects of the commissions, for instance, in the scope of their work, the resources or legitimacy they command, and observers' judgments of their ultimate effectiveness or success. With regard to scope, for example, a few of these commissions, most notably South Africa's, added the term *reconciliation* to their title, pointing to much wider ambitions in the area of post-conflict peacebuilding; in some other cases, the search for truth defines the commission's mandate, but the further task of reconciliation is controversial (as in Peru) or intentionally left out (Yugoslavia). Yet even where the search for truth is highlighted in the commission's name and mandate, some of the commissions have been able to command wide recognition and respect for their relative impartiality and effectiveness (South Africa and Argentina); whereas others have been seen as more compromised (Chile's, where members of the old regime remained influential), as reluctant responses to international pressure (Uganda's 1974 commission), or merely as platforms to criticize the old regime and legitimize the new one (Chad).

Justice

Most of what has been written by academics, supporters and critics both, of these commissions has focused on the problem of how they relate to *justice* (Avruch and Vejarano 2001). The crucial point to remember here is that the vast majority of commissions (Canada's being a noted exception) were established by newly emerging and often very fragile democracies, "transitional governments" in Kritz's (1995) term, which sought or were pressured to present a formal accounting of the violence and civil and human rights violations of the past. The emphasis here is on the production of an *account*. More difficult questions, political and moral ones, of *accountability*, are less adequately addressed by these commissions (Minow 1998; Rotberg and Thompson 2000; Baker 2001). The distinction between providing an account and assessing accountability is vital to what distinguishes such commissions from tribunals or other criminal judicial proceedings, and naturally the questions raised will focus attention on the problem of *justice*, specifically on the ability of the commissions to deliver justice to victims by finding perpetrators formally guilty of their crimes and rendering some sort of appropriate punishment—*retributive justice*, in other words. Kritz (1995) and others have argued instead for forms of transitional justice appropriate to transitional regimes: less adjudicative, formal, and retributive, but in their lesser stringency and flexibility more able to help a new, fragile regime maneuver around the potential resistance posed by former elites and potential "spoilers" and thus achieve a measure of stability (Stedman 1997; van der Merwe, Baxter, and Chapman 2009). This is the necessary political compromise some see built into the nature of the truth commission, especially if, as in the South African and several other cases, the commission lacks the power to prosecute but is able under some circumstances to grant amnesty to further prosecution. In fact, the question of amnesty granted perpetrators is among the most controversial aspects of these commissions' work.

In addition to the sorts of tactical benefits of transitional justice suggested by Kritz, others have gone further—none more eloquently than Bishop Tutu (1999)—in arguing for different *genres* of justice to be recognized as established and validated by the commissions. The sort of justice delivered in a formal criminal judicial proceeding has a long history and appears to most of us (if not always to the philosophers of law) almost self-evident in its definition. It is *retributive* in nature. In distinction to retributive justice, the justice of punishment, vengeance, and *lex talionis*, which is retroactive and focused mainly on the perpetrator, others argue for a different form of justice entirely, which they call *restorative* or *reparative*. This sort of justice, based upon forgiveness, not vengeance, focuses attention on the needs of the victim as well as the punishment of the perpetrator, and points us to the future rather than the past—that is, toward *reconciliation* (see Minow 1998).

Some critics contest the claim that the victim's needs are better served by restorative than retributive justice; and some researchers have interviewed survivors of deadly violence—in South Africa, Rwanda, or Cambodia, for example—where the desire for retributive justice is strongly expressed (for instance, Wilson 2000; Lambourne 2001). About South Africa, van der Merwe (2001:189) argues, "Fundamentally, the TRC was the embodiment of a denial of justice because the amnesty provision … had robbed victims of their right to criminal and civil recourse." Other critics might demur on the question of individual benefit but contest whether the "needs" of society as a whole are best served when perpetrators escape criminal responsibility: whether a so-called culture of impunity is too high a price to be paid for less problematic political transitions. In some conflicts, the search for justice is existentially paramount (as many Palestinians argue), and peace without it is inconceivable (e.g., Rouhana 2004). In any event, the question of the relationship between justice and the TRC is perhaps the central one that these endeavors face. It raises the question, among others, of how far reconciliation can proceed if victims who demand justice feel that it was never attained (or, indeed, ever attempted).

Truth

Although most writing has focused on the problem of justice, attention has also been paid to the notion of truth as featured in the commissions' title. Here, too, the basic distinction is made between the sort of "forensic" truth established as "facts" in courts of law with rules of evidence (often backed up by the standards of scientific proof) and impartial procedure, and the more elusive (but, to advocates, equally valid) sorts of truth sought after and established in truth commissions. In the final report of the South African TRC, four different kinds of truth are set forth. The first is the forensic truth of science and law. The second is "personal" or "narrative" truth, the truth of experience and individual subjectivities. The third is "social" or "dialogue" truth, which emerges through collective discourse and converging *inter*subjectivities. The fourth is "healing" or "restorative" truth, which places truth in a context that consciously affirms individual experience and points toward reconciliation (TRC Final Report 1998:29–45).

Narrative or personal truths especially have been championed as crucial parts of the memory work that these commissions seek to accomplish, ensuring thereby that acts of oppression, violence, and abuse suffered by individuals are inscribed indelibly onto a *public* record and into a *social* memory, and in this way can never be forgotten. (This is why publication of final reports is so important and why the most detailed, descriptive, and experience-near of them—such as Argentina's *Nunca Más*—is so chilling and effective.) Arguably—and here I mean arguably from the psychological point of view—if these commissions are at all truly therapeutic for the victims, a claim made by many supporters, it must be because in the telling of their stories lies some sort of abreactive release (though how a retelling/reliving of terror and abuse can be therapeutic without substantial psychological framing, support, and follow-up, often not so readily available to victims, is an open question).

But the most important claims for these commissions, especially with respect to the goal of reconciliation, necessarily depend on their construction of social dialogue and restorative truths—with the latter presumably dependent on the successful emergence of the former. The emergence of social truth, in turn, requires the convergence of individual memories into a collective memory, of singular narratives onto a grand narrative. (The *meta*narrative then becomes "reconciliation.") There are several reasons to be less than sanguine here. First, one must acknowledge the practical difficulties of crafting shared or collective narratives about deeply contested pasts—pasts, moreover, acted out in acts of horror and violence. Thus Michael Ignatieff wrote that truth commissions can only "reduce the number of lies that can be circulated unchallenged in public discourse" (1996:113). Others face the challenge of formulating social truth by requiring something less than a shared or collective narrative. "Reconciliation," Kelman writes (2004:123), "does not require writing a joint consensual history, but it does require admitting the other's truth into one's own narrative."

Ignatieff's assertion about the reduction of lies notwithstanding, forensic or scientific-historical truths—the facts—however curated, public, or well established, are often of little practical help. Avruch and Vejarano (2001:51) have commented on the "extant massive facticity about the Shoah that yet deters no Holocaust denier." Finally, because facts are never really self-evident, never stand alone, but are always mediated, there is the inevitable problem of the *interpretation* of facts in the creation of narratives. Avruch and Vejarano (2001:52) continue, "Apartheid security forces and the Latin American generals and colonels apparently believed they were fighting Communist subversion under emergency conditions that demanded extraordinary measures to protect national security; and many believe it today, even some among them who appeared before various commissions and admitted their acts and expressed regret for their victims and offered apologies to the survivors. Shared facts do not necessarily conduce to shared truths."

The complexity of establishing *the truth* is hardly limited to the work of TRCs (as centuries worth of philosophical inquiries will attest), but it is a crucial question that they face. Such truth is connected to producing some account of the past, of recent and contested history. Regimes in transition may consciously or explicitly choose not to engage the past in order to safeguard the transition to a more democratic future. This, indeed, was Spain's decision (political elites both on the left and the right in agreement) after Franco's death. But now, more than three decades later, with democracy well established in Spain, calls for some sort of official reckoning with the past—perhaps even a truth commission—are increasing. To many, a past suppressed is a truth repressed, and this constitutes unfinished business for the task of reconciliation, on both the individual and societal levels.

Reconciliation

Reconciliation is a topic of increasing concern in conflict resolution or peace studies, particularly as the former has moved beyond mostly investigating the technical problems involved in getting the parties to the table to sign an agreement or treaty (thus involving technical issues in negotiation or mediation, for example, in peacemaking) and has engaged problems of post-conflict dynamics, of peacebuilding (Ramsbotham et al. 2005:30). The growing literature on reconciliation reflects a wide variety of conceptions of reconciliation as both an ongoing process and an outcome. Some stress structural components such as democratization generally or specific structural arrangements such as the 1951 economic union between France and Germany for coal and steel production that some see as the beginning of postwar European reconciliation. Other researchers have emphasized interpersonal efforts, for instance, through dialogue groups or citizen and student exchanges. But even the structuralists agree that some sort of psychological change among individuals is important in making reconciliation achievable—that formal arrangements at an elite level (a top-down approach) are not by themselves sufficient.[5] Some conceive of reconciliation as the final stage of a continuum of conflict-ending endeavors, beginning with conflict *settlement* (the signing of the treaty, the ending of active violence), conflict *resolution* (addressing the root causes of the conflict, making future violence improbable), and true *reconciliation* (transforming the relationship between the parties so that future violent conflict appears unthinkable). This way of thinking has had a sobering effect for some conflict resolution specialists regarding the likelihood of full reconciliation in cases involving decades of violent conflict or extreme asymmetries of power between the parties, or concerning deeply held values or existential fears about survival. The case in point is often the Israeli-Palestinian conflict (Hermann 2004; Rouhana 2004).

In the literature on reconciliation, truth commissions are usually cited as one component of the larger process, mainly a way of dealing with past violence, with history. Establishing historical truth, as noted, is no small undertaking, and not all such commissions have added the notion of reconciliation to their title or their project—indeed, in a few cases reconciliation was consciously rejected as an aim. Only a minority of them took on this extra task, the best known of which is the South African TRC (1995–1998); not surprisingly, most of that has been written about *truth and reconciliation* has dealt with this case.[6]

If seeking to establish truth—almost any sort of truth—is daunting enough, seeking to go further by adding reconciliation to the aims of the commission is to add a task of immeasurably greater complexity. For in this case, one must necessarily go beyond asserting forensic or even personal individual narrative truth to the collective, the social-dialogic, level. Reconciliation, which is by nature intersubjective and *multiple*, can only emerge with the creation of at least minimally shared—and probably much more than minimally shared—narratives of the past and visions of the future. At least, as Kelman argued, one must be willing to recognize the other's truth as part of one's own narrative. It is hard to imagine a *reconciliation* that is only ever intrapsychic or, if you prefer, it is easier to imagine a personal narrative truth that is autistic, but not a social-dialogic one.

Lederach (1997) has defined reconciliation as requiring the presence of four ingredients: truth, mercy (or forgiveness), justice, and peace. We have already discussed truth and justice in terms of their vicissitudes. By "peace" Lederach intends the notion of positive peace as set forth by Johan Galtung (1969)—a peace beyond the mere absence of direct violence but also of structural violence; one prerequisite here is justice. Mercy or forgiveness is more psychologically complex (see Pruitt and Kim 2004:220–223, on which the following discussion is based). At root, forgiveness entails the relinquishment of the desire for vengeance. Thus it entails changes in self-conception and identity, from *one who wreaks vengeance to one who offers forgiveness*. It is possible then to imagine forgiveness as a wholly intrapsychic or intrapersonal process, a unilateral or inner decision, requiring no action from the offender. (Jesus on the cross is paradigmatic. He also raises some interesting cross-cultural problems for reconciliation, in ethnoreligious traditions wherein forgiveness is less a doctrinal core value than in Christianity—in Buddhism, Islam or Judaism, e.g.; see Abu-Nimer 2003; Gopin 2001; Lambourne 2001.)

But reconciliation (whatever the status of forgiveness) cannot be adequately served by wholly intrapsychic or intrapersonal processes. It requires a transactional process and usually entails apology, and often contrition as well. Much of the work on apology and forgiveness—psychological, pastoral, theological—has stayed close to the interpersonal case, to dialogue in the strict sense of self and alter, I and Thou. But—and here we are getting close to the core of the essay and the central dilemma of the truth and reconciliation commission and issues of identity transformation—how do we get from the one, to the two, *to the many*? The social psychologists Dean Pruitt and Sung Hee Kim (2004:222) pose the problem with deceptive simplicity: "If forgiveness is difficult to achieve at the interpersonal level, imagine how hard it is to achieve between groups. In fact, some authors … have questioned whether group forgiveness is even possible."

Apology and Forgiveness

Apologies offered by one group to another are delicate affairs—whether they are accepted or not is a different question entirely. One way in which such an apology is rendered is by having a representative of the offending group offer an apology to members of the offended group—"the one to the many." Thus Pope John Paul II apologized to the Jewish people, in March 1998, for the Roman Catholic Church's failure to speak out against the Holocaust. This was followed in March 2000 by a more general apology intended explicitly as an act of contrition or "repentance" for "the errors of the Church" in the past two thousand years and for "sins committed" against Jews—but it angered some in that the Holocaust was not singled out.

One-to-many apologies can be tricky. African Americans have long demanded an apology from the United States' government for slavery. President Clinton, on a trip to Africa in March 1998, expressed regret for slavery (but did not quite apologize) and set off a firestorm in the United States between those who claimed he had no right to do so (e.g., then–Republican majority leader Tom De Lay) and those who said his words fell far too short. (Clinton apparently felt an official apology would open the door to reparations, which he opposed.) On the other hand, a remarkable attempt to negotiate the one-to-many model is the establishment in 1998 of a National Sorry

Day in Australia, whereby ordinary Australians took part in ceremonies to mark and apologize to Australia's indigenous people for the crimes and indignities perpetrated against them. This followed an initial rejection of a formal apology from the government of Australia by the Conservative Prime Minister John Howard.

However, the government did establish, on a perhaps politically innocuous "Culture and Recreation" website, "Sorry Books, in which people could record their personal feelings, [which] were presented to representatives of the indigenous communities. Hundreds of thousands of signatures were received. People could also register an apology electronically. You can view the 24,763 apologies to Australia's indigenous people made at *Apology Australia.*" Sorry Day was an annual event between 1998 and 2004. In 2005, it was renamed a "National Day of Healing" with the aim of reconciliation now made explicit. As a result of this bottom-up movement, there was enough popular support by late 2007 for Prime Minister Kevin Rudd to offer, in a motion passed unanimously by the Parliament in February 2008, an official and formal apology to all Aborigines for laws and policies that had in the past "inflicted profound grief, suffering, and loss."[7] One lesson here is the need to build, perhaps over a period of time, wide support at all social levels for such apologies, and not to regard official or elite support alone as sufficient. Another lesson, however, is not to regard such apologies, even if widely supported and enthusiastically received, as panaceas. The apology was not accompanied by any provision for compensation, and this angered some Aborigines, who called it, among other things, a "cut-price sorry."

If mercy or forgiveness is an ingredient to reconciliation, it is difficult to imagine reconciliation occurring in the absence of contrition demonstrated, apologies offered, and acceptance forthcoming. If so, how do truth and reconciliation commissions—South Africa's TRC in particular—fare?

In the course of the TRC's work, there were certainly many instances of victim (or victims' family) meeting perpetrators in situations fraught with emotion. A remarkable film, *Long Night's Journey Into Day* (2000) follows four such cases. One case shows a black policeman who had helped lure seven young activists into a trap where they were killed, confronting and begging forgiveness from the boys' mothers. It is emotionally wrenching and belies any notion that forgiveness is easily given in such cases (to be discussed in more detail on the following pages). But the film also depicts the confession of a white security officer involved in murderous action, and it appears here that remorse or contrition were not so deeply felt—it was certainly resisted by the embittered wife of the victim. Especially in the face of possible amnesty, confessions or apologies may be "tactical" in nature, and therefore, at the *level of self,* apology and confession *need not be transformative.* Such transformation, according to Lederach (1997), *of both self and the relationship between self and other,* sits at the heart of reconciliation. Without it, it is difficult to imagine reconciliation effected. Going further, some critics of the process have raised the question of whether the strong "advocacy of forgiveness" surrounding the TRC has meant that "victims faced with moral pressure [to forgive] by the TRC are further victimized" (Baker 2001:314).

Although no one can deny that many instances of interpersonal reconciliation occurred as a result of the TRC, the goals of the TRC were much grander: They included intrapersonal healing and interpersonal reconciliation—but also healing and reconciliation between communities and at the national level. Intrapersonal or intrapsychic healing is therapeutic and carries implications for self/identity transformation. By extension, an argument can be made for interpersonal reconciliation of the purely dialogic, the I and Thou, type. Here the healing engages two selves, and identity transformation is possible insofar as it is mutually constitutive. But at the level of community, collectivity, and nation-state, the potential for identity transformation becomes much less assured. This is only partly a matter of scale—think of how Clinton's "regret" was not at all unilaterally accepted, for different reasons, by everyone in either community—and the inherent problem in the one-to-many dynamic (see the following text). Fundamentally, it reflects the danger of too easily conflating the individual with the collective, the personal with the political, and therapeutic change with political change (see Rotberg and Thompson 2000; and especially Du Toit 2000). And finally, it runs the risk of underestimating the sorts of deep psychological transformations in selves that had occurred before the TRC begins it work, as a result of years of direct physical violence, or terror and abuse. For in this case we are not dealing with identity transformation in some vector-neutral, or "normally developmental" sense. In the aftermath of violence inflected on selves—and this is the environment in which TRCs attempt to do their work—it is more realistic to think of *identity reconstruction.* And this is indeed a psychologically and politically daunting task, one that underlines the complexity of the one-to-many dynamic.

Manipulating Identities:
From the One to the Many (and Back)

Consider, briefly, two examples highlighting the moral and political complexity of identity transformation in one-to-many situations of assessing accountability in the aftermath of extreme and widespread violence.

Among one of several critiques of Israel's very public trial in 1961 of Adolph Eichmann, Hannah Arendt (1964) took the prosecutors to fault for using the prosecution of one man to stand in for the crimes and atrocities of an entire regime. The scale of the Holocaust, indeed of the entire tragedy of the war in Europe, was beyond the ability of a criminal trial directed against a single individual to contain or to represent. Arendt rejected any trope that had Eichmann stand for Nazism. A trial can only establish the guilt or innocence of, and render punishment to, an individual accused. To go beyond this is to manipulate history for political reasons—and in Israel's case, in part to claim the post-Holocaust right to speak for all of Jewry: for *raisons d'état.*

Now consider another tribunal, held four decades later. Slobodan Milošević appears finally in the Hague and insists on defending himself. In his opening remarks to the court, Milošević is not only not contrite (nor even, as an Eichmann-like technocratic functionary of death, *banal*), but is positively defiant. He accuses the court of being illegitimate and illegal, aiming to rewrite history and find guilty not only himself but the whole nation of Serbia. Here are his opening remarks (February 14, 2001), from the trial's transcript:

> Over the past two years all the prosecutors that we have heard here have uttered one particular sentence—that is to say they were just trying an individual .... So they're trying an individual and not a nation. All three prosecutors said that. But in all the indictments, they are accusing the whole nation, beginning with the Serb intelligentsia .... (http://news.bbc.co.uk/1/hi/world/europe/1820382.stm)

Of course, the Eichmann and Milošević cases are mirror images of one another. Eichmann is held by others (in part against his will: "I was just following orders ... ") to signify Nazism—the one-to-many. Milošević—despite explicit claims by the prosecution that seek to retain the criminal-juridical status of the trial—demands that he signify the many, and therefore to condemn him is to condemn Serbia: now the many become one.

Both of these cases involve criminal trials and not truth commissions, and apology, forgiveness, and reconciliation of any sort are not on the table. Nor is identity transformation in the intrapsychic sense—how Eichmann or Milošević think or feel about themselves—a matter for anyone's concern. But some sort of identity transformation is on the table, though it is decidely political and not therapeutic: The State of Israel claims to represent all of Jewry and make Eichmann represent all of Nazism; and Milošević seeks to become the metonym for all Serbs. In making the political machinations of identity manipulation so explicit, both cases illustrate the sorts of parallel political complexities faced by truth commissions in moving from individual testimony (personal or narrative truth) to shared community or national narrative (social-dialogic truth), to reconciliation (restorative truth).

The success of the South African TRC in this matter is equivocal. On the one hand, Richard Wilson (2000) writes of the TRC trying to recognize and collectivize individual suffering through televising the hearings daily (much as Eichmann's trial was televised). He argues that this succeeded in part, creating a new "national victim" in a "new national collective conscience." On the other hand, Tom Winslow (1997) argues that although the TRC has worked in some ways to effect reconciliation at the collective level, this can occur at the expense of individual, psychological healing—if, for example, the strong "advocacy of forgiveness," noted previously, puts pressure on some victims and forces reconciliation with perpetrators that is ungenuine and perhaps even psychologically hurtful. This is especially true if victims have suffered violence at the hands of perpetrators, in fact the usual environment in which TRCs do their work.

Legacies of Violence and the Reconstruction of Identity

Herbert Kelman (2004:119) has written explicitly of reconciliation as involving a transformation of *collective* identity, of "changing one's collective identity by removing the negation of the other from it." In focusing on collective identity, Kelman once again returns us to the core conceptual problem of negotiating the one (individual personal identity) with the many. But TRCs do their work with identities, personal and collective, that have been traumatized by often extreme and perduring physical violence. This violence complicates immeasurably the identity transformative task of reconciliation. The literature on violence, self, and identity is enormous, and no attempt will be made to summarize it here—beyond the observation that (with the possible exception of unreconstructed cognitive behavioral therapists) most of it focuses in one way or another on how violence is deeply transformative of identity and self, from the shaping of subjectivity (e.g., Das et al. 2000) to the rewiring of the brain (e.g., Niehoff 1999). Likewise, we must accept from the outset that the effects of collective violence are never just about individual psychological functioning, and the "traumatized social self," as Robben and Orozoco-Suarez (2004) maintain, emerges at intersections of self, society, culture, and the globalizing political economies of war and depredation. Though parsed in different terms from "collective identity," with the notion of the "social self" we are once again facing the problem of the one to the many.

Many aspects of social experience or learning, even after the standard "developmental" phases are taken into account, can be transformative. What sets violence apart? Why insist that not only identity transformation is called for in TRC-based reconciliation, but something more precise and emphatic, identity reconstruction? On the one hand, many social psychologists have analyzed the sorts of cognitive and affective changes that occur in individuals after violent conflict has persisted for some time (see Pruitt and Kim 2004:153–160, for a survey.) Mostly (Kelman's work excepted), these stop short of requiring psychological "identity reconstruction" as part of post-conflict reconciliation. On the other hand, "the self," the psychoanalysts Galatzer-Levy and Cohler write, can be taken to mean "the experience of coherence of experience and vitality of will" (1993:28). Here is one way in which extreme violence affects the self precisely, by destroying the subjective experience of coherence and by vitiating subjectivities of agency—vitality—or will.

Here I want to follow the seminal insights of Elaine Scarry (1985) on the consequences of intense and perduring *pain*, and here make pain a signifier of violence more generally. In the world of experience, violence and pain are existential correlates; one can think of them semiotically in the same way. Sara Cobb (2003:294) writes, "Violence marks a place where words no longer fit." Pain, Scarry writes, silences one's voice, constricts one's vision, and effaces the existence of others. The world of the victim is, however, not merely shrunk, for intense and perduring pain "unmakes the world." A world unmade means a self and identity unmade, and "healing" this self and identity requires more than transformation to attain or regain a modicum of agency (enough agency to recognize and *forgive* a perpetrator, the agentic cause of the suffering). A world unmade demands rebuilding, reconstruction.

What is not so clear to me is whether such a reconstruction can take place entirely intrapsychically, with rebuilding focused on one's own subjectivity alone. Here I defer to experienced clinicians, therapists who have treated such victims. But I have my doubts because I believe that part of the unmaking, the *de*construction of self and identity that takes place as a result of violence, ends up somehow incorporating the selves and identities of the perpetrators. In classical psychodynamic terms, their *imago* is introjected; in terms closer to Heinz Kohut's (1971) psychology of the self, a new "selfobject" has been constituted. I think the psychodynamically informed work of Vamik Volkan (2001) on ethnic conflict and hatred, for example, on chosen traumas, is broadly supportive of this way of thinking about self and identity reconstruction (though Volkan focuses importantly on the transgenerational transmission or reproduction of traumatized selves). The implication is this: that the psychological part of identity and self-reconstruction requires the victim to come to terms with that part of the perpetrator that is also him- or herself. This, it seems to me, is the psychological meaning of forgiveness, that first and necessary part that means one has let go of vengeance.

The other implication, less evident in a Kohutian model but crucial for the social scientist seeking to understand reconciliation and the work of TRCs, is that the *other* (the perpetrator, in this way of speaking) collaborates in the reconstruction. We have to be careful here, first because of the deep psychological and therapeutic support that may be required if victim and perpetrator meet face to face (see my earlier reference to the film *A Long Day's Journey Into Night,* or consider Ariel Dorfman's powerful 1991 play, *La Muerte y la Doncella [Death and the Maiden]*). Second, not all commissions deal in as temporally clear a situation as the South African or Argentine TRCs, where victim and perpetrators were contemporaries (in Alfred Schutz's sense of the term) who *could,* indeed, meet face to face. In the Australian case, and especially in the Canadian one, where the wrongs that are focused on are quite specific historical ones (indeed, in both cases critics mention this as a weakness of the process)—a past history of forced placement of children in residential schools—it is more difficult to imagine the possibility for face-to-face meetings with individual *perpetrators,* even though *victims,* including pointedly the children of the residential school students, can be readily found throughout Canada. Who then can stand in for perpetrator as collaborator in the crafting of new narratives? Arguably, it should be Australian or Canadian society as a whole, a psychically embodied body politic. And how likely is this?

Here once again is my skepticism that healing on this scale can be intrapsychic only. And this joins a practical worry that reconciliation processes that do not do *demand* the participation of the perpetrator (in some form) will always be partial. And it is with this observation that the classical language of depth psychology can rejoin other discourses used in this essay, particularly the post-Lacanian discourse of language and narratology—for we are really speaking about the creation of joint therapeutic transcripts, of narratives asserting the social and dialogic truths heralded into existence (perhaps) by the South African TRC. From either perspective relied upon in this work, the psychological or narratological, the therapeutic or political, these are daunting tasks for truth and reconciliation commissions. It is not clear, in their absence, how else the tasks could be accomplished. It is cruel irony to conclude by saying, "The *jury* is still out," but this, in fact, is the case.[8]

9

Conflict Resolution and the Dilemma of Power

Introduction: Power as Other

It is not by chance that David Dunn (2004) entitled his study of John Burton *From Power Politics to Conflict Resolution*, or that Alex Scheinman (2008:240), in his study of the intellectual roots of conflict resolution, referred to power politics as the field's "Other." When conflict resolution is conceived (as it is increasingly) more broadly as "peace and conflict studies," the contrast with power politics becomes even sharper. The reason for this can be found in the "first great debate" that established the hegemony of realism over idealism in the emergent field of international relations, IR (Richmond 2008:21). IR originated in the aftermath of World War I as an enterprise that sought systematically to study the causes of war in order to birth a science of peace. IR in this idealist mode focused on internationalism (today we would say pluralism or world society) "and interdependence, peace without war, disarmament . . . the right of self-determination of citizens, and the possibility of world government or a world federation" (Richmond 2008:22). Its goals found institutional expression mainly in the League of Nations. Had IR continued to develop in this mold, it would, I suggest, very much resemble the field of cosmopolitan "contemporary conflict resolution" as portrayed in the comprehensive textbook of the same name (Ramsbotham et al. 2005). In Foucault's sense of genealogy, conflict resolution, that is, peace and conflict studies, is the descendant of the loser of IR's first great debate. Idealism lost as it was overtaken by events: the rise of fascism and Nazism and the carnage of the World War II. Wilson's idealism and its institutions were judged to have failed. Its goals were derided as utopian, its vision of a world without war inextricably linked to Chamberlain's "peace in our time" and to appeasement. On the eve of that war, E. H. Carr (1939) savagely critiqued idealism's failures as allegedly not seeing the world as it really is, portraying instead the imaginary world idealists would like to see exist. Carr called for an IR that eschewed utopian advocacy in favor of clear-eyed and rigorous analysis.

The winner of the first great debate and the mode of thinking that went on to majorly shape and dominate IR as a discipline for many years was one that purported to see the world as it really is. It arrogated the name *realism* and it was in almost all ways the exact antithesis of idealist—or conflict resolution or peace studies—thinking. Realism (or its refinement in neorealism) made no claims to be a science of peace. It was in fact the opposite, a field devoted to the study of war among nation-states.

The classical realism of Hans Morgenthau's *Politics among Nations* (orig. 1948; cited as Morgenthau and Thompson 1985), Morgenthau himself a refugee from the European barbarism—began with ontology: a conception of Man as "fallen," and a universal human nature characterized by the drive of all for power. Second, he distinguished sharply international from domestic politics: the latter take place within the bounds of some moral community, defined by shared norms, mores or laws. Alongside jural or other levers of control (manifestations of power), such moral principles serve to discipline, as it were, man's dark nature. But no such shared moral community characterizes the international arena, and therefore in international politics the usual moral calculi did not apply. Third, given the *sui generis* nature of international politics, the nation-state was the sole relevant "actor" in this arena, both as player and as object of analysis. States acted to protect or further their national interests. The "main signpost" in following international politics was the concept of national interest "defined in terms of power." Power was "anything that establishes and maintains the control of man over man ... from physical violence to the most subtle psychological ties by which one mind controls another" (1967:9). Though physical violence or force was one manifestation of power, Morgenthau argued that purely political (as opposed to purely military) power was not based on force, because violence obviated the "psychological" domination of mind over mind that formed the essence of political relations. Nevertheless, the conception of power as domination or control was central to classical realism. "All politics," Morgenthau wrote, "domestic and international, reveals three basic patterns; that is, all political phenomena can be reduced to one of three basic types. A political policy seeks either to keep power, to increase power, or to demonstrate power" (1967:36).

For the most part, the main elements that go to make up national power are scalable or can be objectively characterized, measured, and evaluated, treated as variables. They include physical geography (miles of coastline, navigable rivers, deep-water ports, etc.), natural resources (amount of arable land, raw materials, etc.), industrial capacity, military preparedness (including technology and quality/quantity of armed forces), and population. Slightly less scalable are elements of power called national character and national morale—though for the latter Morgenthau approvingly cites Leo Tolstoy's attempt in *War and Peace* at formulating an algorithm for "the spirit of the army" in battle. As for national character, Morgenthau's reference to the "elementary force and persistence of the Russians, the individual initiative and inventiveness of the Americans, the undogmatic common sense of the British, the discipline and thoroughness of the Germans...." (1967:127) should remind us of all that is wrong with the notion of national character (see Chapter 6), and also that in the hands of a realist stylist, even the most elusive elements of power can be made sharply assessable, if not entirely scalable.

The larger point about power is that it emerges in classical realist thinking both as something defined as control and domination, and consisting of relatively objective and countable things—population, GNP, naval tonnage.[1] The first sense of power, as control or domination, has a long history and mainly follows Weber's classic definition.[2] The second sense, objective and mainly material, is more problematic for a Weberian also concerned with meaning (a point taken up mostly by political sociologists; see below), but is central to realist thought. The definition of national interest in terms of power reveals the way in which Morgenthau's politics ultimately dovetailed with his ontology of human nature. Furthermore, for Morgenthau, interests, defined in terms of power ("getting, holding, or increasing") are always self-evident. Boulding made this observation in a review of a later edition of *Politics among Nations*: "To say that a nation follows its national interests is rather like saying that an individual maximizes utility; unless something can be specified about the contents and formation of the values of the decision-maker, the theory amounts to very little more than saying that nations, or persons, do what they do" (Boulding 1964:66). And that is the point: what they (nation or person) do is seek power.[3] How self-evident interests really are is a problem to be discussed below, though it is never a problem in realism.

So the IR that might have been cosmopolitan peace and conflict studies becomes the constricted IR of realist and neorealist theory and research. In the process, peace becomes chimerical, the study of international conflict reduces to the politics of interstate relations by asserting an epistemological disjunction between (domestic) society and state, and finally the whole field is colonized by a mainly materialist conception of power as dominance, coercion, and control. No wonder power becomes the Other for conflict resolution and peace studies. Asserting the relevance of the field means, among other things, asserting a conception of power broader, more nuanced—and yes, more hopeful—than Morgenthau's, and in this way imagining a *praxis* less frightening than Waltz's balance of power (which all too often devolves to a balance of terror) or Herman Kahn's arguments for the feasibility of nuclear war (Kahn 1960).

What makes power a root problem for conflict resolution is the fact that conflict usually occurs between self-evidently more and less powerful parties—

pure power symmetry is the exception rather than the rule—whereas most classical techniques of conflict resolution (including negotiation and mediation) all too often presume a symmetry that does not exist. In the realist's world, as in Thucydides's world of the Melian dialogue, the solution to the problem is self-evident: "The strong do what they have the power to do and the weak accept what they have to accept."[4] This is an axiom essentially unacceptable to conflict resolution or peace studies given its normative base (the very constraint under which realism need not labor). The problem is, if power as dominance or control colonizes the field, what sort of practice can conflict resolutionists in fact follow? Rubin and Salacuse wrote, "Without exaggeration, it can be said that the problem of negotiating under conditions of power inequality is one of the toughest problems currently confronting scholars in this area" (1990:26). No one has put this more strongly than Adam Curle: "Mediators should be very cautious of involvement in conflicts in which one side obviously possesses far more power than the other and is genuinely confident of victory. The reason is not that the weaker, and often oppressed, side should not be forsaken; but that *mediation simply will not work*. The strong are not going to heed any appeal for clemency or compromise. Why should they?" (Curle 1986:12–13, emphasis added).

Taken at face value, Curle seems to render the entire enterprise of conflict resolution, at least of mediation, in conditions of power asymmetry impossible: a field born into stillbirth. But this can't be so: and indeed Curle goes on (as we shall see) to show how a mediator may proceed (Hint: The powerful party appears "genuinely confident of victory"). How can conflict resolution approach, and in fact reduce, the powerful Other of coercive and dominating power? There are at least five options, with several variant strategies. In some ways, the most radical option is to *deny* outrightly the "power of power" as relevant in deeply rooted conflicts (Burton 1987, 1990). In stark contrast, one can *accept* the notion of power as a reality in social relations and seek to accommodate it within "dispute resolution systems" alongside interest-based negotiation and rights-based solutions (Ury, Brett, and Goldberg 1988). Or one can conceptualize power starkly as dominance and control, and work to *undermine* it on its own terms—thus Adam Curle (1986), among others—or go further to identify asymmetry with injustice and inequality and work not just to undermine, but to eradicate (Rouhana 2004). Alternatively, one can *deconstruct* power asymmetry into differentially addressable issues (Mitchell 1993, 2001, 2003) or *broaden* power's scope toward "productive" and prosocial conceptions (Boulding 1956, 1961, 1962, 1964, 1989).[5] In any case, a conflict resolution that fails to engage power in some way forfeits its normative claims and its pragmatic goals, as well as undermines an ethic of practice. The Other cannot be ignored.

This chapter describes the various terms of engagement the field (including its more ADR-oriented practitioners) has undertaken. First, and with some trepidation, I consider some conceptualizations of power beyond Morgenthau and the realists.

Conceptualizing Power

I say trepidation, but honestly the emotion of *Schadenfreude* may be closer to what an embattled culture theorist—used to conceptual assaults on culture; charges of trafficking in "impossible objects"; "empty signifiers" (Brigg 2008; Brigg and Muller 2009); or worse, calls to simply ditch the idea entirely—feels when encountering the debates on the notion of power. Here is Dennis Wrong's brief (and incomplete!) survey of what he called the "definitional chaos" in the field:

> Power is regarded as a form of influence, or influence as a form of power, or they are treated as entirely distinct phenomena. Power is held to rest always on consent, or it must always confront and overcome resistance. Authority is a subtype of power, or power and authority are distinct and opposite. Persuasion is a form of power; it is not a form of power at all. Force is a form of power; it is not power but a sign of the breakdown or failure of power. Manipulation is or is not a form of power. Personal leadership is or is not a form of authority. Competence is a basis for persuasion and has nothing to do with power and authority, or it is the fundamental implicit ground of all legitimate authority. All power is reducible to the unequal exchange of goods and services, or the offering of benefits in return for compliance is simply one form of power. (Wrong 1988: 65 [orig. 1979])

Wrong leaves out of this catalogue approaches to power based mainly on ideas of intentionality (Russell 1962 [orig. 1938]), decision making (Dahl 1957, 1961), capacity (Lukes 2005 [orig.1974]), the power nexus between individual agency and institutions/structures (Giddens 1979), or (looking somewhat ahead), the entire edifice of poststructural thinking about power, notably Foucauldian ideas of discipline, discourse, the carceral, the capillary, governmentality, and the nexus of power/knowledge (Foucault 1980). Out of this definitional chaos power may thus appear simultaneously the central concept in all the social sciences (Russell 1962 [orig. 1938]), vague and better discarded than kept (McClelland 1971), or an essentially contested concept—though indispensable for all that (Lukes 2005:30 [orig. 1974]).[6] Whatever else these different and varied conceptions of power indicate, they point to a more suggestive range of ideas than the rather monodimensional and mainly materialist depiction found in realist IR. Power is an essentially *uncontested* and unproblematic notion for Morgenthau and Waltz, in line with their conception of the rational action demanded from states in an anarchic and amoral international system. Just how flat the realist's conception of power is can be gleaned when one considers the respectful attention—as though something utterly new has been discovered—given by the readership of *Foreign Policy* or *Foreign Affairs* to the idea of extending the notion of power from "hard power" to "soft power," defined as the ability to influence others through "attraction" rather than coercion or "payments," and combining them (mostly in American public diplomacy or for more effective counterinsurgency operations) to create something called "smart power" (Nye 2004).

Political philosophers, political sociologists, and political scientists (those who did not work formally in IR) thought about power differently. Many of these scholars shared with realists the base Weberian definition of power as the ability of individual actors (which meant states, for the realists) to control others ("even in the face of resistance"); but the sociologists, in particular, understood that by the time Weber moved from power to authority and legitimacy, he inevitably invoked institutions ("offices") bestowing authority and meaning (the normative and moral dimensions of legitimacy) beyond the cost-benefit technical rationality that the realists expected of states in the international system. Two major debates characterized discussions of power among sociologists and political scientists before, at least, those discussions were occupied by poststructuralist concerns. The debates overlapped in that the power theory of C. Wright Mills featured in both of them.

The first debate pitted functionalist against conflict sociology. Talcott Parsons defined power as "the generalized capacity to secure the performance of binding obligations by units of a system of collective organization when the obligations are legitimized with reference to their bearing on collective goals and where in case of recalcitrance there is a presumption of enforcement by negative situational sanctions—whatever the actual agency of that enforcement" (in Haugaard 2002:78 [Parsons 1963]). Elsewhere, Parsons characterized the role of political power as facilitating political exchange, and in this way analogous to the function of money in the economic system. The wielder of political power was analogous to a banker. In Parsonian sociology, concepts of power, authority, and legitimacy were thoroughly conflated. Power was presumed always already legitimate, working (like a well-functioning market) to maintain the stability or equilibrium of the social system. The basal state of the social system was consensual. Opposition or resistance to the exercise of power was by this definition always to be considered contra-legitimate, as deviance. "Negative situational sanctions"—say, violence, coercion, or force— were therefore not assumed to be structurally intrinsic to the system (hence, situational), and not part of the exercise of true power, only a temporary, situational corrective to address transient systemic disequilibria.[7]

Although others, like Ralf Dahrendorf (1959), came to oppose Parsons's functionalism in articulating conflict sociology, it was C. Wright Mills who addressed Parsons with the greatest animus (Mills 1959), which was reciprocated (Parsons 1957, 1960). In *White Collar* (1951) and *The Power Elite* (1956), Mills set out a Marxian analysis of power in America as rooted in social class and deployed by an interlocking network of powerful individuals coming from political, military, and economic institutions. This elite group represented the "managerial reorganization of the propertied classes [the traditional Marxist ruling class] into the more or less unified stratum of the corporate rich" (Mills 1956:147). Mills followed Weber in defining power as domination of others even in the face of resistance, and saw (as did Marx) coercion as intrinsic to the system. Against Parsons, he saw manipulation at work where the former adduced legitimacy.

Besides Parsons, other American sociologists doubted Mills's depiction of a corporate ruling class of elites (e.g., Reisman 1956, who found in the American middle class the main locus of power, and this pluralistically distributed), but it was in political science that Mill's elite theory was most productively attacked (and defended). Much of the critique was on the basis of Mills's alleged empirical shortcomings and lack of methodological rigor: He was not value-neutral and certainly hostile to American capitalism![8] The engagement with Mills's elite theory occurred in a series of studies of the politics of American communities. In the earliest and influential of these, methodological rigor and empirical purity were guaranteed by adhering strictly to behavioralist criteria. Power was operationalized by defining it in terms of who controlled decision making over public policy issues, and measured by counting only these observable events—public policy decisions about specific issues made by identifiable individual actors.

In the work of Robert Dahl (1957, 1961), the behavioralist criteria were invoked first in response to a study of community power by Floyd Hunter (1953), which broadly supported Mills's conception of a small local elite, often working behind the scenes, who controlled decision making on matters both public and private. But Hunter had defined his elite group in terms of reputational criteria, by asking locals to name those they believed ran things in the community and then creating a group composed of names that appeared frequently in many locals' lists. Dahl rejected this on the methodological grounds that collating varied lists did not allow a sufficiently "well-defined" group of decision makers to emerge, and that reputation was not a sufficiently robust measure of actual power—power as deployed rather than notional. In a study carried out in the 1950s in New Haven, Connecticut, Dahl argued that across a number of public policy domains—urban renewal, school desegregation, and political party nominations—there emerged no monolithic elite group or hidden ruling class. Instead, different actors, parties, and groups competed with one another based upon their interests or preferences, and power was measured by counting whose preferences prevailed in the end. In this way, a sense of power derived from Weber was operationalized in the arena (one is tempted to say marketplace) of public policy decision making. Rather than being centralized in any single elite group, power was distributed pluralistically. At the same time that this was a methodological critique of Hunter's work, the pluralist's position also set forth a metanarrative in opposition to Mills's depiction of class domination and elite rule. It was, that is, a defense of American democracy, positing a picture of political power in terms of freely and openly competing interest groups.

The several critiques of Dahl and the pluralists that followed came to define much of the pre-poststructuralist discussion of power in American political science and sociology. Schattschneider (1960) introduced the idea of the "mobilization of bias," arguing that organizations were structured with bias built in, allowing some forms of conflict to surface but disallowing others. "Some issues are organized into politics," he wrote, "and some issues are organized out" (1960:71). Following this line of thinking, although rejecting power as reputational or resource based and sticking with the "metric" of decision making, Bachrach and Baratz (1962, 1963) proposed a "second face of power," operationalized by the idea of "non-decision making." This meant: Who had the power to keep some issues from ever coming to the point of decision (the power to ensure some bits of potential politics/conflict are organized out)? Who had the power to control the agenda on which issues did or did not appear for consideration?

Although the idea of controlling the agenda as a form of power looks like common sense—certainly ought not appear obscure or exotic to any academic who has sat through a semester's worth of departmental faculty meetings under a muscular chair—the pluralists nevertheless riposted on methodological grounds: How does one *count* a nonevent? How does one authenticate a counterfactual? It seemed as if the pluralists, relying on an unreconstructed behaviorism—what counts is only what we can see—were invoking The Method in just the way Mills accused, as a way to suppress "out of politics" substantive questions. Bachrach and Baratz, as commonsensical as agenda control seemed, were methodologically disadvantaged by the fact that they also adhered to behavioral criteria in seeking only to count outputs—decisions not to make decisions. Furthermore, behind the critique lay a real difficulty having to do with how we define the nature of interests. Bachrach and Baratz's critics relied on a notion of interests as preferences made visible in the arena of public, competitive political process, and if preferences remained invisible (unvoiced or "un-agenda-ed") in non-decisions, how do we know they represent the parties' "real interests"? Put differently: Are interests only to be defined in subjective terms? As we shall see, this is a crucial question for conflict resolution as well, particularly for those forms of negotiation (and by extension, mediation) conceptualized as digging beneath positions to parties' underlying (divergent) interests and reconciling these with problem-solving modalities. If there are questions about the wholly subjective nature of interests and the possibility of unvoiced interests, as above, can conflict resolution practitioners be confident they know what the parties' interests really are? Do they have an ethical responsibility to find out?

Putting aside these conflict resolution-specific issues for the moment (they'll return with a vengeance around the idea of empowerment), I move to Steven Lukes's contribution to the debate, in his articulation of power's third dimension (Lukes 2005 [orig. 1974]). Lukes argued that Bachrach and Baratz's articulation of power's second dimension was an improvement over Dahl in that it paid attention to power as control of the agenda (and to the organization of bias), in addition to observing decision making in official or public agendas. But they didn't go far enough in keeping with the behaviorist idea of non-decisions as sorts of events, and linking such non-decisions to overt conflict over unarticulated grievances and unexpressed interests (preferences) on the part of the less powerful. Lukes wanted to go beyond the unarticulated to the *unarticulable*:

> To put the matter sharply, A may exercise power over B by getting him to do what he does not want him to do, but he also exercises power over him by influencing, shaping or determining his very wants. Indeed, is it not the supreme exercise of power to get another or others to have the desires you want them to have—that is, secure their compliance by controlling their thoughts and desires? (Lukes 2005:27 [orig. 1974])

Later this question, around wants, was sharpened to refer explicitly to the nonexpression of grievances, that is to the possibility of power and latent, as opposed to manifest, conflict, and to a conception of unarticulated preferences—unarticulated because unarticulable—as the third (and in a sense ultimate) dimension of power:

> [I]s it not the supreme and most insidious exercise of power to prevent people ... from having grievances by shaping their perceptions, cognitions and preferences in such a way that they accept their role in the existing order of things, either because they can see or imagine no alternative to it, or because they see it as natural and unchangeable, or because they value it as divinely ordained and beneficial? To assume that the absence of grievance equals genuine consensus is simply to rule out the possibility of false or manipulated consensus by definitional fiat. (Lukes 2005:28 [orig. 1974])

Lukes's contribution to the community power debate came to be known as completing the "three faces of power" and framed much of the work on power generally in political sociology and political science—even if in critique—throughout the 1970s and 1980s, at least until poststructuralist approaches began to capture the attention of many. His third dimension echoed Gramsci's idea of hegemony, and his conception of power as domination fit most, if not all, varieties of Marxist analyses of power, as it did IR's realism, though with a problematized approach to interests. His idea of unarticulated/unarticulable preferences pointed toward the Marxist notion of real or objective interests as opposed to subjective interests defined (as behaviorists defined all interests) in terms of actors' preferences as revealed by their public (and countable) choices and decisions. However, his "radical" proposition of wants, desires, perceptions, and cognitions shaped by others reminded many (but especially his critics) of Marx's false consciousness, a "discredited idea" some saw as presumptuous, patronizing, or revealing a "deeply condescending conception of the social subject as an ideological dupe ...." (Lukes 2005:149).

In the second edition of *Power: A Radical View* (2005), Lukes responded to various critics, noting the influence of Foucault and other poststructuralist writings on power, in two chapters that taken together were longer than the original text. I want to concentrate here on his response to critics who questioned his formulation of domination in terms of shaping actors' real interests as false consciousness. He responds first by delinking the idea from a Marxist "exclusionary focus on class," as well as disclaiming the "self-assurance and dogmatism with which Marxist thinkers, sectarians, and party secretaries" acted to impute false consciousness to others (2005:145–146). But in the end, he is unwilling—unable—to give up the idea because his conception of power as domination through constraint of interests that are unrecognized by the actors "requires an external standpoint" (2005:146). But if not class, whence that standpoint? His answer demonstrates the impact of poststructuralist critiques of grand theoretical narratives and Archimedean conceits. He sounds almost a relativist as he defines real interests as a function not of some universal and rigid category like class but of the analyst's case-specific "purpose, framework and methods, which in turn have to be justified." He continues in a Foucauldian mode, "There is no reason to believe that there exists a canonical set of such interests that will constitute the 'last word on the matter'—and will resolve moral conflicts and set the seal on proffered explanations, confirming them as true" (2005:148). Thus he wishes to avoid the "unwelcome historical baggage" carried by the idea of false consciousness by reducing it from an "arrogant assertion of a privileged access to *truths* presumed unavailable to others … to a cognitive power of considerable significance and scope, namely, *the power to mislead*" (2005:149, emphasis in original).

Invoking modesty, this response is nevertheless not entirely convincing. Short of adopting a full-blown relativism with respect to identifying objective or real interests and leaving every judgment about interests to the subjectivity of the actors, Lukes's dilemma remains: The very idea of power's third dimension *requires* that "external standpoint."[9] Having jettisoned class, Lukes finds his "empirical basis for identifying real interests" by repeating the argument made in the earlier (1974) edition: One finds real interests in situations of A having power over B not by looking to "A, *but to* B exercising choice in conditions of relative autonomy and … independently of A's power—e.g., through democratic participation" (2005:146, emphasis in original). The external standpoint emerges thus by *imagining* an autonomous agent free of constraints, democratically exercising choice: a Habermasian standpoint. Intent on preserving his conception of power as the capacity to "secure unwilling consent to domination," Lukes is unable to embrace a fully poststructuralist conception of power because of the threat imposed by relativism and the necessity to give up on Archimedes. In denying the existence of a canonical and truthful set of interests but holding on to "real interests" nevertheless, he ends the book, quoting Marcuse, as a sort of critical theorist. Academic labels aside, what matters for the practice of conflict resolution facing the obdurate problem of power is that the dilemma faced by the need to claim an external standpoint for the identification of real interests is the same dilemma faced by third-party practitioners in the field when confronting situations of power imbalance and domination, while rejecting out of hand the realist's Melian solution.

Power and Conflict Resolution in ADR Theory and Practice

This is not to say that practitioners, particularly those working in ADR contexts, explicitly link their practice around power to coherent theories or theorizing in general. Quite the contrary is true. In her insightful study of mediators' perspectives on power, Juliana Birkhoff notes that although mediators are certainly aware of power dynamics in the course of mediation, and are mostly sensitive to power asymmetries, they tend not to think of power in theoretical or abstract terms. In fact, they resisted talking about power as a concept at all. Instead, she writes, mediators' thinking about power "is tacit and contextual. Furthermore, although they have a set of 'seat of the pants' concepts, they do not inductively move from those concepts to link them into a framework. They do not explicitly abstract from those cases to a theory" (Birkhoff 2002:304). Nor do they seem to explicitly deduce from any theory to a case or to a practice.[10] But, of course, they do possess a tacit and implicit theory of power to guide their practice, as Birkhoff finds in her interviews and surveys. It is first of all a theory of power very much focused on the agency part of the structure/agency dynamic. In the tradition of a liberal humanist perspective on power (as distinct from a structuralist or poststructuralist one), it concerns the skills, abilities, or capacities of the individual, or the resources he or she can access and deploy. Combined with this is a sort of ambivalence toward power that Birkhoff characterizes as a distinction between "good power" versus "bad power." Bad power is coercion, repression, or manipulation of one party by another, what many mediators (and others in the field) call "power over." In contrast, there is a way of conceiving of power in positive terms, called "power to" or "power with." Birkhoff finds her mediators consider this positive power "emancipatory or self-actualizing power. By differentiating between negative and positive power, mediators try to distinguish between the results of power dynamics they approve of: effective individuals, democratic processes, fair institutions; and the results of power dynamics they disapprove of: manipulation, coercion, and domination" (2002:124).

This tacit theorizing accounts for how many mediators deal with obvious power imbalance in their practice. Even the change of language from *power over* to *power to/with* implies an understanding of mediation as a process by which disputants engage in problem solving, entailing jointly productive, creative, and collaborative work. Indeed, this is also the way in which interest-based negotiation of the "getting to yes" variety conceives of problem solving in contrast to adversarial positional bargaining. This parsing of power comes across as almost Parsonian in its positive connotations and system-enhancing capacity. Such an approach is particularly to be found in genres of mediation bordering on the therapeutic, like Bush and Folger's (1994) transformative mediation, which views self-actualization as power enhancing and a successful mediation as relationship building or reparative. Collaboration is also central to narrative mediation, an approach, like transformative mediation, not conceived as a problem-solving modality (Winslade and Monk 2000).

But as we know, many mediators concentrate on case-specific details in formulating their approach to power. If in the course of a mediation the *power over* sense of asymmetry is recognized by the mediator then, absent his or her successful transformation of the parties within the case to *power to/with* modalities, to creative and constructive collaboration, what is to be done? Given unyielding *power over*—the domination of one party by another—another strategy may be called for. The general term for such a strategy is "empowerment," which Birkhoff finds many mediators regard as the epitome of "good power." Empowerment is a key idea for a variety of conflict resolution practitioners, and it means different things in different contexts, as we shall see. In the ADR-oriented world of Birkhoff's mediators, it refers to enhancing the position of the less powerful party in the context of the mediation. For most mediators, this begins with a strong commitment to address power imbalance by ensuring the integrity of the *process* itself. This means, for example, setting out and enforcing ground rules that apply equally to all parties, regulating turn taking, preventing personal attacks, guaranteeing within the process a parity of esteem, and ensuring that the parties think about and evaluate potential alternative courses of action. This last reflects the conceptual connection between mediation and negotiation—the former steps in when the latter falters—discussed in Chapter 7. Given mediation's role as stepping into disputes where negotiation between the primary parties has in some way failed, the generating of alternative outcomes is in line with the fundamental advice routinely given to negotiators, namely that the most important source of power in a negotiation is first to know, and then with luck to possess, a good BATNA.[11]

The other sort of *power over* that Birkhoff's mediators recognize results from unequal possession or access to resources. However, the extent to which mediators ought to address disparities of resources, and how to do so, becomes problematic given the commitment to neutrality that many mediators adhere to—understanding that neutrality has long been a point of contention in the field. First, what does one mean by "resources?" If by resources one means providing information or knowledge intrinsic to the *process*—say, what mediators sometimes do for parties in caucuses, such as "reality checking"; or an acknowledgment up front that an agreement need not necessarily emerge and either party is free to leave the mediation at any time; or indeed, guaranteeing parity of esteem for the less powerful party—then providing such resources will not threaten mediator neutrality. But if the information to be given requires expertise about substantive matters relating to the dispute, say technical information currently available to one party but not the other, or if it involves resources in some way entirely external to the process—funds to hire a good lawyer, to take an extreme example—then it is more problematic for a neutrality-committed mediator to intervene. Sara Cobb (1993) has also pointed to incoherence among most mediators with respect to separating "process" from "content." Of course, as we shall see, if neutrality is rejected out of hand, then empowerment carries much more weight, transcending the rigid boundaries of "the process" as most facilitative mediators understand it. For one thing, a decidedly *activist* third-party role is implied. For another, such empowerment may point to a conception of third-party practice reaching beyond a liberal humanist understanding of power as focused on the individual, and toward a critical engagement with structure.

For the ADR-oriented mediators in Birkhoff's study, power is conceptualized mainly in individual, agentic terms, viewed with ambivalence and split into "good" and "bad" varieties. Power asymmetry is certainly familiar, and many recognize it as a potential problem. The "remedy" is mainly to be found in the mediator's skill in guaranteeing the integrity of the process and seeking within the process to transform power as domination, *power over*, to power as creative collaboration: *power to* or *power with*. Within the field generally, the most articulate description of these different varieties of power is found in Kenneth Boulding's *Three Faces of Power* (1989).[12]

Boulding's version of *power over/to/with* begins with classifying forms of power in terms of their social consequences: *destructive, productive, and integrative.* The power to destroy represents the essence of *power over*, epitomized by threats. Productive power, perhaps not surprisingly for an economist, is best represented as exchange power. This is a *power to* manifestation, the power to create goods, services, and resources by engaging in social reciprocity, from formal trade to informal conversation. Boulding invokes Adam Smith's vision of social exchange as a positive and creative process, but the image could just as easily be Parsons's power as a medium of political exchange. Integrative power—here speaks the Quaker rather than the Keynesian—is the *power with* that emerges from valued social relationships, epitomized by love or, "if *love* seems too strong, substitute *respect*" (1989:29). In turn, these three "faces" of power can be found in different major domains of society: destructive threat in the political and military domain, productive exchange in the economic, and integrative love in the social. Finally, there's a little bit of each kind of power in all the three faces. One can find some version of the *power over/to/with* image in much writing on mediation and other third-party processes, dating back to Mary Parker Follett (e.g., Follett 1973; Coleman 2000; Docherty 2004). It infuses some kinds of feminist discourses on conflict and conflict resolution, as well (e.g., Schaef 1981; Taylor and Miller 1994). One can argue that such forms as transformative and narrative mediation—or, indeed, interest-based negotiation of the "getting to yes" variety—all partake in some way or another in the deconstruction of power from modalities of domination, control, and destruction to softer, more hopeful construals of it. After all, Paulo Freire (1970:78) explicitly linked his notion of *conscientization*—a crucial mechanism of empowerment to be considered in greater depth below—to "love"; and Foucault (hardly a Parsonian) often noted power's capacity to create and integrate, even as it simultaneously destroys and divides (Foucault 1980:119).

Within the purely dispute resolution sense of conflict resolution, perhaps the most pragmatic, or least fraught, approach to the problem of power has been offered by Ury, Brett, and Goldberg (1988), who place it in the context of designing complete "systems" to deal with disputes and the "costs of conflict."

Power, defined narrowly as the ability to coerce, is inevitably part of social relationships, and part of a repertoire of choice in dealing with conflict. The other two choices involve paying attention to interests (essentially the "getting to yes" model of interest-based problem solving and negotiation), and appealing to rights (as defined and legitimated contextually). Even while noting that sometimes power is necessarily invoked (e.g., to bring a "recalcitrant party" to the table), or a rights orientation makes sense (to decide on social structural issues, such as school desegregation in the 1954 Supreme Court decision), Ury, Brett, and Goldberg take a pragmatic and cost-benefit approach to assessing the strengths of each choice. They argue that "in general, reconciling interests is less costly than determining who is right, which in turn is less costly than determining who is more powerful.... [F]ocusing on interests ... tends to result in lower transaction costs, greater satisfaction with outcomes, less strain on the relationship, and less recurrence of disputes" (1988:15). They are careful, as noted above, to say that not all disputes involve reconcilable interests (they mention pro-life and pro-choice conflicts around abortion as an example; see Chapter 7), and those that do not often relate to deeper structural issues of social inequality or cultural ones around strongly held values (Forester 2009). These sorts of cases lead us away from narrowly ADR-oriented approaches to power and conflict, and toward a range of conflicts identified variously as deep-rooted, protracted, or intractable ones.

Power in Conflict Resolution Theory and Practice Beyond ADR

In Chapter 2, I discussed the very bright line that John Burton sought to draw between conflict *management* and conflict *resolution*: the former dealing with *disputes* amenable to distributive bargaining or the more advanced interest-based sort, and to mediation techniques that built upon these; the latter dealing with deep-rooted *conflicts* that were often characterized by violence, repression, and human suffering, and caused by the suppression of basic human needs. Within peace studies, meanwhile, a cognate distinction was drawn by Galtung between interventions aimed at reducing or stopping direct violence, bringing a negative peace, and those that sought to address deep-rooted structural violence, eventuating in positive peace. This distinction became the fundamental axiom for peace studies. Because of the nature of the conflicts that Burton and Galtung, among others, attended to, the problem of power—power asymmetry to be precise—was less a technical question to be dealt with in the context of the mediation process and more an overtly political (and for some a moral) question that reflected the very contours and dynamics of what the conflict was about. Power imbalance, in other words, was often one of the key factors at the very root of the conflict, and these protracted and intractable conflicts could be understood almost by definition as the powerful in some way oppressively dominating a less powerful party.[13]

What made this a fundamental problem for these conflict resolution practitioners was twofold. First, the (realist's) Melian solution was not acceptable; indeed, in many cases the more powerful party's attempt to impose one is what led to the conflict's most virulent manifestations. People, Burton argued, would struggle to their deaths in seeking satisfaction of repressed basic human needs. This anti-Melian stance, after all, was what made power, as understood by realists, the Other for conflict resolution and peace studies. Second, almost all of the extant "technologies" of conflict resolution presumed the essential symmetry of the parties; when asymmetry was recognized, it was typically worked around in the context of the negotiation or mediation process, usually in ways wholly internal to the process.[14] Analytically, this was true from the ground up, so to speak: the presumption of symmetry infused even the paradigmatic epitome of two-party negotiation modeled by game theory. Game theory, Balzer wrote, can indeed "describe exertions of power .... The point however, is that it can do so only *in the given frame* of the rules of the game. Since the essence of power consists in changing these rules, game theory fails to grasp the essential feature of power" (Balzer 1992:74, emphasis in original). What we learned from Lukes, among others, is that power is about the capacity to determine (or change) the very rules of the game under which negotiation (or other sites of social interaction) takes place. The problem facing conflict resolution attempting to deal with conflicts characterized by histories of oppression, lethal violence, and suffering—and sometimes with mutual victimization and recrimination—is simply that it may not be up to the task: "What lags behind are the methodologies of conflict resolution that remain stuck in paradigms of symmetrical analysis and avoidance of the core issues and trying to force them into the symmetrical paradigms" (Rouhana 2011:304). It is especially not up to the task, Rouhana continues, if it takes on the burden of achieving Burton's full conflict resolution, Lederach's conflict transformation, or Galtung's positive peace, that is, in moving beyond settlement or management toward the *reconciliation* of the former enemies. Among the core issues Rouhana considers "avoided" by much conflict resolution is justice (Rouhana 2004, 2005, 2008, 2010).

So how is power handled in conflict and peace studies beyond ADR, where it might be accommodated alongside negotiation or recourse to rights as the possibly costliest alternative in a well-designed dispute resolution system? As I wrote earlier, there are several strategies. Underlying all of analytical problem solving, but also fundamental to transformative, narrative, and dialogic approaches, is the idea that one can, as Boulding did, broaden the reach of power beyond dominance and control, *power over*, to conceive of its operating in more benign, integrative, or creative ways—*power to* and *power with*. If, however, one limits the understanding of power more narrowly to *power over*, domination and control, one can seek to undermine these, the basis of *over*, by altering the balance of power between the parties, either relatively and situationally, such that the powerful are induced to suspend, at least contingently, outright domination and come to negotiate, or absolutely, such that all imbalance is removed and "justice" prevails. An unexpected strengthening of the weaker party might make the continuation of the conflict more costly for the stronger party, perhaps even leading to a "hurting stalemate," which some see as a sign of a conflict's "ripeness" and a prerequisite for the stronger party's willingness to negotiate (Zartman 2000b; but see also Pruitt 2005). The question of justice prevailing, meanwhile, entails a far more thoroughgoing structural change, what Curle (1971) calls a "revolution." Collectively these strategies often go by the name of empowerment. (Relatedly, as the problem is conceived in terms of power asymmetry, one can move analysis from focusing mostly on the effects of power, supposedly addressed by empowerment, to focus on the nature of asymmetry, its possible varieties, and the different implications for third-party practice these might entail; see below.)

Before discussing empowerment, I should note the most radical approach to the problem of power offered in our field, by John Burton. Burton's theory of the suppression of basic human needs as the root cause of deep-rooted conflicts denies the very "power of power" to effectively dominate and control. Individuals will struggle unto death as these needs are suppressed, and neither outright repression (à la Marx) nor seemingly benign socialization (the Parsonian solution) is capable of eradicating or significantly altering these needs, which are internal to individuals as ontological givens. This idea was first fully articulated in *Deviance, Terrorism and War* (Burton 1979), and remained unchanged in his later work, such as *Violence Explained* (1997). The denial of the ontological primacy of power naturally put Burton at odds with the dominant trends in IR on both sides of the Atlantic and made him a somewhat marginal figure in that field, if at the same time a central one in peace and conflict studies, which needed to "Other" power in one way or another.[15] Nevertheless, there is an element of legerdemain in Burton's denial of power to the realists, because in another sense his theory of basic human needs has the effect of proposing a metatheory of power, or at least one of displacing ultimate power from actor or nation-state onto biology or ontology. Thus we have not so much done away with power as moved its primary base of operation. In any event, the main third-party *practice* implied by Burton's theory, the analytical problem-solving workshop, was based on the expert panel's guiding the parties to an *analysis* of the conflict as one of suppressed or unmet basic human needs, while *educating* the more powerful party about the limitations of their so-called power, the ultimate dynamics — and fateful outcomes: struggle by the weaker unto death — of such conflicts, and then getting the more powerful to *cost* these outcomes in order to see that resolution is, in the end, the most rational and beneficial course for them to take (Avruch and Black 1990).

The twinned ideas of analysis and education also characterize the widespread notion of empowerment, though with a key difference. In Burton's practice, analysis and education are to be directed primarily toward the more powerful party, to get them to recognize the conflict as one of suppressed basic human needs and to appreciate the costs to their own interests of continuing it. In empowerment, by contrast, the activities of analysis and education are to be directed by the third party to the less powerful, in the service of increasing their power vis-à-vis the more powerful party, leveling the field and bringing some balance to the contest.

This is precisely what Adam Curle meant by empowerment: It is only by leveling the field that one might significantly affect the behavior of the more powerful party, which under normal circumstances has no felt need for "clemency or compromise," much less to negotiate or invite the intervention of mediators. "Why should they? They are confident that they can get what they want without giving an inch" (Curle 1986:13). Here then is the key to empowerment: by increasing the power of the less powerful, one undermines the confidence of the more powerful that victory is assured. Curle takes Schelling's (1966) definition of power as the capacity to create uncertainty, and seeks in empowerment a way to allow the less powerful party to increase the uncertainty (by decreasing the certainty of prevailing) of the more powerful (Curle 1971:6).

Curle sees empowerment as part of the six-stage process through which "peacemakers" operate: research, conciliation, bargaining, development, education, and confrontation. The two most closely associated with empowerment *per se* are the last two. In education, "the weaker party in a low-awareness/ unbalanced relationship gains awareness of its situation and so attempts to change it." Following increased awareness of its plight comes confrontation, "through which the weaker party to an unbalanced relationship asserts itself in the hope of gaining a position of parity, and hence the possibility of reaching a settlement that will lead to a restructuring of the relationship. Confrontation may have many forms, ranging from revolution to nonviolent protest" (Curle 1971:20). Nonviolent protest presents no great dilemma for the Quaker Curle (though see Groom and Webb's [1987] critique that follows). The idea of revolution, involving the overturning of existing power elites and their structures of privilege does, however, present problems. First, is the endpoint simply the replacement of one "oligarchy" by another? This only redistributes the loci of injustice. Second, to what extent does revolution entail the *violent* elimination of those who surely would not welcome the end of their privileges: "If peace can be won only by turning the top dogs into underdogs (or perhaps dead dogs), can it be said to be peace?" The "idea jars," Curle remarks (1971:22). The possibility that confrontation brings with it violence is something Curle takes seriously, and he discusses situations wherein violence makes some sense, in building morale or confidence, for example, or by encouraging "those who might otherwise have remained passive" to join in the struggle (1971:199). He goes so far as to cite Fanon's (1986) argument that freedom achieved "without violence is only half achieved .... I have seen enough of neocolonialism to concede the force of this argument" (1971:199). Not surprisingly, nevertheless, in the end he adduces many reasons why violence is to be avoided at—almost—all costs, not the least being its destructive and usually viral nature. In the end, in keeping with the principles of nonviolence, he argues for a form of "moral confrontation"—though here again such confrontation can potentially turn violent. What is interesting in this argument is that he focuses mainly on violence directed by the underdogs against the top dogs. Groom and Webb (1987), as we shall see, reflecting that most revolutions fail and that in almost any form of confrontation the top dogs are usually better equipped, worry about the vector going the other way.

Curle's understanding of "education" as the making of awareness is directly comparable to Paulo Freire's discussion of "conscientization" in his *Pedagogy of the Oppressed* (1970).[16] Curle and Freire's conceptions are brought together explicitly in Diana Francis's *People, Peace, and Power* (2002), where the ideas are applied to the practice of conflict transformation workshops in conflicts characterized by power asymmetries—Francis here clearly differentiating conflict resolution (which to her leaves power largely unaddressed) versus transformation. Her "dialogue workshops" do not therefore resemble Burton's in important ways, including, for example, an emphasis on meeting the psychological needs of the participants, over and above rational problem-solving analytical work, and through the use of role-plays and simulations to build trust and empathy—two ideas not much regnant in Burton's vocabulary. Francis follows Curle's notion of confrontation (if for her, necessarily nonviolent), "whose essence is to *engage* in conflict in order to resolve it" (2002:40, emphasis in original). What is clear in both cases is that by invoking conscientization, confrontation, and empowerment, the idea of a *neutral* third party has been jettisoned: the "mediator" now more closely resembles the "activist" role outlined by Laue and Cormick (1978). Compare, in fact, this understanding of the "peacemaker's" role with the fiery description of the community organizer in the classic "primer for hell raisers," Saul Alinsky's *Rules for Radicals*:

> The organizer dedicated to changing the life of a particular community must first rub raw the resentments of the people in the community; fan the latent hostility of many of the people to the point of overt expression .... An organizer must stir up dissatisfaction and discontent; provide a channel into which people can angrily pour their frustrations. He [*sic*] must create a mechanism that can drain off the underlying guilt for having accepted the previous situation for so long. Out of this mechanism a new community organization arises .... When those prominent in the status quo turn and label you an "agitator" they are completely correct, for that is ... your function—to agitate to the point of conflict. (Alinsky 1971:116–117)

For Alinsky, perhaps, the awareness of injustice or exploitation lies closer to the surface among his clients than they seem to do for Curle or Francis—not much heavy educating needs to be done; these people *know* they are getting the short end of the stick. Yet in this passage, Alinsky makes clear the distinction between the *latent* conflict that exists and the *manifest* one that must be engaged through rubbing things raw—indeed, he goes further by confidently imputing *guilt* among the community residents for needing an outside organizer to tell them this! Leaving the matter of guilt aside, the ideas of latent and manifest conflict—indeed the whole edifice of empowerment through third-party education or conscientization—bring us back to Lukes's point about articulating objective real interests versus subjective ones, and the dilemma faced by the analyst or other sort of third party in invoking notions (for some) very closely connected to false consciousness. Alinsky, the quintessential outside agitator, faces no dilemmas here: His way is morally clear, and all the real problems are technical ones of organization and mobilization and overcoming resistance. Curle recognizes something else. He notes that once engaged in empowerment, the peacemaker is likely to be considered *parti pris* and then *persona non grata* by the more powerful party, in a sense doing him- or herself out of a job at some point. (This reminds us of the many forms of third parties, and their noninterchangeability, as discussed by Mitchell and in Chapter 7, Figure 3.) More perceptively, he notes that at some point the weaker party, once partially or fully empowered, may well turn on the peacemakers and tell them in effect to go home—this, too, is part of a fundamental restructuring of power relationships. Do not expect undying gratitude, he advises. Perhaps this is Curle's nod to some part of the psychological process, or even to insufficiently processed guilt, that underlies such third-party work.

What one does after the rubbing raw and making manifest is for Alinsky, as noted, not a problem, and being a sort of primer, *Rules for Radicals* is quite detailed about what precedes and follows. In contrast, although Curle and Francis both include case studies (Curle) and close descriptions of workshops (Francis) wherein conscientization and empowerment take place, curiously neither is very precise on what follows confrontation, besides encouraging its nonviolent form. Francis writes of the next steps of group organization and mobilization, and Curle moves quickly (rather too quickly, perhaps) to development, conciliation, and bargaining. Beyond education and the making of awareness, what sorts of concrete resources or capacities are brought to bear for the weaker party, or against the stronger one? Note that realists, given their material and scalable conception of power, have no problems here: One supplies the *mujahaddin* with stinger missiles, for example, or the supported regime with AWAC aircraft or a "nuclear shield." But the nature of empowerment beyond conscientization, and the making explicit of real interests and the latent manifest, is more of a problem for peacemakers or other sorts of conflict resolution/transformation third parties. We are in some sense back to the dilemma of Birkhoff's ADR mediators: Can one empower through (beneficently) controlling the mediation process alone but substantially ignoring the content of the dispute or the outside world with its *material* bases of domination and control?[17]

As mentioned earlier, there is another basis for a critique of empowerment, which takes it seriously as an *experimental* form of "social engineering." Groom and Webb (1987) first differentiate conflicts in which norms and values are essentially shared (nonstructural ones) from those where such sharing is absent and the very rules of the game or such things as the nature of justice are in question (1987:264). It is the latter, structural conflicts that they (like Burton,

Galtung, or Lederach) are concerned with as arenas for empowerment. Like Curle, they note that a third-party functioning as an agent of empowerment will likely lose the trust or credibility of the stronger party, but they go beyond this to argue that should empowerment fail to bring about significant change, the stronger party may view it as simply a nonthreatening "anodynetic activity," and the weaker party come to view it the same way, perhaps even to regard the third party as working (even if unintentionally) for the powerful as a "fifth column." Paradoxically, half-hearted or otherwise unsuccessful empowerment can be "nonempowering." Alternatively, empowerment is seen to be working, and the stronger party, now "challenged in its supremacy" and with much to lose, likely reacts with further suppression or even lethal violence. This places "a very great responsibility on the empowering agent, since it is surely incumbent on that agent to be able to predict at least to some degree the outcome of his [sic] actions.... And, given the current state of knowledge, is there any way in which the interventionist can *predict* the outcome of his intervention?" (1987:275; emphasis in original). Groom and Webb think not, and suggest, given this, that it is "imprudent [and they imply not a little immoral] to select empowerment as a meditational strategy" (1987:246). A Leninist revolutionary probably expects large-scale injury, loss of life, and other high costs to be borne by the *lumpen* as they attain awareness, cast off their chains, and engage in full struggle. Indeed, such things might even be part of the larger plan, welcomed as part of the strategy to energize the masses. If *we*, however, are to be the agents actively bringing this state of affairs about, such suffering is perhaps harder to justify in our field. At the least one thinks of the acid thrown into the faces of young girls bravely attending schools earnestly built with USAID funds and American "social change" encouragement. And one thinks as well of Hannah Arendt's caustic remark that Gandhian nonviolence would have met a different fate—"massacre and submission"—if it opposed Stalin or Hitler rather than the British empire with a liberal and democratic (and increasingly sympathetic) opposition in Parliament and the country at large (Arendt 1970:53).

In offering an alternative methodology to empowerment, Groom and Webb suggest facilitation, based on but going beyond the Burtonian problem-solving workshop. They point out, reasonably, that such "consciousness raising" (they use the term, if in quotation marks) that goes on in this format is directed "to *all* the parties in relation to the costs and benefits of different strategies and different alternatives" (1987:27), and not just to the weaker one. It is true that such facilitation may not work (deep-rooted or structural conflicts are notoriously difficult to resolve under any circumstances), but then they say neither might "unpredictable" empowerment—and the risks in facilitation to the weaker party are in any case greatly reduced. They also point to the fact that "asymmetry" comes in different forms, making power a more complicated notion than empowerment usually suggests. This observation is important, and it points us finally to Christopher Mitchell's attempt to solve the enigma of power within the practice of conflict resolution. As I said, Mitchell strives to reverse figure and ground: Instead of focusing on power, he looks to the rather complicated and multifaceted nature of asymmetry itself.

On Asymmetry

Even discounting Thucydides's insights on the nature of asymmetric conflict—which, indeed, tended toward ending further discussion of the matter rather than encouraging it—it is the case that thinking about the nature of asymmetric conflict has a long history and nowadays even a specialized academic journal or two devoted specifically to the topic. The current concern with "asymmetric warfare" accounts for much of this interest, which stems in turn from trying to understand the outcomes of some twentieth-century postcolonial conflicts occurring in a neocolonial world. Here one question is "why big nations lose small wars" (or what strategies can prevent this?) to quote Andrew Mack's memorable title in an article investigating the topic broadly that was motivated most immediately by the failure of the United States to prevail in Vietnam (Mack 1975). Among his most salient lessons: Do not mistake power, measured as raw military or industrial capability or superiority (i.e., something akin to the fundamental realist's conception of power), for capability as defined by the political will of the less powerful to resist, and to resist long enough to destroy the parallel political will of the stronger power (aided by strong public opposition, typically) to continue to fight. In fact—a second lesson—superior military capability may be not only irrelevant but actually counterproductive for the more powerful party in these wars.[18] Many will recognize in Mack's careful theoretical analysis a précis of Mao's more "practitioner-oriented" thoughts on how to fight an insurgent's war.

Closer to our field, Zartman and Rubin (2002) collected a group of studies on international negotiations between manifestly stronger and weaker parties that demonstrated the "commonsense" hypotheses that the strongest side always wins, or that *perceptions*—already a nuancing of the realist's conception!—of equal power between parties tends to result in more effective negotiations than unequal power, are in fact unfounded. They do agree that stronger parties will often act exploitatively and weaker ones must submit, but this conventional wisdom must be modified by a conditional: unless "certain special conditions prevail" (Zartman and Rubin 2002:16). In a sense, the entire volume of case studies is devoted to exploring the nature of those special conditions, which turn out to be varied and not so special or rare as the ancient Athenians led Thucydides to think. (Presumably, the Melians had no access to them.) Zartman and Rubin offer some lessons as well, complicating the idea of power, such as not mistaking "resource power" (or capability) in general for the exercise of power in the closed context of the negotiation. Another lesson concerns mistaking "aggregate power" entering a negotiation for "issue-specific power" that weaker parties may hold, for example, by taking a firm, resistant stand on an important interest of the stronger party, but one of only marginal importance to the weaker: a variant of now standard familiar interest-based negotiation wisdom. Another lesson is that power is sometimes available to the weaker party via the intervention of third parties, who have their own interests in the outcome of the negotiation and the resulting symmetries of the international arena (all their cases involve negotiation between nation-states or such international blocs as "North–South"). Behind the specific analysis of power, Zartman and Rubin tell us much about the different modality of symmetry/ asymmetry. Which side (the weaker?) can invoke recognized bureaucratic or legal rules of procedure or principles of justice; appeal to the importance of the ongoing relationship; reach out to public opinion; threaten violent (or nonviolent) resistance; enlist the help of external parties? All of these shift us from looking directly at power, however nuanced, toward examining more closely the nature of symmetry/asymmetry.

Mack's analysis already pointed us toward one very important dimension of symmetry that broadened our conception of "power imbalance" beyond power as control and domination—beyond power as coercive capacity. In discussing the U.S. failure to prevail in Vietnam despite overwhelming traditional military and technological superiority, he notes that American political leadership faced an increasingly divided citizenship at home in support of the war, in fact an increasingly skeptical and finally demonstrably critical one. In Mitchell's (1995) terms, the "intraparty cohesion" of the American side was low. The Vietcong and their North Vietnamese supporters, in contrast, possessed high intraparty cohesion (they had been fighting an anticolonial war for decades). So there were several different dimensions of symmetry/asymmetry present in this conflict, and they varied differently and with different effects. In terms of coercive capacity, asymmetry was clearly in favor of the United States. In terms of intraparty cohesion—which it turns out had significant implications for such other dimensions as "leadership security," or "leadership legitimacy" (Lyndon Johnson was the only incumbent president in American history who chose not to run for reelection), the asymmetry that existed clearly favored the Vietcong and North Vietnamese. In the end, the lack of intraparty cohesion (of the American public), with its implications for leadership security, legitimacy, and (in mounting opposition to the war) a growing constituent mobilization on the part of antiwar protest, counted for more than American dominance in military and technological domains.

Recognizing that most conflicts are unlikely to be perfectly symmetrical, much has been written about asymmetry in general, and particularly what asymmetry implies for conflict resolution practice (e.g., Aggestam 2002; Zartman and Rubin 2002; Agusti-Panareda 2004; Quinn et al. 2006; Arreguin-Toft 2007; McAuley, Glynn, and Tonge 2008; Kriesberg 2009; Pruitt 2009).[19] But the topic has been most systematically addressed in a series of papers by Christopher Mitchell (1991, 1995, 2009), which importantly connect his earlier discussion of the variety of third-party roles and functions (see Figure 3 in Chapter 7) with conditions of symmetry and asymmetry best suited to achieve conflict reduction.

Recognizing that the field of conflict resolution has often implicitly assumed symmetry in formulating its techniques, but eschewing a simple conception of asymmetry as power imbalance, Mitchell outlines thirty-one dimensions of variation along symmetric/asymmetric lines (1995:28–29). These include such dimensions as *constituent mobilization*; the *access* possessed by weaker parties to "get on the agenda" of political process (cf. Bachrach and Baratz's second face of power); *bargaining ability* (capacity to undertake skillful negotiation); *survivability* (extent to which a party can survive a major setback or defeat); and *legitimacy* (the accepted legal—or moral—standing of each party). These are reduced to seven key dimensions connected to the necessary conditions for conflict reduction (1995:46):

- Coercive ability ("classical power")
- Intraparty cohesion (degree of internal divisions or unity)
- Leadership insecurity (challenges leadership is facing)
- External dependency (extent to which patrons are pursuing their own interests)
- Goal salience (whether conflict goals are essential or nonnegotiable)
- Elite entrapment (leadership attachment to current goals or strategies)
- Acceptance (recognition of other party's leadership or right to exist)

Mitchell generally supports the hypothesis that "all other things being equal," conditions of symmetry between parties is more conducive to conflict reduction than is asymmetry, implying that intervening third parties should try to enhance symmetry when possible (see also Quinn et al. 2006). But, of course, all other things are never equal. Certain sorts of symmetry are bad for conflict reduction: for example, if each party is so internally divided that no coherent policies of mutual engagement can be agreed to and no appropriately representative negotiating teams can be put together and put forward. The same would be true if the leadership or elites of both sides were symmetrically insecure. Likewise, if the goals salience of both parties is symmetrically high—if, for example, both parties view the conflict in existential terms as a matter of group survival (Israelis and Palestinians?)—then the room third parties have to disaggregate key issues and interests in aid of problem solving or even compromise is much reduced.[20] But on the whole, the idea that near equals can better enter negotiation toward problem solving or compromise holds (the brutal epitome is perhaps Zartman's "mutually hurting stalemate"), and this suggests a number of ways third parties can strategize interventions. The key here is to remember the extreme multidimensionality of symmetry and that some sorts of symmetry (e.g., symmetrically high intraparty unity) are good, whereas other symmetries (high goals salience or low intraparty unity) are bad. Mitchell remarks that "no simple relationship between symmetric conflict structure and conflict reduction" is likely to emerge, and therefore third parties should consider "a multiplicity of strategies" (some aimed at increasing symmetry, some at lessening it or increasing asymmetry) must be considered

(1995:44). Given the great diversity of strategies, it is also likely that no single individual third party or institution can reasonably be expected to play all the roles through all phases of a conflict. This is the point that came through most emphatically in thinking about the role of a third-party "empowerer" (assuming a much simpler conception of power than Mitchell uses), soon to be regarded as outside agitator and *persona non grata* by the stronger party and sometimes eventually by the weaker one as well.[21]

Mitchell harbors no illusions as to the ease with which third parties can usefully intervene even given the most perspicuous analysis of differential asymmetries and their entailments for conflict escalation or reduction. But it seems to me that his is thus far the most systematic and nuanced approach to power in the field of conflict and peace studies. It is a far cry from understanding power as the *machtpolitik* of realists. By extension, however, it also gives to potential third parties a huge role beyond purely facilitative mediation, indeed even beyond the suggestion of formulas or provision of technical advice. It is clearly activist and interventionary, moving beyond guaranteeing "the integrity of the process" to interference in the content of the conflict. It therefore raises modalities of analysis beyond interests as recognized by the parties themselves, into the realm of telling the parties what their real interests may be. (To the stronger: "It is actually in your interest to allow me to empower your presently weaker opponents. Stand aside.") In doing all this it approaches the model of directive or *manipulative mediation* as defined by Touval and Zartman (1985; also Princen 1992).[22] As I now move to consider poststructuralist conceptions of power and conflict resolution, the question it raises is whether Mitchell's intervention into the nature of intervention has had the effect of replacing Power as the field's Other with the third party—that is, with the field itself: a self-reflexive and mimetic Othering.

This bit of constructed irony is an appropriate way to introduce poststructural concerns with power.

Poststructuralism and Power

Although thus far I have referred only in passing to postructuralist approaches to power, their impact on the way in which many social scientists have dealt with the topic should not be underestimated. There is, of course, no single poststructuralist take on power, any more than one would expect a single understanding to be found in community studies or conflict sociology, although the level of dissension internal to poststructuralists, given their individual pretensions to virtuosity, may be much higher. It is nevertheless indisputable that the dominant scholar in the field has been Michel Foucault, whose influence in many areas of the human sciences has been profound. Yet even if we focus on Foucault, it is hard to find a definitive statement or definition (he seemed particularly averse to definitions), because his views on power changed as he took on new topics—punishment, prisons, histories of medicine and psychiatry, sexuality, epistemes and discourse, sovereignty and governmentality, to name a few—and refined, backtracked, expanded, and sometimes contradicted himself. Depending on the period to which one refers, Foucault appears to locate power within institutions and their associated discourses, in the relations between persons (and institutions), in techniques or mechanisms—practices—by which individuals are disciplined and their subjectivities are constituted, in discursive formations wherein truth is legitimated and power operates through exclusion. The metaphors with which to capture power change as well: power/knowledge, capillary movement, microphysics, biopower, Bentham's panopticon. Power is never just one thing in Foucault's writings, which perhaps is one reason they have proven so attractive to so many other theorists of power. With careful reading of the texts, one need not choose any one understanding of power exclusively over others. Power is dominating and destructive (Marx) but also productive or creative (Parsons or Boulding); it oppresses but also facilitates; it is sometimes concentrated but also dispersed; it comes from a sovereign (especially in premodern times) but also "from below"; it coerces compliance but simultaneously generates resistance. As it "governs" the conduct of individuals, it determines—but is also indeterminate. Power is inseparable from economic, religious, knowledge-producing/consuming (educational, scientific) domains and, as the body is a site for the operation of power, from sexuality. Power is both cause and effect, constituting and constituted. It is everywhere, all the time: as they say, always already.

Perhaps Foucault's major contributions to theorizing power (though he prefers the idea of "analytics" to "theory") lies in the elucidation of *discourse* (separate from the technical sense of the term as sociolinguists had used it, to indicate chunks of connected text or speech larger than a single sentence or utterance) as a locus of power through exclusion; the notion of the *power/knowledge* nexus; and the idea that the exercise of power simultaneously engenders *resistance*. The notion of resistance, as in the idiom of "hidden transcripts" in the widely read work of James Scott (1985) on peasants confronting the state, has enjoyed wide acceptance but also trenchant critique (see, e.g., Barrett 2002:39–40). In some ways, the appeal of resistance to students of power is similar to the appeal of empowerment to students of mediation and conflict resolution. Both, say critics, have the effect of making the analyst or third party feel better. Both feature the romanticized illusion that "small-scale subversions" are a substitute for "recognizing that large-scale rebellion and revolutionary change are luxuries of the past" (Barrett 2002:40).[23]

But the Foucauldian parsing of *discourse* and all its adjectival derivatives— discursive formations, discursive practices, discursive regimes, and so on— has had a wider and on the whole more sympathetic reception. Discourse is where and how the power/knowledge nexus operates. It is not only that Foucault locates power within discourses, and discourses within structures of exclusionary institutional practices of domination or hierarchy (and resistance!). It is that he *historicizes* discourse—that is after all the point of his genealogical method—locating discourse in specific epistemic communities or epochs. And, of course, the effect here is to deny an atemporal universality of any particular discourse, including those built around such foundational texts as sovereignty or class or the realist's idea of the state. The same goes for dominant discourses in education, science, or disciplines "of the clinic." By genealogizing them (anthropologists having long established that all genealogies are socially constructed, usually with local political aims in mind), Foucault also relativizes them, de-anchoring and decentering them, setting them adrift from any forever stable external standpoint. Just as it does for the practice of medicine, this has implications for our understanding of power in IR or peace or conflict studies, and for thinking about conflict resolution practice as itself a discourse and a site for the operation of power. Before moving specifically to practice, consider first the implications for scholars in theory in IR and peace and conflict studies.

Both Lukes (2005) and Vasquez (1998), neither of them poststructuralist in orientation, take Foucault and poststructuralism seriously, and each devotes a chapter to postructuralism (notably to Foucault) in the second edition of their widely read books on power.[24] Oliver Richmond (2008) considers it one among six major orientations to peace in the field of IR, along with liberal, realist, structuralist, peace and conflict studies, and critical theory. In contrast, Ramsbotham and colleagues (2005:295–298) relegate Foucault's discursive approach to Habermasian critical theory, and probably wisely so, because at base poststructuralism would subvert many of their claims to a "cosmopolitan conflict resolution," under a distrust of the very idea of the cosmopolitan and a suspicion that it stands mainly as a cipher for Western neocolonial neoliberal penetration.

Yet even Lukes and Vasquez's respectful treatment of poststructuralist approaches carefully delimit what they are willing to accept or concede particularly with regard to poststructuralism's profound distrust of universal theories or grand narratives. Lukes, for example, rejects interpreting Foucault's writings on power as "ultraradical," proposing, in effect, a "fourth face." Even in his later writings on *governmentality*, Lukes argues that Foucault never gave up on an "emancipatory ideal." He cites a later essay:

> Foucault's … writing strike a more voluntaristic note. In 'the Subject and Power' power is said to be 'exercised only over free subjects and only insofar as they are free. By this we mean individual or collective subjects who are faced with a field of possibilities in which several ways of behaving, several reactions and diverse comportments may be realized' [Foucault 1982:221]. (Lukes 2005:96 [orig. 1974])

For Vasquez, the several gains to be got from poststructuralism's commitment to critical self-reflexivity, its subversion of "positivist conceits," its Wittgensteinian approach to language games and their relation to truth and power, among others, are to be balanced by the costs of rejecting the Enlightenment project whole cloth: with Lyotard (1984), accepting the notion that all theory is tyrannical, "totalitarian and terroristic," and with Baudrillard (1990) "the idea of representing the world is entirely overturned and replaced with the notion that only simulation is possible, because there is no truth and reality to be represented; indeed the distinction between truth and falsity is blurred" (Vasquez 1998:220–221 [orig. 1993]). The problem, in other words, lies in the costs incurred in accepting radical relativisms: moving from the promise of methodological relativism (positivism is not the only way) to full-blown moral relativism (the values of the Enlightenment are not only one set among many but are also associated with Western hegemony and domination) and epistemological relativism (there is no really real, only the really political). For Vasquez, some of these costs are insupportable, particularly those whose epistemological implications have the effect of rendering empirical work and all attempts at theory building in the social sciences misdirected, or worse: useless, null, and void. Lukes, concerned as he is with freedom and an emancipatory ideal, joins this with an explicit concern for the costs that unbridled moral relativism may impose (though he is reassured that Foucault, at least, never went this far).

Oliver Richmond's chapter on the poststructuralist approach to peace studies is most telling on this point. Acknowledging, as do the others, the robust poststructuralist critique of modernism, grand theory, master narratives, and the neocolonial "liberal empire" created by rational choice theory and realist conceptions of states and power, Richmond goes on to question whether

> peace is a concept or framework that can have any currency at all in poststructural theory, [because] it clearly points to the inadequacies of theory developed to explain IR and the world (let alone peace) via white, Western, male, Christian, developed, liberal and neoliberal settings. Given its resistance to meta-narratives, poststructuralism does not offer a theory, approach, or *concept of peace*. (Richmond 2008:135, emphasis added)

He notes that although one can, in effect, reduce even critical theory to a form of liberalism as it holds fast—*pace* Lukes—to the Enlightenment project of identifying and bringing to bear a universal morality (such as human rights), the same cannot be said of poststructuralism, which "offers a powerful critique of this [Enlightenment] project, without necessarily offering an alternative" (1998:145). Richmond goes on to speculate what such an alternative—multiple "ontologies of peace"—might look like. I believe this is less an alternative than it is a restatement of the context and pretext problems that we in the field face (see Chapter 2). For *we* are not operating in the service of continental philosophy or literary studies, fields conducive and hospitable to all relativism all the time. We (like Marcuse or Adorno or Walter Benjamin) are operating in realms saturated with normative concerns. And so Richmond has left us with what seems to be a real dilemma facing a normative practice like conflict resolution or peacebuilding. First, we are presented with a strong critique, but with less than robust alternative courses of action. Second, given a poststructuralist world featuring multiple contexts of peace (not to say justice), what is *our* pretext for favoring some conception of peace over others? Whence our hubris in assuming a warrant for intervening as third parties to help others resolve their conflicts? What, in other words, can possibly justify our praxis?

Power, Culture, and Conflict Resolution Practice

Among others, this dilemma has been highlighted in the work of Morgan Brigg and Kate Muller (Brigg 2008; Brigg and Muller 2009), both as a critique of my notion of Type I and Type II errors in conflict resolution practice (Chapter 5), and more broadly of the notion of culture itself. Brigg and Muller object to the distinction I make between "cultural analysis" and "culturalism," between what I call technical or scientific understandings of culture and political uses of it by political actors: ethnic or nationalist entrepreneurs, or worse. I cautioned that the benefit to be gained from avoiding a Type I error, charges of cultural insensitivity or underestimating the effects of intercultural differences on causing communicational impedance, and so on, is to be balanced by the potential costs of making a Type II error: taking the actors' case for invoking privileges in terms of "our culture demands, requires, or justifies" as unproblematic and veridical, where such demands in a liberal multicultural context may bring political privileges, and in other settings such requirements sometimes justify or call forth a rationale for ethnic cleansing or genocide. They especially take exception to my argument that the third party must "diagnose" the impact of cultural differences between the parties on the conflict—say on communication or due to differing cognitive maps or symbolic grammars—and not simply accept the parties' assertion of ethnic (politically tactical and strategic) differences as deep cultural ones. Their critique collapses my science/politics distinction (so-called science being yet another discursive site for the operation of power), and I am chided for possessing the hubris to suggest anything as determinative (and imperious) as diagnosis. Behind all this is a deeper critique of the notion of culture, even parsed, as I do, in cognitive or interpretive rather than superorganic or trait-behavioral terms.

Culture is faulted first for its original sin, a genealogical relationship to the colonialism of the past as well as (when used in development work for instance) the neocolonial present. Second, there is a fundamental problem with the notion of culture itself, the pretense that culture has any ontological standing whatsoever, much less a scientific one! It is an invention (Wagner 1975); a constructed category; or as Geertz (1983) once put it, a practice enacted by ethnographers looking over the shoulders of informants as they in turn try to make sense of themselves and their practices. Finally, combining culture's original sin with the fact that, like any practice, to employ it is to engage in an exercise of power, ought to give one pause. "When culture met power in the 1980s and 1990s," Stanley Barrett tartly observed, "culture was the first to blink" (Barrett 2002:113). Given all this, in despair one may want simply to lose culture entirely. As I wrote earlier, this position has its advocates.

And yet, and yet, can we really do without it? After setting out his critique, Brigg, joining others who have disparaged the idea of culture only to admit its necessity, writes, "We cannot dispense with the term 'culture' because it is a powerful and deeply meaningful concept and force in peoples lives and conflict" (2008:42). At the same time it is also an "impossible object, something which needs representation but cannot be easily signified in our systems of signification" (2008:43). And so Brigg and Muller turn to Erneso Laclau's (2001) idea of the "empty signifier," by which culture, though in some sense "real," nevertheless "escapes signification *because* it is too important to be filled or controlled" (Brigg and Muller 2009:133, emphasis added). Geertz was willing to admit that culture was an essentially contested concept (as Lukes did for power). Yet it is some distance to go from a contested concept to an empty one. And what then have we gained?

Brigg and Muller are quite right to remind us (yet again) that culture is a construction, perhaps more confidently used as an adjective than a noun. And it serves me right for bringing science into the discussion, though I am in the end, as they charge, a "modernist social scientist." They are also correct to point that the practice of conflict resolution is also an exercise of power. Building on Foucault's neologism of *governmentality* ("the conduct of conduct," the governance of *mentalité*), Brigg writes: "Conflict resolution governs" (2008:50). One cannot argue with this. It is, in fact, another way of expressing a longstanding critique of the field mounted by legal scholars and social scientists of the *Law and Society* group from the 1970s on (see Chapter 2). Laura Nader was a sharp critic. ADR and its associated practices, she wrote, was just second-class justice, a way to deny have-nots their rights under the law and, preferring the American demotic of con men and carnies to the high gloss (*governmentalité*) of Parisian French, a way to "to cool out the mark" (Nader 1980:44).

There is no denying that recognizing power in the discourse of conflict resolution yields critical insights. For example, Conley and O'Barr (1998) adopt such an approach to their analysis of the "microdiscourses" (understood in the sociolinguistic sense) at work in transcripted mediation sessions of divorce cases. Instead of finding, as Juliana Birkhoff's mediators claimed they would find, the empowerment of the weaker party (usually the woman) going on as integral to "the process," their close conversational analysis revealed a variety of techniques used by mediators (turn taking and rules of procedure, using active listening to reframe and re-represent what the woman was saying, devaluing and disprivileging expressions of emotion while overvaluing rationality, pushing cooperation and dependency as a prime goal, among them) that collectively had the effect of disadvantaging and ultimately dominating the women. The dynamics of the (sociolinguistic) microdiscourse, they argued, had the perhaps unintended effect of reinscribing a macrodiscourse (here, discourse in the Foucauldian sense): and that is the discourse of patriarchy.

But here lies the ethical paradox at the heart of this poststructuralism: Given the lack of a definitive external standpoint from which to render judgment, *what's wrong with patriarchy?* Who gets the right to define oppression—those who advocate against education for young girls, or those who advocate for it? Brigg concedes that in losing a commitment to the "modernist tradition" (and the Enlightenment) "no moral compass" now exists "about how to evaluate whether particular invocations of culture might be appropriate or inappropriate. But it is also true," he continues, "that (an additional one) is not necessary. There are already plenty of moral compasses in circulation" (Brigg 2008:48). Indeed there are, and some of them prescribe some truly awful things be done to other people.

We are back to Lukes's dilemma and momentary embarrassment about claiming an external standpoint with which to formulate power's third dimension, to identify "real interests." Lukes, as we saw, shied away from such fraught phrases as false consciousness and class at the Archimedean crux, unwilling to be accused of treating his subjects as "dupes." He moved to a more indeterminate and perhaps even fuzzy conception of real interests. On the other hand, Trina Grillo (1991) and Penelope Bryan (1992), among other critics discussing "process dangers to women" in mediation, pointed out that women's often very high subjective satisfaction with the outcome of mediation in divorce proceedings often belied real costs to them down the line. Their real interests lay somewhere else, to be objectively assessed in such fiduciary terms as alimony, child support, and so on. But cannot one turn the tables on this thinking? Perhaps the "real interest" of the woman was objectively satisfied by avoiding a drawn-out and brutal fight that bore heavy emotional costs on herself—or on her children. To declare any sort of external standpoint is to take the risk of appearing directive, dominating, or worse. And of course, one ought never act as a third party in any setting insulated from the "subjects" by arrogance or defended by a professionally honed autism. But if, as third parties or peacebuilders, we do not take this risk, what use are we? What we do owe absolutely is a clear and transparent sense, to ourselves as well to the parties, of where our definition of interests come from and, in articulating our external standpoint (knowing full well we are no longer wholly external as soon as we enter the situation), a clear statement about where we stand. To be sure, this is hardly an entire ethics of practice, but it is surely the beginning of one.

Finally—and briefly—back to culture and ontology. Lukes argues that Foucault in effect pulled himself back from the brink of radical relativism when, in the essay "The Subject and Power" (1982), he identifies the idea of "free individual or collective subjects" who are free precisely to the extent that they can exercise choice of diverse possibilities of acting: thus an ontology of freedom. If culture lacks ontological standing, a signifier too important to signify anything and thus empty, signifying nothing, can we say that Brigg has liberated himself via Laclau from all the sovereign tethers of modernism? Perhaps not. In advocating for a new politics of conflict resolution, Brigg relies at last on the value of "recognition," and where this falters, on "relatedness." The latter is defined as "the fundamental being together of humans." Relatedness is necessary because, he continues, "Where recognition [alone] risks returning to the sovereign self, relatedness invokes a *pre-cognitive given-over-ness* which makes each of us vulnerable to others" (Brigg 2008:21, emphasis added). I am unsure what to make of any quality that is "precognitive" and at the same time as fundamental and essential as "given-over-ness." But it does sound suspiciously ontological to me and, nodding to Archimedes, more than a little like a communitarian redaction of human nature.

Conclusion: Dealing with Power in Conflict Resolution

From its beginnings, power has been a problem for students and practitioners of peace and conflict resolution, given the dominant discourse of power that emerged with the rejection of idealism in international relations and its replacement by realism and neorealism, focused as they are on the mainly military-industrial power of the state linked to self-evident national interests. Opposed to the Melian assumption of realist thinking—the strong do what they want and the weaker what they must, that is accede (or form alliances of the weak to balance and thus resist)—power became the Other for peace and conflict studies, even as a "cosmopolitan conflict resolution" strove to become the "IR that might have been." Power became a particular problem for the practice of conflict resolution because most of the traditional practices, from game-theoretic on up, presume an essential symmetry of the contestants in a world where power is mostly distributed unevenly. The purpose of this chapter was first to review some of the main ways in which power, taken abstractly, has been theorized in the social sciences, and then to concentrate on its uses in conflict resolution practice. Not surprisingly, although any particular theorist or researcher approaches the notion of power with an attitude of epistemological self-assurance, when reviewed across a number of different theoretical approaches, definitions proliferate. One theorist's self-assurance becomes another's wrongheadedness; one researcher's operational definition, another's methodological artlessness—and the whole idea of power is soon rendered an essentially contested concept.

On the practice side of things, the fact that power asymmetry presented some sort of dilemma in managing their process was recognized by all but the most unreflective of third-party practitioners (i.e., those who unself-consciously believed in and hid behind the mask of neutrality), even among those who never seriously questioned the conceptual underpinnings of the techniques that they had been trained to use (Avruch 2009). Some practitioners went much further and made addressing power the centerpiece of their practice. The main ways in which power has been dealt with in conflict resolution practice include the following:

- Recognize that power and power asymmetries exist, and seek to integrate power alongside recourse to negotiation and rights in a well-designed dispute resolution system (Ury, Brett, and Goldberg 1988).

- Acknowledge power's "functional" (Parsons 1963) or creative as well as destructive potential, and encourage the former in fashioning prosocial deployments of power: moving from *power over* toward *power to* and *power with* (Boulding 1989).
- Recognize power's mainly repressive or dominating character, and seek to undermine its deployment in a particular encounter (the mediation session and beyond) by seeking to *empower* the weaker party and level the field toward power equality, thereby hastening a mutually hurting stalemate and the more powerful party's willingness to come to the table, and heightening the chance for a successful negotiation or dialogue (now between near-equals) to take place. The locus and nature of empowerment vary widely, from fixing it firmly within the mediation process (Birkhoff 2002) to social settings far beyond it. Empowerment usually implies (for the weaker party) education, creating self-awareness, or conscientization, up to (regrettable) revolutionary violence (Curle 1971).
- Separate the twinned notions of power and asymmetry—focus on the latter, and reverse figure and ground. In this way, one loses some of the contestedness and metaphysics surrounding discussions of power, to concentrate on the more concrete manifestations of asymmetry such as stability of leadership, amount of legitimacy enjoyed, intraparty unity or factionalism, and so on. This also helps a third party focus contextually and situationally, matching third-party function and role closely to the different sorts of asymmetry identified and their tactical implications for successful intervention (Mitchell 1991, 1995).
- Most radically, deny the power of power to forever dominate over unmet or repressed basic human needs in situations of deep-rooted, protracted social conflicts, in effect writing power entirely out of relevance for conflict resolution practice (Burton 1979, 1990, 1997).

Reviewing these, it seems to me that Mitchell's reversal of figure and ground with respect to separating power from asymmetry and concentrating on the latter is the most promising strategy for practice. It is, of course, far less radical than Burton's denial, and also less dependent on assuming prosocial conceptions power; that is, it conserves the basic and widely accepted Weberian approach to power as controlling and dominating while (to use a phrase Mitchell would likely find discomfiting) usefully deconstructing it.

To these five approaches to power, one may add the sixth I discussed, the poststructuralist perspective. This perspective concentrates on generating critical skepticism; it is high on critique but rather low on suggestions for conflict resolution practice, because the main point here is to direct attention to conflict resolution practice as itself comprising techniques of power in a discursive regime intended to discipline contestants into accepting the rationality of neoliberal governance (Brigg 2008). The focus on the unequal power of the parties is transmuted into one on the (unequal, perhaps greater) power of the intervener. Although it is hard to believe that any sentient conflict resolution practitioner was ever totally unaware of his or her power "within the process," what poststructuralism represents is a skepticism with regard to what is seen as the unrestrained meliorism of traditional conflict resolution and peacebuilding—this it shares with the older Marxian critique coming out of the Law and Society group.

In its strongest form, tending toward a full embrace of relativism, the poststructuralist perspective deeply problematizes the approach to power featured as Steven Lukes's third dimension or face. This refers to a structural conception of power, located beyond the power allocated to decision-making individual actors as assumed by neoclassical economics, liberal politics, or realist IR (where states are treated as undifferentiated individual actors as well). The dilemma here comes not with value-neutral analysis, but when one tries to turn from theory to some form of praxis. In doing practice, an acknowledgment of larger structures in which individuals are embedded (or of grand narratives into which they are implicated) necessarily leads one to some sort of Archimedean site, an external standpoint from which, structure now recognized, power is interpellated and praxis can be launched. Afraid of being called a vulgar Marxist, Lukes shied away from class and false consciousness, but in the end he failed to evade the dilemma, something no *normative* theory directed to supporting social change can anyhow afford to do (no more than mediators in North America can hide behind specious claims to neutrality or impartiality for keeping their practice virginal). Without presuming an external standpoint, ideas of empowerment and conscientization are rendered meaningless—truly empty signifiers.

The burden of conflict resolution is that in recognizing power, it must simultaneously acknowledge its commitment to some moral calculus, that is, a calculus beyond the behaviorist's counting decisions made in city council meetings or the merely Machiavellian cunning to rig meeting agendas. For this reason, a poststructuralism that fully embraces relativism, that goes all the way, can only offer critique to our field—*a necessary and invaluable thing to be sure*—but little in the way of suggesting alternatives for practice (Avruch 2001:644–646).

A Brief Postscript: Vasquez on the Power of Power Politics ("Othering" the Other)

Unlike the concept of culture, a complicated word of relatively recent provenance grievously tainted by the original sin of Western colonialism, the idea of power appears to us ancient (hence Thucydides), universal, and redolent of common sense: One knows it when one sees it. These qualities surely helped to make power the central concept of realist and neorealist theories for understanding the international system and for guiding decades of research. But have the classical realist and neorealist theories proved adequate for ensuring this research was productive according to positivist canons and standards, the standards by which IR scholars in that tradition judge their own and others' work?

In *The Power of Power Politics* (1983, second edition 1998) John Vasquez set out to assess the adequacy of the realist and neorealist paradigm. Without attempting to rehearse all of his arguments and methods, I will summarize them by saying that in conclusion he found that paradigm inadequate. The second, expanded edition of the work added a chapter on poststructuralism and constructivist approaches to IR and, following Imre Lakatos (1970), a further critique of the paradigm and its associated research as "degenerating" rather than "progressive." He goes on to say that much of this stems from realism's making of power the central and dominant variable of its paradigm. This finding is consistent across both editions of the book. In discussing the implications for providing practical advice on foreign policy, which adequacy can be assessed in large measure by applying the positivist criterion of its predictive adequacy to past events, Vasquez remarks on

> the empirical unsoundness of neorealist advice ... because the main variable, used to understand the future, focuses on shifts in the distribution of power.... Yet the evidence shows that power variables are not often as strongly correlated with the onset of war and peace as one would expect given the central focus of them in the paradigm.... This evidence which has been persistent since the mid-1960s should give realists and neorealists some pause. (1998:314)

In the main, it hasn't given them pause, which brings us perhaps to different questions in the sociology and political economy of knowledge—not our main concern here. We are here faced with a situation similar to the one I discussed in Chapter 6, on Huntington's clash of civilizations thesis: a bad theory as judged empirically and conceptually, but with wide appeal and nowadays conceptually regnant nonetheless. The point I wish to draw from Vasquez's critique of power is that in offering examples of *better theories* for explaining the behavior of states in the international system, he turns to what he calls a variety of "nonrealist theories." These "focus not on power variables, but on learning, changes in cognitive belief systems and the efficacy of cooperative acts" (1998:338). Elsewhere he points to world-society and conflict resolution approaches as strong theories in the nonrealist tradition. Discussing the fundamental conflict resolution notion of striving to attain a "harmony of interests" toward a nonviolent resolution of conflict, Vasquez remarks,

> [T]he fact that harmonies of interest are rare does not mean that they never exist; nor does it follow that all conflicts of interest are such that they are equally prone to violent solution. The realist paradigm has a difficult time seeing this, however. Such distinctions make realists nervous; they are like traumatized victims who are quick to see the world as a jungle and would rather be wrong about seeing threats where none exist, than being taken as a 'sucker'. (Vasquez 1998:302)

What this tart characterization suggests to me is that although power may remain an Other for conflict resolution, it should not be imbued with preternaturally powerful and determinate qualities for explaining the world or prescribing action in it. Perhaps we have all oversubscribed to the power of power politics. David Dunn (2004) was right in calling his study of John Burton *From Power Politics to Conflict Resolution*. For me, more than Burton's reliance on ontological basic human needs as the central engine of his practice, it was his pioneering writings on what was called, mainly in Britain, the "world society" approach to IR that makes him a central figure in our field. If we have good reason to doubt the "natural" hegemony of power politics, it should give us reason to believe in the promise of conflict resolution. It is time we faced power but with confidence, not defensively, and made of it *our* Other on our terms.

Afterword

With the exception of the final chapter, on power, all of the chapters in this book began as articles or essays that appeared in the decade following *Culture and Conflict Resolution*. Better than any but the most perspicuous and critical reviewer, an author knows, or should know, all the parts of a finished book that stand up less well under close scrutiny. These may consist of questions posed but left unanswered, assertions disguised as arguments, arguments held together more by grace than logic, logic more glissando than syllogism, or just plain loose ends and nagging doubts. Then, too, fields of inquiry and modes of practice develop and move on, raising questions and concerns that were not seemingly germane at the time. The preceding chapters were my attempt to address some of these gaps, evasions, or field developments. They cohered around a quartet of concerns central to conflict resolution (or peace and conflict studies, as the field now increasingly appears to call itself): culture, identity, power, and how all of these implicate practice. The first three, culture, identity and power, are as well interconnected—indeed, they interpenetrate—and that is one of the points these chapters make. But they are also not synonyms for one another, nor are they mutually reducible; that is another point.

The title of this book reflects my belief that questions of *context* are central to our understanding of culture and identity. Questions of *pretext*, meanwhile, focused especially on how to conceptualize (and deploy) power, are central to understanding our practice—how we engage ethically in the work of conflict resolution or peacebuilding in the first place. In calling this collection *Context and Pretext in Conflict Resolution,* I was also thinking about some of the ways in which both the notion of culture (so important to the development of my own work in the field) and the very idea of conflict resolution have been the objects of academic critique. Academic critiques of the concept of culture came, as it were, from the "right" or the "left." From the right—behaviorists, positivists and quantifiers to the core—culture appears to be congenitally fuzzy, mysterious, and ineffable: essentially unoperationalizable. From the poststructural left, culture is permanently burdened by its colonial past and not sufficiently ineffable, committing such sins as totalizing social life and essentializing the Other.

In a parallel way, the concept of conflict resolution attracts critics who come at it from very different directions. To one set—the diehard hawks, academic neorealists, or other devotees of *machtpolitik*—conflict resolution, insofar as it distinguishes itself (*pace* John Burton and Chapter 2) from conflict management and acts as a cipher for peace studies—is but a wishy-washy liberal's dream of a new world–ordered utopia that never was and never can be, irrelevant and blind to the "tough neighborhoods" that comprise the international system of states (real, fragile, failed, or imagined). To the other set, those invested heavily in ideas of peace or justice, conflict resolution is either cold-hearted and technocratic (if it distinguishes itself too explicitly from peace studies) or is but a way of instilling a false consciousness of "harmony ideology" (Nader 1991 [1998]) in the service of preventing real social change—or worst of all, it sins by imposing neoliberal ideas of order and governance on neocolonial Others (Brigg 2008). The first critique, mainly academic, aims to delegitimize the context of conflict resolution; the second, looking to practice and its consequences, questions its intentions, its pretext.

The book's subtitle reflects four broad areas that the field has engaged in the past decade. Of the four, I am most closely associated with culture, being one of several scholars and practitioners beginning in the middle and late 1980s who sought to introduce a concept of culture to a field and practice that had thus far developed, for reasons I related in Chapter 1, free of any coherent culture theory. *Culture and Conflict Resolution* aimed to critique a conflict resolution field ignorant or dismissive of culture and at the same time to advance a way of looking at culture less essentialist and totalizing, more nuanced than national character. My aim in the first chapter was to carry this line of argument further, generalizing culture as a way of thinking and talking about context and meaning in conflict analysis and resolution, while introducing many of the other themes in the chapters that followed. These included disaggregating culture from identity *per se,* problematizing rationality and rational choice, and connecting culture theory to conflict resolution practice. Rational choice was taken up in Chapter 7 as part of a critique of interest-based negations and related forms of mediation in the case of conflicts involving deeply held values. Interests themselves, so fundamental to our understanding of many kinds of conflict resolution practice, turn out to be not as self-evident as rational choice makes them appear, and the problem faced by third parties in actually defining interests, and the ethical implications involved in how they do so, was the main concern of Chapter 9, on power.

The problem of power, increasingly important in later chapters, was not much featured in this first chapter, except incidentally (and here conflated with authority) on describing cockpit culture in the opening sketch on the Air Florida tragedy. Consideration of power was not entirely absent in *Culture and Conflict Resolution,* but I never felt I gave the topic its due there. Although *culture* has become a respectable term in our vocabulary and cultural differences demand our attention—perhaps overly respected and sometimes wrongly attended to, as I argued in Chapter 5—and though "identity" has been enshrined as the *sine qua non* of most deeply rooted conflicts, which are now in fact synonymous with "identity conflicts" (although astute skeptics, such as Brubaker [2005], have appeared), the problem of power is only now gaining prominence in our field. In this as in other ways, the field has lagged behind some of its cognate social science disciplines. In the late 1980s and throughout the 1990s, just as the field of conflict resolution (peace and conflict studies) was discovering the importance of culture, other social and human sciences—my "home" discipline of anthropology in particular, now Foucauldian—were busy questioning culture's legitimacy and relevance or, as in cultural studies, were collapsing the idea of culture into a discourse of power. A similar tendency can be seen in the work of younger scholars and practitioners writing critically about culture and power in our field today (Brigg and Muller 2009).

Although associated mainly with culture, my own earliest work in the field, alone and with Peter Black, recognized that culture, identity, and power were always mutually implicated (e.g., Avruch and Black 1991; Avruch 1991). With respect to identity and culture, it was at first a matter of disentangling the two. In setting out our original list of "inadequate ideas about culture," Black and I cautioned against seeing culture as either "uniformly distributed across a group" or as merely "synonymous with group identity," reducing it to a label for ethnic groups or a cipher for ethnic identity (Avruch and Black 1991:29). I took up the potential cost to "efficient" and ethical practice in conflating culture and identity in Chapter 5, which, along with Chapter 6 on Huntington, reflected my longstanding interest in the relationship between theory and practice in conflict resolution (Avruch and Black 1990; Avruch 1991:3–4). Separating culture and identity allows a practitioner to imagine the difference between *cultural analysis* and *culturalism.* The former refers to shared norms, encodements, symbols, and practices that underwrite social life and individual experience; the latter refers to the ideological uses of "culture" in identity politics. (This difference between the two is also germane to my discussion of cultural relativism in human rights.) But making the distinction led some poststructuralist critics to accuse me of scientism (*analysis* is probably the suspect term) and the hubris to diagnose other people's lived experience and instruct third parties to approach their narratives with a diagnostician's clinical caution.

I stand by the distinction but at the same time admit to some sympathy with the critique. The "diagnostician" (third party) is of course assuming a position of power and authority. That's why an ethics of practice (another relatively neglected part of our discipline), including a clear-eyed view of "interests," is so important. I argued for this long ago (Avruch 1991:5–9). In discussing Kochman's (1981) exposition of African-American and white conflict styles for conflict resolution practice, for example, I zeroed in on the importance of perceiving power—power asymmetry—for understanding the *political* (rather than simply the paralinguistic and stylistic) context of interracial negotiation. I returned to this in *Culture and Conflict Resolution* by casting Fisher and Ury's interest-based negotiation as an ethnopractice raised to ethnotheory, apotheosized in *Getting to Yes* into an expert's system, one wherein North American middle-class (and male gender) styles were awarded "home court advantage," which is to say political advantage, in negotiating encounters (Fisher and Ury 1981; Avruch 1998:79–80).

The other reason for my sympathy with my critics is that although I appreciate the power to deconstruct other people's heuristics, such as the "buyer-seller" of rational choice and interest-based negotiation (Chapter 7), I should be prepared to do the same to my own use of heuristics—Type I and Type II errors—with its assumption that social life (much less social conflict) can be reduced to a two-by-two matrix. Of course it can't. But beyond the obvious burden of simplification—this is, after all, the great virtue of any heuristic and fully consonant with its major defect—the problem lies in the obdurately fuzzy relationship between culture and identity, particularly social (ethnic, racial, national, etc.) identity. On the one hand, they are not the same thing. For example, ethnic identity, as Barth (1969) argued long ago, uses socially constructed elements of culture to create boundaries between groups, whereas cultural differences *per se* may well cut across these group boundaries; indeed, they often do. The fact that culture and social identity are not isomorphic means that it is easy to assume an instrumentalist or constructivist position with respect to understanding "identity politics," the position I take in Chapter 4 and presume in Chapter 5. One therefore asks in a situation of social conflict invoking cultural differences (ethnic, racial, national, etc.) the instrumentalist's question: *Cui bono?* Who benefits, politically or economically, by invoking culture (the nationalist politician, the ethnic broker, the male elders)? Or perhaps one poses the constructivist's query: In evoking narratives of constructed difference, whose discursive hegemony prevails? These are the questions my two-by-two heuristic guides third parties to ask. I maintain, still, that they are important questions. But I also alluded to their limitation. Do not mistake heuristics for the world. The problem with identity is that social constructions and ideologies, whatever their instrumental provenance or accompanying political functions, can and do become internalized such that social identities and personal identities are not easily separable. As Eriksen (2001) has put it, in focusing on choice, strategy, and the social construction of identity, don't forget the self. "Ethnicity," particularly if the ethnic conflict is violent and longstanding, can in time become "cultural." Social heuristics, my own or anyone else's, have trouble trading in subjectivity or dealing with the effects of social trauma. This is one of my conclusions in thinking about truth and reconciliation commissions, where my understanding of identity was closer to the world of lived (damaged) experience (phenomenology) and farther from the world of cold strategic choice (the market), where "errors" can be rationally reduced to buy, hold, or sell.

All of this implicates power while striving to connect "theory" with "practice," the fourth concern of this book. In its beginnings in international relations (IR) after World War I, seeking ways to prevent the next war, ours was conceived as a normative discipline, and so the connection between conflict theory and conflict resolution practice—nowadays one might say between peace theory and peacebuilding—was present from the onset. In the development of IR, however, the normative dimension was quickly sloughed off as the new field embraced positivism and turned behaviorist; if there was an implicit normativity, it was that of Machiavelli's Prince (Richmond 2008). One can see some of this princely moral calculus at work in Samuel Huntington's post–Cold War (and post-9/11) grand theory of globalization, the so-called clash of civilizations. Here the concept of culture, hypertrophied and essentialized, implicates sets of practices not so consonant with the goals of our field. It takes cultural difference very seriously, perhaps too seriously.

In Chapter 3, in contrast, I was concerned with a different consequence of taking culture seriously for normative involvement in the world: universal human rights in the shadow of cultural relativism and local knowledge. The growth of a universal human rights discourse and its subsequent enfolding within the broad concerns of conflict resolution or peacebuilding points to one of the several ways in which the field has grown and ramified since the 1970s, as does for that matter the interest in truth and reconciliation commissions. Early on, the more pragmatic orientation of the field was to the technicalities and dynamics of "getting to the table" and reaching agreement and settlement, through integrative bargaining, interest-based and principled negotiation, advanced problem solving, or mediation, for example. In time, post-settlement (mistakenly called "post-conflict") concerns came to dominate, and these in turn ramified the field, now to include such topics as conflict prevention, trauma healing, peacekeeping, DDR (disarmament, demobilization, and reintegration), reconciliation, human security, sustainable development, peacebuilding, transitional justice, and humanitarianism as well as human rights. At the same time, the range of conflict resolution techniques or modalities widened, now to include (often under the rubric "conflict prevention" or early warning) fragile states or peaceful societies indices; or (often under the rubric "conflict transformation") new forms of mediation and third-party work, such as "public conversations," dialogue, discourse-, narrative-, insight-, and memory-work, as well as peace education. Some aspects of the growth of the field, and some early controversies around the growth, were covered in Chapter 2. Here I also examined the normative dimension in our pretext for treating conflict resolution as an exportable commodity and engaging in practice in cultures and societies not our own, a problem I returned to in the context of power.

Framing many of the book's chapters was attention to how the field has changed as it has been institutionalized in university postgraduate programs. The field today is hardly recognizable from what was taught in 1982 to ICAR's (now S-CAR) first master's class in conflict management. In fact, the change of name in our degree from "management" to "resolution," prompted by John Burton's arrival at ICAR (see Chapter 2), represented a key step toward the eventual rapprochement of American "pragmatist" concerns with conflict's regulation or management (epitomized by some as the "Harvard" approach to negotiation) with the traditionally European emphasis on structural change and transformation (associated with Johan Galtung; see Ramsbotham et al. 2005:39–47). The change in the degree's name was, in fact, a step toward the continuing rapprochement of conflict resolution with peace studies, and one reason why scholars today often refer to the field as "peace and conflict studies." Whether as conflict resolution or peace studies, the importance of paying attention to the contexts in which we work (other people's serious conflicts), and our various pretexts for doing so, as well as concerns with culture, identity, and power, are now recognized as indispensable and fundamental, and so must remain central to our research, scholarship, and ethical practice.

Finally, if I began these concluding remarks by referring to gaps, elisions, and territories left behind and unexplored in *Culture and Conflict Resolution*, it should now be clear that elisions in my own work still remain. Other parts of the field were not covered here. Among them, peace studies and peace research were not fully engaged, nor were the fertile ideas of constructive conflict resolution, nonviolence, conflict and development, or human security. In relation to the last area, the changes, real or potential, wrought in our field by its entanglement on the part of some practitioners with the military in "stability and reconstruction" work in Iraq and Afghanistan may prove as fateful for us as any other development of the past decade or so (Rubenstein 2009). Conflict resolution is now a "skill set" valued by defense contractors and "Beltway bandits" working alongside the military and USAID professionals. The question for others in our field is whether what the military and USAID mean by "conflict resolution" is closer to the sense of "conflict management"—and a mainly tactical part of a mostly military exit strategy—and further from the sense of *transforming* deeply rooted conflicts that others had seen, hopefully, the field evolving toward. In an essay titled "Conflict Resolution as a Political System," later published in *Conflict: Resolution and Provention* (1990), John Burton imagined a future wherein conflict resolution, understood as critical analysis of the ways in which basic human needs were suppressed by the powerful, and problem solving in the aid of making the powerful understand (and "cost") this as well, would be fully institutionalized in a transformed political system and "in ways that do not create dominant interest groups that only seek to preserve institutions" (Burton 1990:268). Burton understood this would be a radically different sort of political system from the ones then (and now) predominant. The question is whether "stability and reconstruction" points to the same imaginary or whether it points toward a "conflict resolution" that has been merely co-opted into the existing political system, and not one that proposes a significant alternative to it.

These are open questions. And in the end, however answered, they all conduce to questions about the contexts in which we do our work and our pretexts for doing so. With all that this implies, it not surprising that there is no fully coherent history of our field, much less a critical assessment, as it is too early for either to convey much authority. The one certainty is that matters of context and pretext in conflict resolution are now fundamental to how we conceive the field; that conflict resolution has changed greatly in the years since monolithic and unreflective notions of "getting to the table" and "getting to yes" were its *sine qua non*, and that this change is a good thing.

Notes

Chapter 1

1. "A Crash's Improbable Impact: '82 Air Florida Tragedy Led to Broad Safety Reforms," by Del Quentin Wilber, *The Washington Post*, January 12, 2007, pp. A1, A8.

2. It is important in this context to differentiate an older "cross-cultural psychology" from the later movement called "cultural psychology" and to exempt the latter from my critique. In cross-cultural psychology, culture is a variable used to test the presumed universality of Western psychological categories or processes. In contrast, cultural psychology seeks to elucidate the ways in which different cultures parse the domains of self and mind, enlarging our entire repertoire of psychological categories and processes. For work in this tradition, see, for example, Bruner (1990); Shweder and LeVine (1984); and Nisbett (2003).

3. But see the discussion invoking Bourdieu (1987), below.

4. A *schema* is a networked cognitive structure that makes possible the identification of objects or situations along with variably "canned" procedures for behaving with respect to them.

Chapter 2

1. Many of these are to be found in business or management guides to working in other cultures, for example, W. Hall (1995); Harris and Moran (1996); and Salacuse (1998).

2. K. Lewin (1948); Deutsch (1949); A. Rapaport and A. Chammah (1965); Burton (1969); Boulding (1961, 1962); Schelling (1960); R. Fisher and W. Ury (1981); and H. Raiffa (1982).

3. I'm stressing the differences, but in the field generally there seems to be convergence, as evidenced by the merger in September 2001 of the Academy of Family Mediators, the Conflict Resolution Education Network, and the Society for Professionals in Dispute Resolution, into the umbrella Association for Conflict Resolution. The Association's new journal, *Conflict Resolution Quarterly*, replaced *Mediation Quarterly* and seeks to represent this convergence. Equally, the older journal of Harvard's Program on Negotiation, the *Negotiation Journal: On the Process of Dispute Settlement* (founded in 1984), never limited itself to topics in negotiation but ranged broadly in conflict resolution theory and practice from its beginnings. Nevertheless, some of the individuals whom I later refer to as "restricted" conflict resolution theorists/practitioners, would insist that the differences I outline are valid and ought to be sustained.

4. I make no pretense in this chapter at offering a comprehensive history of the field; see Ramsbotham et al. (2005:32–54) and Kriesberg (2007a) for brief "histories in process."

5. Even today, in the Johns Hopkins School of Advanced International Studies (SAIS)—an institution closer to the pulse of policy making (it supplies many of the policy makers) in Washington than most academic conflict resolution of peace studies programs, the cognate program is called Conflict Management. For a view from SAIS on the "management/resolution" distinction—he calls it one between the "negotiators" and "dialoguists"—see Zartman (2000a:227–235).

6. For example, see Dugan (1989); Katz (1989); and Lopez (1989). More on ICAR's early years can be found in Black and Avruch (1993).

7. *The Journal of Peace Research* was founded in 1964 and published works critical of the American "pragmatic" approach. See Schmid (1968); and Reid and Yanarella (1976).

8. Accounts of Burton's approach can be found in Dunn (2004) and (more critically) in Avruch and Black (1987); Väyrynen (2001); and Sandole (2006).

9. The similarity to Galtung's (1969) distinction between ("surface") direct violence and (deeply rooted) "structural violence," correlated to the distinction between "negative peace" and "positive peace," is evident. Burton elaborates the idea of "provention" in his *Conflict: Resolution and Provention*, 1990. Here he also presents his vision of "conflict resolution as a political system," revealing his faith in the totalizing and socially transformative potential of his theory and method.

10. J. W. Burton (1987).Two of his younger colleagues subsequently produced a less orthodox (but pedagogically much more useful) version: Mitchell and Banks (1996). The analytical workshop technique is described more broadly and contextualized as a genre of third-party intervention by Fisher (1997). Francis (2002) offers a more "experience-near" account of using workshops in intercultural settings.

11. The first analytical problem solving workshop— then called a "controlled communication workshop"—was held in London in December 1965, to work on then rising tensions among Indonesia, Malaysia, and Singapore. One of the expert panelists at that time was Roger Fisher. In October 1966, Burton convened another panel to consider Cyprus. This time, Herbert Kelman was a panelist. Both Kelman and Fisher ended up at Harvard, but each pursued a very different conception of conflict resolution practice. (See also Fisher 1997:21–25.)

12. Azar (1985, 1990). Burton's first major articulation of basic human needs theory and its relation to deep-rooted conflict is in *Deviance, Terrorism, and War: The Process of Solving Unsolved Social and Political Problems* (1979), and he continued to mine this vein (Burton 1997).

13. Indeed, this is why Burton insisted that conflict resolution was a total "political system." Of course, yesterday's radical ideas can become today's clichés—or at least lose their "punch." By the late 1990s, some scholar-practitioners argued that "mere" resolution didn't go far enough and that one must aim for conflict *transformation*. In a sense, "resolution" was becoming devalued coinage—it began to resemble "management." John Paul Lederach (1995:17) writes, "Unlike resolution and management, the idea of transformation does not suggest we simply eliminate and control conflict, but rather points descriptively toward its inherent dialectic nature." The locus for transformation work is in the dynamics of the social relationships among individuals in conflict. Not all scholars, however, are ready to concede the validity of the distinction asserted between "resolution" and "transformation" (see Ramsbotham et al., 2005).

14. Distinctions among different sorts of practice arising from this are set out in Burton and Dukes (1990). With respect to negotiation theory and practice, Burton (and others) believed that interest-based principled negotiation, as identified with Harvard's Program on Negotiation (PON), was appropriate for addressing many, that is, non-deep-rooted, conflicts, especially interpersonal ones or those in commercial settings. But deep-rooted conflicts (especially around identity issues) were not susceptible to interest-based bargaining, because though interests may be "negotiable," basic human needs were not. Thus, both Roger Fisher and Herbert Kelman were early participants in Burton's analytical problem-solving workshops, and both ended up at Harvard. But their respective practices were very different, the former at the center of Harvard's PON and negotiation work, the latter working more closely in the Burtonian tradition. (See also footnote number 6, above, and Zartman's distinction between what he calls the "negotiators" and the "dialoguists" [Zartman 2000a]). The *locus classicus* for principled negotiation is Fisher and Ury's *Getting to Yes* (1981), though one should now consult the second edition, 1991. Mitchell (2001) describes the setting of the original 1965 Burton workshop. Kelman discusses his workshop theory and practice, especially with Israelis and Palestinians, in many places. A basic source is Kelman (1996). Neither Fisher nor Ury share Burton's views on the range of applicability of principled interest-based negotiation, as evidenced by their wide-ranging third-party practice, domestically and internationally, over the years.

15. Many of the classic articles that appeared in the *Law & Society Review,* the journal of the Law and Society Association, can be found reprinted in R. Abel (1995).

16. In North America the anthropologist E. Hoebel collaborated with the law professor K. Llewellyn in the retrospective analysis of Cheyenne law through "trouble cases." (Llewellyn and Hoebel 1941). For Africa, see M. Gluckman (1955) and Schapera (1938).

17. These principles underlay her work with graduate students on a series of comparative projects that were part of the Berkeley Village Law Project from 1965–1975. Some of these were reported by Nader and Todd (1978).

18. Scholarship moves on, of course, and eventually the focus on "dispute" was critiqued for its narrowness and abandoned for even more expansive concerns with larger-scale historical process (such as colonialism), or with political economy—for example, by Starr and Collier (1989). Nowadays, a Foucauldian concern with language and discourse, as well as feminist theorizing, dominate the field; see, for example, Conley and O'Barr (1998). Human rights and aspects of transnationalism and globalization also feature strongly in today's legal anthropology, for example, Starr and Goodale (2002) and Goodale (2008, 2009).

19. For instance, Abel (1973) and Felstiner (1974). In seeing deep conflict as beyond the reach of mere dispute processing, many of these works reflect the dramaturgical analysis of structural conflict—and its ritualized "resolution"—set out by Turner (1957).

20. Galanter (1974); Harrington and Merry (1988); Nader (1980); Harrington (1985); and Sarat (1988).

21. Grillo (1991); Bryan (1992); and Conley and O'Barr (1998). On the costs to women of psychotherapeutics (including mediation) generally, see Fineman (1991).

22. On the nature of these skills in ADR, see the chapter on "Mediation and Arbitration," by Cheldelin, and on "Facilitation and Consultation," by Cheldelin and Lyons, in Cheldelin, Druckman, and Fast (2003). On ethics and third parties generally, see Laue and Cormick (1978); on neutrality, see Cobb and Rifkin (1991); Mayer (2004); and Chapter 9 in this volume.

23. On transformative mediation see Bush and Folger (1994); on narrative approaches, see Winslade and Monk (2000); and Chapter 8, this volume. Some vicissitudes of empowerment are discussed in Chapter 9.

24. At www.courts.state.va.us/main/htm.

25. Foucault (1980) and Bourdieu (1987).

26. Among the USIP studies are Cohen (1997); Schecter (1998); Solomon (1999); Snyder (1999); Blaker, Giarra, and Vogel (2002); Smyser (2002); Cogan (2003); and Wittes (2005). See also works by Blaker (1977); Binnendijk (1987); Weiss (1994a and 1994b); Druckman (1996); McDonald (1996); and Salacuse (1998).

27. For example, from the Lester B. Pearson Canadian International Peacekeeping Training Centre, *Mediating with Muscle: The Use of Force in International Conflict Resolution,* Morrison, Fraser, and Kiras (1997). See also George (1991).

28. We are latecomers and take a back seat to our colleagues in development on this score; see Gardner and Lewis (1996). Nowadays, post-9/11 military interventions in Iraq and Afghanistan have connected some of conflict resolution's concerns with "stability and reconstruction missions" and with a host of for-profit Beltway contractors. Such interventions have also sought new ways to make "culture" and "culture subject area experts" useful adjuncts to more "kinetic" combat operations in the field. This presents us yet a different take on "culture and conflict resolution."

29. The combination of interventionary incompetence and extant corruption is a special case; see Wedel (1998). The question of the impact of the mega ideas of the West—capitalism and democracy—on world stability, peace, and conflict, is the encapsulating one; see Chua (2002). When these mega ideas are to be imposed by force (bomb them into democracy), we get the debacle of the George W. Bush presidency. See also Chapter 8 in this volume.

30. The chapter appears in Lederach and Jenner (2002:225–233). Her now classic work on aid, development, and conflict is *Do No Harm: How Aid Can Support Peace—Or War* (1999).

31. The general study of civil wars is Licklider (1993). The quote comes from Licklider (1999:24).

Chapter 3

1. Submitted to the UN committee at the time drafting the Declaration, the Statement was published in June 1947 in the *American Anthropologist* 49(4):539–543. A key objection, almost directly from Herskovits, stated: "Standards and values are relative to the culture from which they derive so that any attempt to formulate postulates that grow out of beliefs or moral codes of one culture must to that extent detract from the applicability of an Declaration of Human Rights to mankind as a whole" (*American Anthropologist* 49(4):542).

2. The 1999 version can be found at www.aaanet.org/stmts/humanrts.htm Goodale (2009) traces at length the fate of culture and human rights in anthropology's varied discourses on the topics.

3. The work of the International Criminal Court (ICC), founded in 2002, and its chief prosecutor, Luis Moreno-Ocampo, has come under such criticism, for example in Uganda and the indictment of Joseph Kony and other leaders of the Lord's Resistance Army just as they appeared willing to come out of the bush and negotiate. They chose not to come out and killing continued. See Branch (2007) for a critical perspective on the work and effects of the ICC in this case.

4. At least until poststructuralist critiques emerged to challenged notions of using culture in exercising "technical rationality" whole cloth; see Chapter 9.

5. Rorty explicitly rejects "a mindless and stupid cultural relativism … the idea that any fool thing that calls itself culture is worthy of respect" (Rorty 1999:276).

6. For an outsider's understanding of caste, see Beteille (1983); for an angry insider's view, Ilaiah (1996).

7. See, for example, De Bary and Weiming (1998) and Meijer (2001).

8. On Islam, for example, see Tibi (1990) or Silk (1990).

9. For example, Stoll (1997); D. Gellner (2001); and Samson (2001).

Chapter 4

1. The completist impulse, which roots ethnicity in evolutionary psychology—here ethnicity is a vessel stuffed with DNA—never disappears completely; see van den Berghe (1987).

2. Isaacs coined the term *basic group identity* partly to escape obsessive typologizing (differentiating race from religion from ethnicity from nationalism, etc.) and to underline the common nature of what are today called by many "identity conflicts." Race, religion, history, and so on, were for Isaacs building blocks or components of the basic group identity but—as Abner Cohen's early and Richard Handler's later work showed—conflict could over time morph from one identity form to another as the local political environment shifted.

3. Another even more specialized and brutal site of identity construction is the political prison, resulting in the Guantanamoization of selves. These sites in turn produce altogether more specialized individuals, refugees of another sort, who may react on their respective "centers" in altogether more emphatic ways. See Feldman (1991) for an account of this in terms of the creation of resistance, subjectivity, and the exercise of violence and biopower on political prisoners by the British in Northern Ireland. "Guantanamo" is only a parochial metaphor for what occurs in many other places.

Chapter 5

1. A partial exception to this is sensitivity to African-American culture demonstrated in the work—much it of crisis-driven—of the Community Relations Service (CRS) of the U.S. Department of Justice of the late 1960s and 1970s.

2. See www.brad.ac.uk/acad/confres/dislearn/3_part3.htm.

3. It is important to emphasize the political potency of culture because it is hardly the only term in the social sciences that also does double-duty in ordinary speech. Consider the term

market. As used technically by economists it represents something that is (among other things) abstract, complex, multidetermined, and translocal—the entire enterprise of setting prices, buying and selling commodities, and so on. As used by a shopper, it may well refer to a specific place where particular things are sold. It is the difference between an utterance such as "The market is jittery after large-scale financial scandals are revealed," and "I'm going to the market to buy fish." There may be an *e/n* and *e/d* dimensionality to *market,* but it hardly seems conceptually problematic or politically dangerous. Not so with that "hyper-referential" word *culture* (Kuper 1999).

4. It is precisely the *modernist* thrust of this sort of culture theory that has earned the opprobrium of poststructuralist theorists and practitioners—see Chapter 9.

5. See Chapter 6.

Chapter 6

1. The differences between classically *realist* (from Morgenthau and Thompson 1985) and *neorealist* theories (Waltz 1979) are, of course, important ones, but both in the end treated culture in much the same way, as unimportant, and I shall therefore use the terms here interchangeably.

2. See Avruch (1998:31–35) for a discussion and critique of this work.

3. Kaplan himself claims this influence in the preface to the second edition of the book (Kaplan 1996:x). Secretary of State Warren Christopher also referred to the "centuries-old" hatreds that convinced him, earlier in the 1990s, that American or NATO intervention to end the fighting would have been futile.

4. In the words of Dale Eickelman, a widely respected Middle East anthropologist, Patai can be assigned in introductory undergraduate classes at best as "an anti-text to indicate the pitfalls of using psychological projections to elicit characteristics of society and nation." Another anthropologist, Sondra Hale, said, "He can no longer be taken seriously." The quotes from Eickelm and Hale and information on the continued use of the book and the JFK Special warfare Center and School are from an article by Emram Qureshi, "Misreading 'the Arab Mind,'" which appeared in the *Boston Globe* on May 30, 2004, www.boston.com/news/globe/ideas/articles/2004/05/30/misreading_the_arab_mind/.

5. Seymour Hersh, "The Gray Zone: How a Secret Pentagon Program Came to Abu Ghraib," *The New Yorker*, May 24, 2004, www.newyorker.com/archive/2004/05/24/040524fa_fact. How closely should *The Arab Mind* be linked with interrogation practice is a matter of dispute among anthropologists: compare Gonzales (2007) with McNamara (2007).

6. Kaplan, in the preface to the book's second edition, almost says as much: that he wrote "a travel book" not a "policy work" (1996:x).

7. Concerns about the uses of cultural knowledge in "kinetic" (i.e., combat) operations in Iraq and Afghanistan, and about anthropology's engagement with the military in post-9/11 times, are much discussed these days. A selection of articles and position papers, particularly on the so-called Human Terrain teams begun by the military and staffed with "area expert" social scientists, can be found at http://sites.google.com/site/concernedanthropologists/articles sites.google.com/site/concernedanthropologists/articles.

8. See Sandole (2005) for a discussion of the George W. Bush presidency's contribution to this state of affairs.

9. Additionally, realism makes states the main actors; individuals hardly count, and individual agency of any sort is hard to find. This contrasts sharply with conflict transformation theory and practice.

10. Hence Lord Palmerston, famously: Nations have no permanent friends or allies; they only have permanent interests. Huntington, in contrast, speaks of the power of "kin-country" feelings between and among intracivilizational states, who can in effect form alliances through a sort of "kinship sentimentality," the maintenance of which, in turn, becomes a "national interest." He might thus claim that Palmerston could speak dismissively only of friends and allies—not of kin!

11. Text found at the UN University website: www.un.org/dialogue. A speech by President

Khatami in September 2000 before the United Nations, laying out his idea of civilizational dialogue, can be found at www.iranian.com/Opinion/2000/September/Khatami. Among other things, it can be read as an explicit rebuttal of Huntington's interpretation of Islamic civilization.

12. See, for example, the Public Conversation Project: http://publicconversations.org; also the Public Dialogue Consortium: www.publicdialogue.org; and various projects around dialogue undertaken by the nonprofit Search for Common Ground: www.sfcg.org.

13. This remark is attributed to then Secretary of State James Baker, advising President George H. W. Bush in 1991.

14. Here my conception of culture owes much to Bourdieu's notion of habitus (Bourdieu 1977, 1990).

15. See CNN.com report entitled, "Bush Vows to Rid the World of Evil-Doers," September 15, 2001: http://archives.cnn.com/2001/US/09/16/gen.bush.terrorism. The State of the Union Address took place on September 20, 2001. The use of "crusade" in the speech was reported as impromptu by the press; it does not appear in the official transcript of the speech. For a report by the British press on its use and Arab reaction, see www.telegraph.co.uk/news/worldnews/middleeast/1340914/Ill-chosen-word-fuels-claims-of-intent-to-wage-war-on-Islam.html.

Chapter 7

1. Fortgang (2000) provides some data (based on "informal though extensive interviews") on how negotiation is taught in four different professional fields: law, business, public policy and planning, and international relations; conflict resolution or peace studies curriculua are not considered. There are core similarities but also differences in the four fields' respective approaches. Public policy and planning, given the "scale and complexity" of the problems, as well as institutional and political pressures, the multiplicity of parties and interests and—not least—that "the unique role planners themselves play dramatically shapes how negotiation is taught" is perhaps closest to the conceptualization of negotiation in conflict resolution and peace studies (Fortgang 2000:331).

2. I stress "traditionally" here because this figure does not include such newer forms as dialogue, transforming relationships, or reconciliation. Note also that self-help responses to conflict, at the far left of the continuum, are almost never considered part of conflict resolution proper and are in fact often disdained as inferior or failures.

3. Mediation itself turns out to be a complicated category, as I examine in the next section. We have already considered in Chapter 2 Nader's critique of ADR from a political perspective as "second-rate justice" and the Burtonian critique of ADR-type mediation, namely that although it may suffice for resolving interest-base *disputes,* it has little to offer the resolution of deep-rooted *conflicts* over basic human needs; hence his advocacy of the interactive problem-solving workshop form (Burton 1987; Burton and Dukes 1990; see also Kelman 1996; Fisher 1997). A similar critique is mounted by poststructuralism (e.g., Brigg 2008).

4. For a comprehensive account of how negotiating skills are crucial to the work of humanitarians acting as third parties in securing access, assistance, and protection for civilians in situations of armed conflict, see Mancini-Griffoli and Picot (2004); also Avruch (2004).

5. But note that "hidden" interests may still be subjective ones. The distinction between subjective and objective, or "real," interests, often unexamined in ADR practice, is taken up in Chapter 9.

6. So, too, are various boundary-role issues (the potentially problematic relationship of organizationally embedded negotiators to their constituencies) different for third parties. When one negotiates on behalf of oneself, principal and agent are one and the same. See Mnookin and Susskind (1999).

7. Mayer (2004) offers a similar critique of neutrality in terms of its hurting the relevance of conflict resolution—or its attractiveness to potential clients—in addressing their needs.

8. Riskin (1996) differentiated purely *facilitative* mediation from *evaluative,* wherein the

third party plays a more active, advisory, or "reality-tester" role, possibly compromising strict neutrality (see also Gewurz 2001).

9. The project is outlined more fully in the introduction, written by Honeyman and Schneider, to the special issue of the *Marquette Law Review*, vol. 87, no. 4, Special Issue 2004, "The Emerging Interdisciplinary Canon of Negotiation." The project continues and has resulted in a number of conferences and publications since then, including Schneider and Honeyman (2006); a special issue of *Negotiation Journal* on Second Generation Global Negotiation Education (Honeyman, Coen, and De Palo 2009b); and a volume focused on "rethinking" teaching negotiation (Honeyman, Coben, and De Palo 2009a).

10. Fisher and Ury (1981 [1991]); Raiffa (1982); Walton and McKersie (1965).

11. For example, Raiffa (1982). A contemporary example is Thompson (2009). Jonathan Cohen (2003) has written perceptively of the many metaphors, reflecting the essential tension between competition and cooperation, that we use in thinking and speaking about negotiation (and by extension, mediation). I maintain—at least so far as interest-based negotiation is concerned— that the buyer-seller metaphor most fundamentally captures the tension of "mixed motive" interdependency.

12. In the Prisoners Dilemma version of game theory, central to so much early negotiation research in the experimentalist tradition, after all, the "prosecutor" has something to "sell" the "prisoners," with clear payoffs (costs and benefits), and they must decide whether and how to "buy" it. See Pruitt and Carnevale (1993).

13. Nicholson (1963:71, 77). For a view underlining the cultural construction of such a conception, see Avruch 1998:39ff).

14. For example, Bazerman (1983). For a discussion of such regular or "predictable" distortions to be found in international negotiation at the state level, see Jervis (1976). An early insight in this direction, with implications for peace and conflict studies, can be found in Kenneth Boulding's *The Image: Knowledge of Life and Society* (Boulding 1956).

15. A sample of recent works in this vein: Eich (2000); Forgas (2000); Fridja, Manstead, and Bem (2000).

16. Richard Rubenstein reminds me that there is another dimension to the problem over and above imperfect information and emotional biases in decision making, namely that rational choice theory is not as "coldly analytical" as it seems. Rubenstein argues that it is in many ways "a disguised normative theory, instantiating certain *values* such as a commitment to a certain sort of freedom and a certain sort of social order." He adds parenthetically: "One might even be tempted to call these 'bourgeois values' if one weren't concerned with being thought of as a Marxist dinosaur" (personal communication, July 1, 2004). I would note that one needn't be a Marxist (nor a saurian) to recognize the normative dimension (and social functions) of what theorists from Max Weber to Jurgen Habermas, among others, sometimes called "technical rationality" (*Zweckrationalität*).

17. On the "tragedy of the commons," start with the classic work of the same name by Hardin (1968). Hardin's theory has garnered a fair share of criticism (e.g., Appell 1993) often based on a reading of it as offering an ideologically inspired brief in favor of private property (e.g., Ostrom et al. 1999). This is not my intention here. Rather, I am concerned with the more prosaic lesson: that individual rationality may produce unintended consequences for larger systems.

18. The economist Kenneth Arrow (1963) proposes the "impossibility theorem." For skepticism directed at a sociological "invisible hand" capable of maximally organizing social collectivities, see Hechter (1987). I have hardly scratched the surface of this literature in rational choice and exchange theory, ranging from ecology and economics to sociology and political science.

19. Aaron Wildavsky (1987) argues against the universality and for the cultural variability of "preferences" (utilities). Recall also, as noted in Chapter 1, Ross's caution on conflating *interests* with *motives* when working cross-culturally (Ross 1997:50).

20. Outside of the more formal negotiation literature, the *locus classicus* of this argument is Fisher and Ury's *Getting to Yes* (1981). A critique of the position-interest distinction has been advanced by Provis (1996). Although I have critiqued this book from a cultural perspective in the past, it is mildly distressing to see *win–win* turned so decisively into a cliché. I have been in the field long

enough to remember first encountering the term *win–win* as a genuine and thought-provoking insight. Now one can hear it used routinely by Pentagon spokespersons or on unwary consumers by unscrupulous mortgage bankers or in the finance departments of automobile dealerships all over the country.

21. An important caveat to all these sorts of models, especially hierarchical ones, is that interests and values are never uniformly distributed in social groups—some may hold interests and values that others in the group do not—and that interests and values, even if socially shared, are always differentially internalized by different individuals. For some individuals, to take an example, the value of "Christian charity" may be held, but only at the level of cultural cliché; other individuals might organize their whole lives around it.

22. Burton had an interesting and to some counterintuitive conception of power relations. He assumed that one party—the weaker, disenfranchised, or oppressed one—suffers disproportionately suppressed needs, and its social agitation "causes" the conflict, with the stronger party (often the State) then responding repressively and violently, leading to escalation and conflict spirals. But Burton always recognized that the stronger party has irrepressible needs, too—often around security—and these must be addressed as well if resolution is to occur. A striking example of this was Burton's arguing, throughout the 1970s, 1980s, and early 1990s, that any nonviolent solution to South African Apartheid and the transition to majority black rule would necessitate addressing white, and particularly Afrikaner, concerns. In that era, in the liberal-to-radical university, peace studies, and conflict resolution settings in which he moved, this was a politically incorrect and for some a distasteful position to espouse. Always the iconoclast, political correctness of any sort was never Burton's concern. Nevertheless, most "experts" predicted the end of Apartheid in a racial bloodbath, borne mostly by whites, and a few in radical circles were prepared to welcome it. Now reflect on the genius of Nelson Mandela's guiding South Africa's nonviolent transition to majority black rule and the end of Apartheid—precisely, how the fears of white South Africans *were* addressed, materially and symbolically—and the wisdom of Burton's insights about protecting the needs of apparently stronger parties in deep-rooted conflicts cannot be ignored. There are lessons here for, among others, the Palestinian-Israeli conflict, especially for those more vehement critics of Israel or Zionism who tend toward demonification.

23. How to deal with strong emotions/affect also demands attention. Emotions like anger were dismissed in early negotiation and mediation work by seeing the parties' affect as inimical to rational problem solving and therefore as something to get past, through "venting" for example. The field has moved beyond this. Working from within the broader "Harvard" model of interest-based negotiation, Daniel Shapiro explicitly addresses the problem of how strong affect complicates negotiation. In Fisher and Shapiro (2006), five "core concerns" capable of generating powerful emotions are described: appreciation, affiliation, autonomy, status, and role. These bear a strong resemblance to Burton's basic human needs, also in their presumed universality, and serve the same function as sources of motivation. Like its illustrious predecessor *Getting to Yes*, the book (*Beyond Reason*) is pragmatically oriented, and the reader is told how to address and satisfy these needs and taught how to *use* emotions to get back to the rational part of the negotiation process and toward agreement. Readers are taught, "beyond venting," how emotions can be, in effect, leveraged and controlled.

24. Granted, although I suspect that another reason exists for this assertion, regarding trust in general, if not disclosing one's BATNA, has to do with the presumption (particularly in simulation or experimentalist settings) that buyer-seller negotiations are one-off, "cash-and-carry," nonrepetitive encounters. If one assumes a continuing relationship, even in strictly surplus-maximizing, cost-benefit encounters, then perhaps the notion of trust looms larger—it becomes another utility? The one-off nature of the buyer-seller heuristic is, of course, not a necessary element, but a commonly assumed one. More broadly, Thompson is forgetting that even the most coldly rational or economistic negotiation between buyer and seller depends upon the existence of some shared norms, for example, a consensual legal framework that valorizes contracts. In this sense, one might assume there is a basic level of trust in "the system" if not in the (other) individual. Finally, markets in other cultures may well parse trust in different ways: see Clifford Geertz's chapter on the Moroccan *suq* in Geertz, Geertz, and Rosen (1979).

25. Perhaps the paradigmatic negotiation in both rights and power (more the latter!) is the plea bargain: the prisoners' dilemma in a different light.

26. See especially articles by Jayne Seminare Docherty (2001, 2006); and Christopher Honeyman and Andrea Schneider (in Honeyman and Schneider [2004] and Schneider and Honeyman [2006]).

27. "Recognizable," but not necessarily "identical." Other markets in other places ("cultures") provide evidence of this. Among other things—*pace* Leigh Thompson on "trust"—Geertz writes of buyer-seller interaction in the Moroccan *suq*: "Bargaining does not operate in purely pragmatic, utilitarian terms, but is hedged in by deeply felt rules of etiquette, tradition, and moral expectation" (Geertz 1979:122). For an account that breathlessly assimilates all this to the interest-based negotiation model, see Senger (2002).

28. Other features of this social setting may include notions of gender equality (for heterosexual couples), egalitarianism, the absence of an official state-sponsored religion, or at least the effective legal separation of church and state.

29. This "solution" is the one most in keeping with the highly individualized and religiously privatized nature of the society itself. It *is* rational. Does it make any sense to you?

30. One can even try to run a nation-state in this way, for example, Lebanon: thus, "rational choice."

31. In contrast, consider the *millet* system of the Ottoman empire, which protected the prerogatives of minority religious communities by allowing them jurisdiction over legal matters involving personal status—marriage, divorce, adoption, and so on. But all matters arising between communities, especially those involving Muslims, fell under the jurisdiction of Muslim *qadis* and courts: the clear intersection of rights with power.

32. Wallace Warfield, personal communication, June 30, 2004.

Chapter 8

1. Peacekeeping itself underwent significant change in this period, from UN Charter's traditional–type interventions (see Chapter 6), where UN forces are invited by conflicting states to form a demilitarized buffer zone (or act as observers) while official peacemaking continues, to interventions without formal invitation and with a more muscular or "kinetic" (armed combat—see Chapter 7) potential. For a discussion of peacekeeping written before the failed interventions in 1993 in Somalia and Haiti, see Diehl (1994). For analysis of later interventions, see Bellamy, Williams, and Griffin (2004); and Durch (2007). Rubinstein (2008) discusses cultural aspects of peacekeeping operations.

2. A correlate of this has been the United States' post-9/11 military involvement in Iraq and Afghanistan, particularly with the debacle of the post-invasion disintegration of Iraqi society. This has led to interest and massive funding on the part of the Pentagon in so-called stability and reconstruction work, parts of which are parsed as a form of conflict resolution. The huge amounts of money, in turn, have attracted federal contractors and "Beltway bandits" of all sorts into the field in large numbers. Their impact on the field is controversial, because for many it represents an unfortunate militarization of the field's goals and character.

3. See Kritz (1995) for an early view of what transitional justice entailed, and Kaminski and Nalepa (2006) for a later assessment.

4. The figure of twenty-five to thirty commissions is conservative; on some counts the number rises to more than seventy. This reflects the diversity of definitions of such commissions. For example, are NGO-run commissions the same as "official" state-run ones? Are ones that investigate only corruption the same as ones investigating violations of human rights? It also reflects the fact that some commissions have been announced but have never appeared, as in the case of Mexico.

5. For a sense of these perspectives, see Ackerman (1994); Abu-Nimer (2001); Rigby (2001); Chayes and Minow (2003); Bar-Simon-Tov (2004); and Kriesberg (2007a).

6. The literature is large and growing; see Avruch and Vejarano (2001) for an overview, and

Boraine (2001); Christie (2000); and Stanley (2001) for representative pieces. Mendeloff (2004) is more skeptical.

7. For the full text, see www.smh.com.au/articles/2008/02/13/1202760379056.html.

8. Work *empirically* (as opposed to normatively) assessing the impact of truth commissions with respect to a number of their claims—promoting democratization, strengthening protection of human rights, furthering justice and reconciliation, to name the more prominent ones—is in many ways just beginning or awaiting publication; but see Brahm (2009); Wiebelhaus-Brahm (2010); and van der Merwe et al. (2009).

Chapter 9

1. The neorealism of Kenneth Waltz (1959) differs from the classical variety in, among other things, jettisoning any ontology of human nature and focusing only on the intrinsic "anarchy" of the international system that forces states (now as rational actors) into a perpetual security dilemma and has them seeking either hegemony or association to effect a balance of power. Vasquez (1998) sees neorealism as an extension of the classical paradigm and not a new or radically different theory. Richmond quotes Barry Buzan to this effect: "Realism represents an 'ever-changing discourse about the nature, application, and effect of power in an ever-changing historical environment'" (Richmond 2008:41). In fact, power remains central to all varieties of realist IR.

2. Weber defines power (*macht*) as "the probability that one actor in a social relationship will be in a position to carry out his own will despite resistance, regardless of the basis on which this probability rests" (Weber 1994:23); but see below.

3. Boulding's recourse to the language of economics, utilities maximizing, reminds us of the strong reliance on rational choice theory in all the varieties of realism (accounting for its hostility to values-based decision making), and he points to some of the problems with this: "The national interest, indeed, is what nations are interested in, and historically they have been interested in innumerable things besides power; so that power is a very poor measure of interest" (Boulding 1964:66). On interests and rational choice, see also Chapter 7 and the further discussion in this chapter.

4. Thucydides, *History of the Peloponnesian* War, Book V (85–113).

5. There's a sixth option, implied by poststructuralist conceptions of power, to be discussed below.

6. This last quality, essential contestedness, it shares with culture; see Geertz (2000) among others.

7. Parsons shared this view of power with Hannah Arendt. Writing of coercion or force as violence, Arendt says, "Power and violence are opposites; where the one rules absolutely the other is absent ....Violence can destroy power; it is utterly incapable of creating it" (Arendt 1970:56).

8. Parsons (1960:225). Mills himself favored "craft" over methodology, deriding an attachment to "The Method" as but an "attempt to cover up the triviality of its results" (Mills 1959:71). In the atmosphere of high positivism and scientist aspirations that came to characterize American sociology in the 1960s and early 1970s, Mills paid for this stance. He taught in the undergraduate College at Columbia University. Some graduate students were drawn to him, but the senior faculty in the graduate program discouraged that.

9. So much for the subjectivity of the actors. Thinking seriously about the subjectivity of the analyst or third party is mainly a poststructuralist concern, as discussed below.

10. Perhaps they resemble, here, many sorts of practitioners in different fields—"theory" learned in graduate school is forgotten as soon as examinations are passed, theses written, diplomas awarded, and credentials achieved. The gap between academic researchers and scholars, and practitioners is proverbially wide. Addressing this gap is what made the idea in conflict resolution of the "scholar-practitioner" so attractive.

11. See, for example, Fisher (1983) and Thompson (2009).

12. Remarkably, Boulding's title reflects no connection whatsoever to the extensive literature on the "three faces of power" that dominated so much political science and sociology for decades

and continues today. His meaning is utterly different. Indeed, he wrote in the book's introduction, "Since essentially completing the contents of the volume, a somewhat uneasy conscience has pushed me into reading some of the literature in the field outside my own specialties, and I have to report, perhaps with some embarrassment, that this experience has not changed my mind" (1989:10–11). Whether one finds this admission ineffably arrogant or charmingly eccentric depends, I suspect, on whether one spent any time at all in his company. (I had this pleasure, in the late 1980s.)

13. I do not mean to imply that every ADR-oriented practitioner left these concerns out of his or her practice: a glance at Laue and Cormick's (1978) impassioned defense of the interests of the less powerful, their rejection of doctrinaire neutrality, and their outright refusal to intervene in a way that benefits the powerful would belie this. But Laue was a practitioner strongly guided by Christian ideas of justice, by a profound moral and normative sense of what an ethical conflict resolution was supposed to be about (see Black and Avruch 1999).

14. An early critique of *Getting to Yes* was made on the basis that it offered "no direct analysis of the role of power" (McCarthy 1985:64). Fisher responded to such critiques by proposing six "categories of power" and suggesting ways to address each in a negotiation. Most of the six remedies deal with factors fully internal to the negotiation, such as establishing a good relationship, seeking an "elegant solution," and of course, the tremendous power that comes from possessing a good BATNA (Fisher 1983).

15. This is made clear in Dunn's (2004) study of Burton's work. Burton was not shy in proclaiming his theory an entirely new "paradigm" for international studies (see, e.g., Burton and Sandole 1986). When Avruch and Black (1987) questioned the "revolutionary" status of the theory, it was on the basis of recognizing a long-standing tradition of methodological individualism combined with basic human needs theorizing, as well as on Burton's dismissal of culture—they wrote that little was innovative in this and that Burton's claims for "paradigm busting" were overstated. On the other hand, they underestimated the challenge Burton presented to the dominant trends in IR on the central question of *power*. On this, see Sandole (2006) and Vasquez (1998), below.

16. Curle notes that he read Freire after completing his book, and that Freire's analysis, "more than anything else I have read, is directly and penetratingly concerned with education for awareness, as a tool for moving societies toward peace" (1971:195).

17. As noted previously, this is the dilemma Sara Cobb (1993) raised with respect to mediator empowerment. Her solution, given that power asymmetry resided in discursive processes within mediation, was essentially a narrative one. Although ingenious (and probably right), this does not, however, take us far outside the mediation process itself and into the recalcitrant, material, and resourceful world.

18. A third lesson, still relevant today, is that as the stronger party's military responds to the steady resistance of the weaker part *and* the growing loss of political will to fight at home, it may escalate and resort to increasingly brutal methods to win as quickly and decisively as possible. Mack cites General Massu's use of torture in Algeria, opposition to which soon widened and deepened general opposition to the war in France.

19. Nadim Rouhana's work, cited previously, focused on the Israeli-Palestinian conflict, emerges as a consistent critic of conflict resolution that (in his view) fails to recognize asymmetry, here conceived as the far greater military and coercive power possessed by Israel compared to the Palestinians. He argues that such blindness has the effect of conflict resolution forfeiting a normative commitment to "justice" in favor of "settlement." It is a powerful critique, but it suffers precisely from the monodimensionality of asymmetry conceived only as coercive capability. A more multidimensional view, *pace* Mitchell for example, would recognize (among other things) the increasing asymmetry (increasing in favor of the Palestinian side) on the stage of world opinion, going so far as to undermine or question the very legitimacy of the Jewish state—something Israelis deeply fear.

20. Indeed, McAuley and colleagues (2008) argue that agreement in Northern Ireland came partly as a result of decreasing the symmetry of both Republicans and Loyalists as to the threat to their existential survival that any agreement would pose.

21. See also the discussion of third party roles in Chapter 7, especially Figure 3. Mitchell (1995) attempts to link some of these roles or functions explicitly to conflict reduction strategies toward

achieving (or in some cases preventing) symmetries along the different dimensions in specific conflicts.

22. In Touval and Zartman's (1985) terminology, the facilitative mediator, closest to the classic model of mediator in ADR and the Burton/Kelman models, concentrates on process matters such as enhancing communication, handling logistics, "reality-checking" the parties and so on. There is little interference in substantive matters in the conflict: the parties "own the conflict and its resolution." The mediator as formulator is more involved in substance and participates in the process in this way, such as actively proposing "formulas" leading to resolution ("land for peace"), that is, in suggesting possible outcomes. The manipulator is deeply involved in process and substance, bringing resources to the parties, both carrots and sticks, and using persuasion, leverage, or "muscle" to move the parties toward particular resolutions or outcomes.

23. Scott's peasants mostly lack their Saul Alinskys, and their "transcripts" mostly remain hidden. If they do rebel, rising in overt resistance, they are mostly bloodily put down.

24. Vasquez (1998:214) terms the poststructuralist approach "postmodernism," and identifies it as an "epistemologically more radical form of 'postpositivism.'" As *postmodern* was always in dispute (as a term of opprobrium by detractors and considered inappropriately applied by those most likely to be called postmodernist), and is less in use nowadays, I use the term *poststructuralist.*

References Cited

Abel, R. "A Comparative Theory of Dispute Institutions in Society." *Law & Society Review* 12:217–347, 1973.

———. *The Politics of Informal Justice*, vols. 1 and 2. New York: Academic Press, 1982.

——— (ed.). *The Law & Society Reader.* New York: New York University Press, 1995.

Abu-Lughod, L. "Writing Against Culture." In R. G. Fox (ed.). *Recapturing Anthropology.* Santa Fe: School of American Research Press, 1991.

Abu-Nimer, M. "Conflict Resolution Approaches: Western and Middle Eastern Lessons and Possibilities." *American Journal of Economics and Sociology* 55:35–52, 1996.

———. *Reconciliation, Justice, and Coexistence: Theory and Practice.* Lanham MD: Lexington Books, 2001.

———. *Nonviolence and Peacebuilding in Islam: Theory and Practice.* Gainesville: University Press of Florida, 2003.

Ackermann, A. "Reconciliation as Peace-Building in Postwar Europe." *Peace & Change* 19:229–250, 1994.

Aggestam, K. "Mediating Asymmetric Conflict." *Mediterranean Politics* 7(1):69–91, 2002.

Agusti-Panareda, J. "Power Imbalance in Mediation: Questioning Some Common Assumptions." *Dispute Resolution Journal* 59(2):24–31, 2004.

Ajami, F. "The Summoning." *Foreign Affairs* 72(4):2–9, 1993.

Akenson, D. H. *Small Differences: Irish Catholics and Irish Protestants, 1815–1922.* Dublin: Gill and Macmillan, 1991.

Alinsky, S. *Rules for Radicals.* New York: Random House, 1971.

American Anthropological Association. "Statement on Human Rights." *American Anthropologist* 49(4):539–543.

Anderson, B. *Imagined Communities,* rev. ed. London: Verso, 1991 [1983].

Anderson, M. B. *Do No Harm: How Aid Can Support Peace—Or War.* Boulder CO: Lynne Rienner, 1999.

Appadurai, A. *Modernity at Large: Cultural Dimensions of Globalization.* Minneapolis: University of Minnesota Press, 1996.

Appell, G. N. "Hardin's Myth of the Commons: The Tragedy of Conceptual Confusions." *Working Paper Number 8.* Phillips ME: Social Transformation and Adaptation Research Institute, 1993. http://dlc.dlib.indiana.edu/dlc/handle/10535/4532.

Arendt, H. *Eichmann in Jerusalem: A Report on the Banality of Evil.* New York: Viking Press, 1964.

———. *On Violence.* New York: Harcourt, Brace & Company, 1970.

Aronoff, M. *Israeli Visions and Divisions: Cultural Change and Political Conflict.* New Brunswick NJ: Transaction Books, 1989.

Arreguin-Toft, I. "How the Weak Win Wars: A Theory of Asymmetric Conflict." *International Security* 26(1):93–128, 2007.

Arrow, K. *Social Choice and Individual Values.* New York: John Wiley and Sons, 1963.

Augsburger, D. W. *Conflict Mediation Across Cultures.* Louisville KY: Westminster/ John Knox Press, 1992.

Avruch, K. *American Immigrants in Israel: Social Identities and Change.* Chicago: University of Chicago Press, 1981.

———. "On the Traditionalization of Social Identity." *Ethos* 10(2):95–116, 1982.

———. "Making Culture and Its Costs." *Ethnic and Racial Studies* 14(4):614–626, 1992.

———. *Culture and Conflict Resolution.* Washington DC: United States Institute of Peace Press, 1998.

———. "Culture and Negotiation Pedagogy." *Negotiation Journal.* 16(4):339–346, 2000.

———. "Notes Toward Ethnographies of Conflict and Violence." *Journal of Contemporary Ethnography* 30(5):637–648, 2001.

———. "Culture." In S. Cheldelin, D. Druckman, and L. Fast (eds.). *Conflict: From Analysis to Intervention.* London and New York: Continuum, 2003a.

———. "Type I and Type II Errors in Culturally Sensitive Conflict Resolution Practice." *Conflict Resolution Quarterly* 20:351–371, 2003b.

———. "Culture as Context, Culture as Communication; Considerations for Humanitarian Negotiators." *Harvard Negotiation Law Review* 9:391–407 (Spring), 2004.

———. "Of Time and the River: Notes on the Herrman, Hollet and Gale Model of Mediation." In M. Herrman (ed.). *The Blackwell Handbook on Mediation: Bridging Theory, Research, and Practice.* Malden MA: Blackwell, 2006, pp. 384–394.

———. "What Is Training All About?" *Negotiation Journal* 25(2):161–169, 2009.

Avruch, K., and P. W. Black. "A Generic Theory of Conflict Resolution: A Critique." *Negotiation Journal* 3(1):87–96, 99–100, 1987.

———. "Ideas of Human Nature in Contemporary Conflict Resolution Theory." *Negotiation Journal* 6(3):221–228, 1990.

———. "The Culture Question and Conflict Resolution." *Peace and Change* 16(1):22–45, 1991.

———. "Conflict Resolution in Intercultural Settings: Problems and Prospects." In D. J. D. Sandole and H. van der Merwe, (eds.). *Conflict Resolution Theory and Practice.* Manchester, UK: Manchester University Press, 1993.

———. "ADR, Palau, and the Contribution of Anthropology." In A. Wolfe and H. Yang (eds.). *Anthropological Contributions to Conflict Resolution.* Athens: University of Georgia Press, 1996.

Avruch, K., P. W. Black, and J. Scimecca (eds.). *Conflict Resolution: Cross-Cultural Perspectives.* New York: Greenwood/Praeger, 1991 [1998].

Avruch, K., and B. Vejarano. "Truth and Reconciliation Commissions: A Review Essay and Annotated Bibliography." *Social Justice* 2(1–2):47–108, 2001.

Azar, E. "Protracted Social Conflicts: Ten Propositions." *International Interactions* 12:59–70, 1985.

———. *The Management of Protracted Social Conflict: Theory and Cases.* Brookfield VT: Gower, 1990.

Bachrach, P., and M. Baratz. "The Two Faces of Power." *American Political Science Review* 56:941–952, 1962.

————. "Decisions and Non-Decisions: An Analytical Framework." *American Political Science Review* 57:641–651, 1963.

Bailey, F. G. *Stratagems and Spoils: A Social Anthropology of Politics.* Boulder CO: Westview Press, 2001.

Baker, J. "Truth Commissions." *University of Toronto Law Journal* 51(3):309–326, 2001.

Baker, P. H. "Conflict Resolution versus Democratic Governance: Divergent Paths to Peace?" In C. Crocker, F. Hampson, and P. Aall (eds.). *Managing Global Chaos: Sources of and Responses to International Conflict.* Washington DC: United States Institute of Peace Press, 1996.

Balibar, E. "Is There a 'Neo-Racism'?" In E. Balibar and I. Wallerstein (eds.). *Race, Nation, Class: Ambiguous Identities.* London: Verso, 1991.

Balzer, W. "Game Theory and Power Theory: A Critical Comparison." In T. E. Wartenberg (ed.). *Rethinking Power.* Albany: State University of New York Press, 1992, pp. 56–78.

Bar-Simon-Tov, Y. *From Conflict Resolution to Reconciliation.* Oxford: Oxford University Press, 2004.

Barrett, S. *Culture Meets Power.* Westport CT: Praeger, 2002.

Barth, F. (ed.). *Ethnic Groups and Boundaries.* Boston: Little, Brown, 1969.

Baudrillard, J. *Seduction.* New York: St. Martin's Press, 1990.

Bazerman, M. "Negotiator Judgment: A Critical Look at the Rationality Assumption." *American Behavioral Scientist* 27(2):211–228, 1983.

Beer, J., and E. Stief. *The Mediator's Handbook.* Gabriola Island BC: New Society Publishers, 1997.

Bellamy, A., R. Williams, and S. Griffin. *Understanding Peacekeeping.* London: Polity Press, 2004.

Bercovitch, J., "Mediation in International Conflict." In I. W. Zartman and J. Rasmussen (eds.). *Peace Making in International Conflict: Methods and Techniques.* Washington, DC: United States Institute of Peace Press, 1997.

Beteille, A. *The Idea of Inequality and Other Essays.* Delhi: Oxford University Press, 1983.

Bidney, D. "On the Concept of Culture and some Cultural Fallacies." *American Anthropologist* 46(1):30–44, 1944.

Bieber, F. "The Conflict in Former Yugoslavia as a 'Fault-Line War'? Testing the Validity of Samuel Huntington's 'Clash of Civilizations.'" *Balkanologie* 3(1):33–48, 1993.

Binnendijk, H. (ed.). *National Negotiating Styles.* Washington DC: Foreign Service Institute, U.S. Department of State, 1987.

Birkhoff, J. *Mediators' Perspective on Power: A Window into a Profession?* Unpubl. Ph.D. dissertation, ICAR, George Mason University, 2002.

Black, P. W., "Social Identities." In D. Druckman, S. Cheldelin, and L. Fast (eds.). *Conflict: From Analysis to Resolution,* 2nd ed. London and New York: Continuum, 2008.

Black, P. W., and K. Avruch. "Culture, Power, and International Negotiations: Understanding Palau-U.S. Status Negotiations." *Millennium* 22(3):379–400, 1993.

————. "The Role of Cultural Anthropology in an Institute for Conflict Analysis and Resolution." *Political and Legal Anthropology Review* 16:29–38, 1993.

————. "Cultural Relativism, Conflict Resolution, and Social Justice." *Peace and Conflict Studies* 6(1):21–36, 1999.

Blaker, M. *Japanese International Negotiating Style.* New York: Columbia University Press, 1977.

Blaker, M, D. Giarra, and E. Vogel. *Case Studies in Japanese Negotiating Behavior.* Washington DC: United States Institute of Peace Press, 2002.

Bobbitt, E., and E. Lutz (eds.). *Human Rights and Conflict Resolution in Context.* Syracuse: Syracuse University Press, 2009.

Bolman, L. G., and Deal, T. E. *Reframing Organizations: Artistry, Choice, and Leadership,* 3rd ed. San Francisco: Jossey-Bass, 2003.

Boraine, A. *A Country Unmasked: Inside South Africa's Truth and Reconciliation Commission.* Oxford: Oxford University Press, 2001.

Boulding, K. *The Image: Knowledge and Life in Human Society.* Ann Arbor: University of Michigan Press, 1956.

———. *Perspectives on the Economics of Peace.* New York: Institute for International Orders, 1961.

———. *Conflict and Defense: A General Theory.* New York: Harper & Row, 1962.

———. "The Content of International Studies in College." *Journal of Conflict Resolution* 8(1):65–71, 1964.

———. *Three Faces of Power.* Beverly Hills CA: Sage, 1989.

Bourdieu, P. *Outline of a Theory of Practice.* Cambridge: Cambridge University Press, 1977.

———. *Distinction: A Social Critique of the Judgment of Taste.* Cambridge: Harvard University Press, 1987.

———. *The Logic of Practice.* Stanford: Stanford University Press, 1990.

Boutrous-Ghali, B. *Agenda for Peace.* New York: United Nations, 1992.

Brahm, E. "What Is a Truth Commission and Why Does it Matter?" *Peace & Conflict Review* 3(2):1–14, 2009.

Branch, A. "Uganda's Civil War and the Politics of ICC Intervention." *Ethics & International Affairs* 21(2):179–198, 2007.

Brigg, M. *The New Politics of Conflict Resolution: Responding to Difference.* London and New York: Palgrave Macmillan, 2008.

Brigg, M., and K. Muller. "Conceptualising Culture in Conflict Resolution." *Journal of Intercultural Studies* 30(2):121–140, 2009.

Bringa, T. "Haunted by the Imaginations of the Past: Robert Kaplan's *Balkan Ghosts.*" In C. Besteman and H. Gusterson (eds.). *Why America's Pundits Are Wrong.* Berkeley: University of California Press, 2005.

Brown, D. *Human Universals.* New York: McGraw Hill, 1991.

Brubaker, R. "Ethnicity without Groups." In J. Adams, E. Clemens, and A. S. Orloff (eds.). *Remaking Modernity: Politics, History, and Sociology.* Durham: Duke University Press, 2005.

Bruner, J. *Acts of Meaning.* Cambridge: Harvard University Press, 1990.

Bryan, P. "Killing Us Softly: Divorce Mediation and the Politics of Power." *Buffalo Law Journal* 40:441–523, 1992.

Burns, T. R. "Human Agency and the Evolutionary Dynamics of Culture." *Acta Sociologica* 35(3):187–200, 1992.

Burton, J. W. *Conflict and Communication: The Use of Controlled Communication in International Relations.* London: Macmillan, 1969.

———. *Deviance, Terrorism, and War.* New York: St. Martin's, 1979.

———. *Resolving Deep-Rooted Conflict: A Handbook.* Lanham MD: University Press of America, 1987.

———. *Conflict: Resolution and Provention.* London: Macmillan and New York: St. Martin's, 1990.

———. *Violence Explained.* Manchester, UK: Manchester University Press, New York: St. Martin's, 1997.

Burton, J. W., and F. Dukes (eds.). *Conflict: Practices in Settlement, Management, and Resolution.* New York: St. Martin's, 1990.

Burton, J. W., and D. J. D. Sandole. "Generic Theory: The Basis of Conflict Resolution." *Negotiation Journal* 2:333–344, 1986.

Buruma, I., and A. Margalit. *Occidentalism: The West in the Eyes of its Enemies.* New York: Penguin, 2005.

Bush, R., and J. Folger. *The Promise of Mediation: The Transformative Approach to Conflict.* San Francisco: Jossey-Bass, 1994.

Caplan, P. (ed.). *Understanding Disputes.* Oxford, UK: Berg, 1995.

Carnevale, P. "Strategic Choice in Mediation." *Negotiation Journal* 2:41–56, 1986.

Carr, E. H. *The Twenty Years' Crisis.* London: Macmillan, 1939.

Carrier, J. G. (ed.). *Occidentalism: Images of the West.* New York: Oxford University Press, 1995.

Charters, D. (ed.). *Peacekeeping and the Challenge of Civil Conflict Resolution.* Halifax: Center for Conflict Studies, University of New Brunswick, 1994.

Chayes, A., and M. Minow (eds.). *Imagine Coexistence: Restoring Humanity after Violent Ethnic Conflict.* San Francisco: Jossey-Bass, 2003.

Cheldelin, S. "Engaging Law, Community, and Victim in Dialogue: From Conflict to Shared Understanding." *Ohio State Journal on Dispute Resolution* 22(1):9–36, 2006.

Cheldelin, S., D. Druckman, and L. Fast (eds.). *Conflict: From Analysis to Intervention.* London and New York: Continuum, 2003.

Chew, P. K. (ed.). *The Conflict and Culture Reader.* New York: New York University Press, 2001.

Christie, K. *The South Africa Truth Commission.* London: Palgrave/Macmillan, 2000.

Chua, A. *World on Fire: How Exporting Free Market Democracy Breeds Ethnic Hatred and Global Instability.* New York: Doubleday, 2002.

Citrin, J., C. Wong, and B. Duff. "The Meaning of American National Identity: Patterns of Ethnic Conflict and Consensus." In R. D. Ashmore, L. Jussim, and D. Wilder (eds.). *Social Identity, Intergroup Conflict, and Conflict Reduction.* Oxford: Oxford University Press, 2001.

Clarke, W., and J. Herbst. *Learning from Somalia: The Lessons of Armed Humanitarian Intervention.* Boulder: Westview Press, 1997.

Clifford, J. *The Predicament of Culture.* Cambridge: Harvard University Press, 1988.

Cobb, S. "Empowerment and Mediation: A Narrative Perspective." *Negotiation Journal* 9(3):245–259, 1993.

———. "Fostering Coexistence in Identity-Based-Conflicts: Towards a Narrative Approach." In A. Chayes and M. Minow (eds.). *Imagine Coexistence.* San Francisco: Jossey-Bass, 2003.

———. "Witnessing in Mediation: Toward an Aesthetic of Practice." *Working Paper No. 22.* Fairfax VA: Institute for Conflict Analysis and Resolution, 2004.

Cobb, S., and J. Rifkin. "Practice and Paradox: Deconstructing Neutrality in Mediation." *Law and Social Inquiry* 16:35–62, 1991.

Cogan, C. *French Negotiating Behavior: Dealing with La Grande Nation.* Washington DC: United States Institute of Peace Press, 2003.

Cohen, A. *Custom and Politics in Urban Africa.* Berkeley: University of California Press, 1969.

———. *Two Dimensional Man.* Berkeley: University of California Press, 1974.

———. "Debating the Globalization of U.S. Mediation: Politics, Power, and Practice in Nepal." *Harvard Negotiation Law Review* 11:295, 2006.

Cohen, J. R. "Adversaries? Partners? How about Counterparts? On Metaphors in the Practice and Teaching of Negotiation and Dispute Resolution." *Conflict Resolution Quarterly* 20(4):433–440, 2003.

Cohen, R. *Culture and Conflict in Egyptian-Israeli Relations: A Dialogue of the Deaf.* Bloomington: Indiana University Press, 1990.

———. *Negotiating Across Cultures*, rev. ed. Washington DC: United States Institute of Peace Press, 1997.

———. "Language and Conflict Resolution: The Limits of English." *International Studies Review* 3(1):25–51, 2001.

Coleman, P. "Power and Conflict." In M. Deutsch and P. Coleman (eds.). *Handbook of Conflict Resolution: Theory and Practice*. San Francisco: Jossey-Bass, 2000, pp. 108–130.

Conley, J., and W. O'Barr. *Just Words: Law, Language, and Power.* Chicago: University of Chicago Press, 1998.

Connor, W. *Ethnonationalism: The Quest for Understanding.* Princeton: Princeton University Press, 1994.

Cowan, J. K., M-B. Dembour, and R. A. Wilson (eds.). *Culture and Rights: Anthropological Perspectives.* Cambridge, UK: Cambridge University Press, 2001.

Cupach, W., and D. Canary. *Competence in Interpersonal Conflict.* Prospect Heights IL: Waveland Press, 1997.

Curle, A. *Making Peace.* London: Tavistock, 1971.

———. *In the Middle: Non-Official Mediation in Violent Situations.* Oxford: Berg, 1986.

Dahl, R. "The Concept of Power." *Behavioral Science* 2:201–215, 1957.

———. *Who Governs? Democracy and Power in an American City.* New Haven: Yale University Press, 1961.

Dahrendorf, R. *Class and Class Conflict in Industrial Society.* London: Routledge & Kegan Paul, 1959.

D'Andrade, R. "Schemas and Motivation." In R. D'Andrade and C. Strauss (eds.). *Human Motives and Cultural Models* (Cambridge: Cambridge University Press, 1992.

———. *The Development of Cognitive Anthropology.* Cambridge: Cambridge University Press, 1995.

Danzig, R. "Toward the Creation of a Complementary, Decentralized System of Criminal Justice." *Stanford Law Review* 26:1–54, 1973.

Das, V., A. Kleinman, M. Ramphele, and P. Reynolds (eds.). *Violence and Subjectivity.* Berkeley: University of California Press, 2000.

De Bary, T., and W. Weiming (eds.). *Confucianism and Human Rights.* New York: Columbia University Press, 1998.

Deutsch, M. "A Theory of Cooperation and Conflict." *Human Relations* 2:129–152, 1949.

Diehl, P. *International Peacekeeping.* Baltimore: Johns Hopkins University Press, 1994.

Docherty, J. *When the Parties Bring their Gods to the Table: Learning Lessons from Waco.* Syracuse: Syracuse University Press, 2001.

———. "Power in the Social/Political Realm." *Marquette Law Review* 27:862–866, 2004.

———. "The Unstated Models in Our Minds." In A. Schneider and C. Honeyman (eds.). *The Negotiator's Fieldbook.* Washington DC: American Bar Association, 2006.

Dominguez, V. *White by Definition: Social Classification in Creole Louisiana.* New Brunswick: Rutgers University Press, 1986.

Donnelly, J. *Universal Human Rights in Theory and Practice.* Ithaca: Cornell University Press, 1989.

Druckman, D. "Is There a U.S. Negotiating Style?" *International Negotiation* 1(2):327–334, 1996.

D'Souza, D. *The Enemy at Home: The Cultural Left and Its Responsibility for 9/11.* New York: Doubleday, 2007.

Du Toit, A. "The Moral Foundations of the South African TRC: Truth as Acknowledgment and Justice as Recognition." In R. Rotberg and D. Thompson (eds.). *Truth vs. Justice: The Morality of Truth Commissions.* Princeton: Princeton University Press, 2000.

Dugan, M. "Peace Studies at the Graduate Level." *Annals of the American Academy of Political and Social Sciences.* 504:72–79, 1989.

Dunn, D. J. *From Power Politics to Conflict Resolution: Assessing the Work of John W. Burton,* rev. ed. London: Palgrave/Macmillan, 2004.

Durch, W. (ed.). *The Evolution of UN Peacekeeping.* New York: St. Martin's, 1993.

———. *Twenty-First-Century Peace Operations.* Washington DC: United States Institute of Peace Press, 2007.

Dwyer, K. *Arab Voices: The Human Rights Debate in the Middle East.* Berkeley: University of California Press, 1991.

Eich, E. *Cognition and Emotion* New York: Oxford University Press, 2000.

Eller, J. D. *From Culture to Ethnicity to Conflict.* Ann Arbor: University of Michigan Press, 1999.

Eriksen, T. H. "Ethnic Identity, National Identity, and Intergroup Conflict: The Significance of Personal Experiences." In R. D. Ashmore, L. Jussim, and D. Wilder (eds.). *Social Identity, Intergroup Conflict, and Conflict Reduction.* Oxford: Oxford University Press, 2001.

Erikson, E. "The Problem of Ego Identity." *Psychological Issues* 1:101–164, 1959.

Evans, J. "Fitting Extremism into the Rational Choice Paradigm." *Government and Opposition* 39(1):110–118, 2004.

Fanon, F. *The Wretched of the Earth.* New York: Grove Press, 1986.

Feldman, A. *Formations of Violence: The Narratives of the Body and Political Terror in Northern Ireland.* Chicago: University of Chicago Press, 1991.

Felstiner, W. "Influences of Social Organization on Dispute Processing." *Law & Society Review* 9:63–94, 1974.

Fineman, M. H. *The Illusion of Equality: The Rhetoric and Reality of Divorce Reform.* Chicago: University of Chicago Press, 1991.

Finkielkraut, A. *The Defeat of the Mind.* New York: Columbia University Press, 1995.

Fisher, R. "Negotiating Power: Getting and Using Influence." *American Behavioral Scientist* 27(2):149–166, 1983.

Fisher, R. J. *Interactive Conflict Resolution.* Syracuse: Syracuse University Press, 1997.

Fisher, R. J. and L. Keashley. "The Potential Complementarity of Mediation and Consultation within a Contingency Model of Third Party Intervention." *Journal of Peace Research* 28:29–42, 1991.

Fisher, R., and D. Shapiro. *Beyond Reason: Using Emotions as You Negotiate.* New York: Penguin Books, 2006.

Fisher, R., W. Ury, and B. Patton. *Getting To Yes*, 2nd ed. New York: Penguin Books, 1991 [Orig. Fisher and Ury, 1981].

Folberg, J., and A. Taylor. *Mediation*. San Francisco: Jossey-Bass, 1984.

Follett, M. Parker. "Power." In E. M. Fox and L. Urwick (eds.). *Dynamic Administration: The Collected Papers of* Mary *Parker Follett*. London: Pitman, 1973.

Forester, J. *Dealing with Differences: Dramas of Mediating Public Disputes*. Oxford: Oxford University Press, 2009.

Forgas, J. (ed.). *Thinking and Feeling: The Role of Affect in Social Cognition*. Cambridge: Cambridge University Press, 2000.

Fortgang, R. "Taking Stock: An Analysis of Negotiation Pedagogy across Four Professional Fields." *Negotiation Journal* 16(4):325–338, 2000.

Foucault, M. *Discipline and Punish*. New York: Pantheon Books, 1978.

———. *Power/Knowledge*. New York: Pantheon, 1980.

———. "The Subject and Power." In H. Dreyfus and P. Rabinow (eds.). *Michel Foucault: Beyond Structuralism and Hermeneutics*. Chicago: University of Chicago Press, 1982, pp. 208–226.

Fox, R. G. (ed.). *Nationalist Ideologies and the Production of National Cultures*. Washington DC: American Anthropological Association, 1990.

Francis, D. *People, Peace, and Power: Conflict Transformation in Action*. London: Pluto Press, 2002.

Freire, P. *Pedagogy of the Oppressed*. New York: Continuum, 1970.

Fridja, N., A. S. Manstead, and S. Bem (eds.). *Emotions and Beliefs: How Feelings Influence Thought*. Cambridge: Cambridge University Press, 2000.

Fry, D., and K. Björkqvist. *Cultural Variation in Conflict Resolution: Alternatives to Violence*. Mahway NJ: Lawrence Erlbaum, 1997.

Gadamer, H. G. *Truth and Method*, 2nd ed. New York: Continuum, 1993.

Gadlin, H. "Conflict Resolution, Cultural Differences, and the Culture of Racism." *Negotiation Journal* 10(1):33–47, 1994.

Galanter, M. "Why the 'Haves' Come Out Ahead: Speculations on the Limits of Legal Change." *Law & Society Review* 9:95–160, 1974.

Galatzer-Levy, R., and B. Cohler. *The Essential Other: A Developmental Psychology of the Self*. New York: Basic Books, 1993.

Galtung, J. "Violence, Peace, and Peace Research." *Journal of Peace Research* (3):167–191, 1969.

———. "Cultural Violence." *Journal of Peace Research* 27(3):291–305, 1990.

Gardner, K., and D. Lewis. *Anthropology, Development, and the Post-Modern Challenge*. London: Pluto Press, 1996.

Geertz, C. *The Interpretation of Cultures*. New York: Basic Books, 1973.

———. "Suq: The Bazaar Economy in Sefrou." In C. Geertz, H. Geertz, and L. Rosen. *Meaning and Order in Moroccan Society*. Cambridge: Cambridge University Press, 1979.

———. *Local Knowledge*. New York: Basic Books, 1983.

———. *Available Light*. Princeton: Princeton University Press, 2000.

Geertz C., H. Geertz, and L. Rosen. *Meaning and Order in Moroccan Society*. Cambridge: Cambridge University Press, 1979.

Gellner, D. "From Group Rights to Individual Rights and Back: Nepalese Struggles over Culture and Equality." In J. K. Cowan, M-B. Dembour, and R. A. Wilson (eds.). *Culture and Rights: Anthropological Perspectives*. Cambridge, UK: Cambridge University Press, 2001.

Gellner, E. *Nationalism.* London: Weidenfeld & Nicolson, 1997.

George, A. *Forceful Persuasion: Coercive Diplomacy as an Alternative to War.* Washington DC: United States Institute of Peace Press, 1991.

Gewurz, I. "(Re)Designing Mediation to Address the Nuances of Power Imbalances." *Conflict Resolution Quarterly* 19(2):135–162, 2001.

Gibbs, J. "The Kpelle Moot: A Therapeutic Model for the Informal Settlement of Disputes." *Africa* 33:1–11, 1963.

Giddens, A. *Central Problems in Social Theory.* London: Macmillan, 1979.

Glendon, M. A. *A World Made New: Eleanor Roosevelt and the Universal Declaration of Human Rights.* New York: Random House, 2001.

Gluckman, M. *The Judicial Process among the Barotse.* Manchester, UK: Manchester University Press, 1955.

Gonzalez, R. "Patai and Abu Ghraib." *Anthropology Today* 23(5):23, 2007.

Goodale, M. *Dilemmas of Modernity: Bolivian Encounters with Law and Liberalism.* Stanford: Stanford University Press, 2008.

———. *Surrendering to Utopia: An Anthropology of Human Rights.* Stanford: Stanford University Press, 2009.

Gopin, M. "Forgiveness as an Element of Conflict Resolution in Religious Cultures." In M. Abu-Nimer (ed.). *Reconciliation, Justice, and Coexistence.* Lanham MD: Lexington Books, 2001.

Gramsci, A. *Selections from Prison Writings.* Oxford: Oxford University Press, 1985.

Greenhouse, C. *Praying for Justice: Faith, Order, and Community in an American Town.* Ithaca NY: Cornell University Press, 1986.

Grillo, T. "The Mediation Alternative: Process Dangers for Women." *Yale Law Review* 100:1545–1610, 1991.

Groom, A. J. R., and K. Webb. "Injustice, Empowerment and Facilitation in Conflict." *International Interactions* 13(3):263–280, 1987.

Gudykunst, S., L. Stewart, and S. Ting-Toomey (eds.). *Communication, Culture, and Organizational Processes.* London: Sage, 1985.

Gulliver, P. H. "Introduction to Case Studies of Law in Nonwestern Societies." In L. Nader (ed.). *Law in Culture and Society.* Chicago: Aldine, 1969.

———. *Disputes and Negotiations: A Cross-Cultural Perspective.* New York; Academic Press, 1979.

Gusterson, H. "The Seven Deadly Sins of Samuel Huntington." In C. Besteman and H. Gusterson (eds.). *Why America's Pundits Are Wrong.* Berkeley: University of California Press, 2005.

Habermas, J. *The Theory of Communicative Action.* Cambridge: Polity, 1981

Hall, E. *Beyond Culture.* New York: Anchor Books, 1976.

Hall, W. *Managing Cultures: Making Strategic Relationships Work.* New York: Wiley, 1995.

Hancock, G. *Lords of Poverty: The Power, Prestige & Corruption of the International Aid Business.* New York: Atlantic Monthly Press, 1989.

Handler, R. *Nationalism and the Politics of Culture in Quebec.* Madison: University of Wisconsin Press, 1988.

Hardin, G. "The Tragedy of the Commons." *Science* 162:1243–1248, 1968.

Harrington, C. *Shadow Justice: The Ideology and Institutionalization of Alternatives to Court.* New York: Greenwood Press, 1985.

Harrington, C., and S. Merry. "Ideological Production: The Making of Community Mediation." *Law & Society Review* 22:709–735, 1988.

Harris, M. *Theories of Culture in Postmodern Times.* Walnut Creek CA: Alta Mira Press, 1999.

Harris, P., and R. Moran. *Managing Cultural Differences,* 4th ed. Houston: Gulf Publishing 1996.

Hatch, E. *Culture and Morality: The Relativity of Values in Anthropology.* New York: Columbia University Press, 1983.

———. "The Good Side of Relativism." *Journal of Anthropological Research* 53:371–381, 1997.

Haugaard, M. (ed.). *Power: A Reader.* Manchester: Manchester University Press, 2002.

Hayner, P. "Truth Commissions—1974–1994: A Comparative Study." *Human Rights Quarterly* 16(4):597–655, 1994.

———. *Unspeakable Truths: Facing the Challenge of Truth Commissions.* New York: Routledge, 2002.

Hechter, M. *Principles of Group Solidarity.* Berkeley: University of California Press, 1987.

Herder, J. G. *Reflections on the Philosophy of the History of Mankind.* F. Manuel, tr. Chicago: University of Chicago Press, 1968.

Hermann, T. "Reconciliation: Reflections on the Theoretical and Practical Utility of the Term." In Y. Simon-Bar-Tov (ed.). *From Conflict Resolution to Reconciliation.* Oxford: Oxford University Press, 2004.

Herrman, M. (ed.). *The Blackwell Handbook of Mediation: Bridging Theory, Research, and Practice.* Malden MA: Blackwell, 2006.

Hersh, S. "The Gray Zone: How a Secret Pentagon Program Came to Abu Ghraib." *The New Yorker.* May 24, 2004.

Herskovits, M. *Cultural Dynamics.* New York: Knopf, 1964.

Hobsbawm, E., and T. Ranger. *The Invention of Tradition.* Cambridge: Cambridge University Press, 1983.

Hodgson, D. L. "Comparative Perspectives on the Indigenous Rights Movement in Africa and the Americas." *American Anthropologist* 104:1037–1045, 2002.

Hofstede, G. *Culture's Consequences: International Differences in Work Related Values.* Beverly Hills CA: Sage, 1980.

Honeyman, C., J. Coben, and G. De Palo (eds.). *Rethinking Negotiation Teaching: Innovations for Context and Culture.* St. Paul MN: DRI Press, 2009a.

——— (eds.). "Second Generation Global Negotiation Education." *Negotiation Journal* 25(2), 2009b.

Honeyman, C., B. C. Goh, and L. Kelley. "Skill Is Not Enough: Seeking Connectedness and Authority in Mediation." *Negotiation Journal* 20(4):489–511, 2004.

Honeyman, C., and A. Schneider (eds.). "The Emerging Interdisciplinary Canon of Negotiation." *Marquette Law Review* 87(4), 2004.

Hopmann, P. T. "Two Paradigms of Negotiation: Bargaining and Problem Solving." *The Annals of the American Academy of Political and Social Sciences.* 542:24–47, 1995.

Horowitz, D. *Ethnic Groups in Conflict.* Berkeley: University of California Press, 1985.

Hunter, F. *Community Power Structure: A Study of Decision Makers.* Chapel Hill: University of North Carolina Press, 1953.

Huntington, S. "The Clash of Civilizations?" *Foreign Affairs* 72(3):22–49, 1993.

———. *The Clash of Civilizations and the Remaking of the World Order.* New York: Simon and Schuster, 1996.

Hyatt, M. *Franz Boas, Social Activist: The Dynamics of Ethnicity.* New York: Greenwood Press, 1990.

Ignatieff, M. *Blood and Belonging: Journeys into the New Nationalism.* New York: Farrar, Straus and Giroux, 1994.

———. "Overview: Articles of Faith." *Index on Censorship* 5:110–122, 1996.

Ilaiah, K. *Why I Am Not a Hindu: A Sudra Critique of Hindutva Philosophy, Culture, and Political Economy.* Calcutta: Samya, 1996.

Isaacs, H. *Idols of the Tribe: Group Identity and Political Change.* Cambridge MA: Harvard University Press, 1975.

Jenks, Chris. *Culture.* London: Routledge, 1993.

Jervis, R. *Perception and Misperception in International Politics.* Princeton: Princeton University Press, 1976.

Kahn, H. *On Thermonuclear War.* Princeton: Princeton University Press, 1960.

Kahneman, D., P. Slovich, and A. Tversky (eds.) *Judgment under Uncertainty: Heuristics and Biases.* Cambridge: Cambridge University Press, 1982.

Kaminski, M., and M. Nalepa. "Judging Transitional Justice." *Journal of Conflict Resolution* 50(3):383–408, 2006.

———. *Balkan Ghosts: A Journey Through History,* 2nd ed. New York: St. Martin's Press, 1996 [orig. 1993].

———. *The Coming Anarchy: Shattering the Dreams of the Post Cold War.* New York: Vintage Books, 2001.

Kaplan, R. *The Coming Anarchy: Shattering the Dreams of the Post Cold War.* New York: Vintage Books, 2001.

Katz, N. H. "Conflict Resolution and Peace Studies." *Annals of the American Academy of Political and Social Sciences* 504:14–21, 1989.

———. "Enhancing Mediator Artistry: Multiple Frames, Spirit, and Reflection in Action." In M. Herrmann (ed.). *Blackwell Handbook of Mediation: Bridging Theory, Research, and Practice.* Malden MA: Blackwell, 2006.

Keller (Dougherty), J. "Salience and Relativity in Classification." *American Ethnologist* 5:66–79, 1978.

Kelman, H. "The Interactive Problem Solving Approach." In C. Crocker, F. Hampson, and P. Aall (eds.). *Managing Global Chaos.* Washington DC: United States Institute of Peace Press, 1996.

———. "Social-Psychological Dimensions of International Conflict." In I. W. Zartman and L. Rasmussen (eds.). *Peacemaking in International Conflicts.* Washington DC: United States Institute of Peace Press, 1997.

———. "Reconciliation as Identity Change: A Social-Psychological Perspective." In Y. Simon-Bar-Tov (ed.). *From Conflict Resolution to Reconciliation.* Oxford: Oxford University Press, 2004.

Kochman, T. *Black and White Styles in Conflict.* Chicago: University of Chicago Press, 1981.

Kohut, H. *The Analysis of Self.* New York: International Universities Press, 1971.

Kressel, K. *Labor Mediation: An Exploratory Survey.* New York: Association of Labor Mediation Agencies, 1972.

Kriesberg, L. "The Conflict Resolution Field: Origins, Growth, and Differentiation." In I. W. Zartman (ed.). *Peacemaking in International Conflict,* rev. ed. Washington DC: United States Institute of Peace Press, rev. ed., 2007a.

———. *Constructive Conflicts: From Escalation to Resolution.* 3rd ed. Lanham MD: Rowman & Littlefield, 2007b.

———. "Reconciliation: Aspects, Growth, and Sequences." *International Journal of Peace Studies* 12 (1):1–21, 2008.

————. "Changing Conflict Asymmetries Constructively." *Dynamics of Asymmetric Conflict* 2(1):4–22, 2009.

Kriesberg, L., T. A. Northrup, and S. J. Thorson (eds.). *Intractable Conflicts and their Transformation.* Syracuse: Syracuse University Press, 1989.

Kritz, N. *Transitional Justice.* 3 volumes. Washington DC: United States Institute of Peace Press, 1995.

Kroeber A., and C. Kluckhohn. *Culture: A Critical Review of Concepts and Definitions.* Papers of the Peabody Museum of American Archaeology and Ethnology, vol. 47, Harvard University, 1952.

Kuper, A. *Culture: The Anthropologists' Account.* Cambridge: Harvard University Press, 1999.

Laclau, E. "Why Do Empty Signifiers Matter to Politics?" In M. McQuillan (ed.). *Deconstruction: A Reader.* Edinburgh: Edinburgh University Press, 2001.

Lakatos, I. "Falsification and Methodology of Scientific Research." In I. Lakatos and A. Musgrave (eds.). *Criticism and the Growth of Knowledge.* Cambridge: Cambridge University Press, 1970, pp. 91–196.

Lakoff, G., and M. Johnson. *Metaphors We Live By.* Chicago: University of Chicago Press, 1980.

Lambourne, W. "Justice and Reconciliation: Postconflict Peacebuilding in Cambodia and Rwanda." In M. Abu-Nimer (ed.). *Reconciliation, Justice, and Coexistence.* Lanham MD: Lexington Books, 2001.

Latour, B. *We Have Never Been Modern.* Cambridge: Harvard University Press, 1993.

Laue, J., and G. Cormick. "The Ethics of Intervention in Community Disputes." In G. Bermant, H. Kelman, and D. Warwick (eds.). *The Ethics of Social Intervention.* Washington DC: Halstead Press, 1978.

Lederach, J. P. "Of Nets, Nails and Problems: The Folk Language of Conflict Resolution in a Central American Setting." In K. Avruch, P. W. Black, and J. Scimecca (eds.). *Conflict Resolution: Cross-Cultural Perspectives.* New York: Greenwood/Praeger, 1998 [orig. 1991].

————. *Preparing for Peace: Conflict Transformation Across Cultures.* Syracuse: Syracuse University Press, 1995.

————. *Building Peace: Sustainable Reconciliation in Divided Societies.* Washington DC: United States Institute of Peace Press, 1997.

Lederach, J. P., and J. M. Jenner (eds.). *A Handbook of International Peacebuilding: Into the Eye of the Storm.* San Francisco: Jossey-Bass, 2002.

Lee, R. B. *The Dobe !Kung.* New York: Holt, Rinehart & Winston, 1984.

Lewin, K. *Resolving Social Conflicts.* New York: Harper & Brothers, 1948.

————. *Field Theory in Social Science.* New York: Harper, 1951.

Lewis, H. "The Passion of Franz Boas." *American Anthropologist* 22:221–245, 1993.

Licklider, R. (ed.). *Stopping the Killing: How Civil Wars End.* New York: New York University Press, 1993.

————. "Negotiating an End to Civil Wars: General Findings." In T. Sisk (ed.). *New Approaches to International Negotiation and Mediation: Findings from USIP-Sponsored Research.* Peaceworks No. 30. Washington DC: United States Institute of Peace, 1999.

Llewellyn, L., and E. A. Hoebel. *The Cheyenne Way: Conflict and Case Law in Primitive Jurisprudence.* Norman OK: Oklahoma University Press, 1941.

Long Day's Journey into Night. Documentary film directed by Frances Reid and Deborah Hoffmann. Iris Films, 2000. www.irisfilms.org.

Lopez, G. "Trends in College Curricula and Programs." *Annals of the American Academy of Political and Social Sciences* 504:61–71, 1989.

Lukes, S. "Five Fables about Human Right." In S. Shute and S. Hurley (eds.). *On Human Rights: The Oxford Amnesty Lectures, 1993.* New York: Basic Books, 1993.

———. *Power: A Radical View,* 2nd ed. New York: Palgrave Macmillan, 2005 [orig. 1974].

Lyotard. J.-F. *The Post-Modern Condition.* Minneapolis: University of Minnesota Press, 1984.

Lytle, A., J. Brett, and D. Shapiro. "The Strategic Use of Interests, Rights, and Power to Resolve Disputes." *Negotiation Journal* 15(1):31–51, 1999.

Macduff, I. "Decision-Making and Commitments—Impact of Power Distance in Mediation." In J. Lee and T. H. Hwee (eds.). *An Asian Perspective on Mediation.* Singapore: Academy Publishing, 2009, pp. 111–144.

Mack, A. "Why Big Nations Lose Small Wars: The Politics of Asymmetric Conflict." *World Politics* 27(2):175–200, 1975.

Maiese, M. "Dialogue." In G. Burgess and H. Burgess (eds.). *Beyond Intractability.* Conflict Research Consortium, University of Colorado, Boulder, 2003. www.beyondintractability.org/essay/dialogue.

Malkki, L. *Purity and Exile: Violence, Memory, and National Cosmology among Hutu Refugees in Tanzania.* Chicago: University of Chicago Press, 1995.

Mancini-Griffoli, D., and A. Picot. *Humanitarian Negotiation: A Handbook for Securing Access, Assistance, and Protection for Civilians in Armed Conflict.* Geneva: HD Centre for Humanitarian Dialogue, 2004.

Maren, M. *The Road to Hell: The Ravaging Effects of Foreign Aid and International Charity.* New York: The Free Press, 1997.

Martin, J. *Culture in Organizations: Three Perspectives.* Oxford: Oxford University Press, 1992.

Mayer, B. *Beyond Neutrality: Confronting the Crisis in Conflict Resolution.* San Francisco: Jossey-Bass, 2004.

McAuley, J., C. McGlynn, and J. Tonge. "Conflict Resolution in Symmetric and Asymmetric Situations: Northern Ireland as a Case Study." *Dynamics of Asymmetric Conflict* 1(1):88–102, 2008.

McCarthy, W. "The Role of Power and Principle in *Getting to Yes.*" *Negotiation Journal* 1:59–66, 1985.

McClelland, C. "Power and Influence." In J. R. Champlin (ed.). *Power.* New York: Atherton Press, 1971, pp. 35–65.

McDonald, J. W. (ed.). "Defining a U.S. Negotiating Style." Special Issue of *International Negotiation* 1(2), 1996.

McNamara, L. "Notes on an Ethnographic Scandal: Seymour Hersh, Abu Ghraib and The Arab Mind." *Anthropology News* 48(7):4–5, 2007.

Meijer, M. (ed.). *Dealing with Human Rights: Asian and Western Views on the Value of Human Rights.* Bloomfield CT: Kumarian Press, 2001.

Mendeloff, D. "Truth-Seeking, Truth-Telling and Post-Conflict Peacebuilding: Curb the Enthusiasm." *International Studies Review* 6(3):355–380, 2004.

Menkel-Meadow, C. "The Trouble with the Adversary System in a Post-Modern, Multi-Cultural World." *William and Mary Law Review* 38:5–44, 1996.

———. "Correspondences and Contradictions in International and Domestic Conflict Resolution: Lessons from General Theory and Varied Contexts. *Journal of Dispute Resolution* 2003(2):319, 2003.

Merry, S. "Disputing without Culture." *Harvard Law Review* 100:2057–2073, 1987.

———. *Getting Justice and Getting Even: Legal Consciousness among Working Class Americans.* Chicago: University of Chicago Press, 1990.

Messer, E. "Anthropology and Human Rights." *Annual Review of Anthropology* 22:227–232, 1993.

Mills, C. W. *White Collar.* New York: Oxford University Press, 1951.

———. *The Power Elite.* New York Oxford University Press, 1956.

———. *The Sociological Imagination.* New York: Oxford University Press, 1959.

Minow, M. *Between Vengeance and Forgiveness: Facing History after Genocide and Mass Violence.* Boston: Beacon Press, 1998.

Mitchell, C. R. "Classifying Conflicts: Asymmetry and Resolution." *Annals of the American Academy of Political and Social Science* 518:23–38, 1991.

———. "The Process and Stages of Mediation: Two Sudanese Cases." In D. Smock (ed.). *Making War and Waging Peace: Foreign Intervention in Africa.* Washington DC: United States Institute of Peace Press, 1993.

———. "Asymmetry and Strategies of Regional Conflict Reduction." In I. W. Zartman and V. Kremenyuk (eds.). *Cooperative Security: Reducing Third World Wars.* Syracuse: Syracuse University Press, 1995.

———. "From Controlled Communications to Problem Solving: The Origins of Facilitated Conflict Resolution." *International Journal of Peace Studies* 6(1) 2001.

———. "Mediation and the Ending of Conflicts." In J. Darby and R. MacGinty (eds.). *Contemporary Peacemaking: Conflict, Violence, and Peace Processes.* London: Palgrave/Macmillan, 2003.

———. "Persuading Lions: Problems of Transferring Insights from Track-2 Exercises Undertaken in Conditions of Asymmetry." *Dynamics of Asymmetric Conflict* 2(1):32–50, 2009.

Mitchell, C. R., and M. Banks. *Handbook of Conflict Resolution: The Analytical Problem-Solving Approach.* London: Pinter 1996.

Mnookin, R., and L. Susskind (eds.). *Negotiating on Behalf of Others.* Thousand Oaks CA: Sage, 1999.

Moore, C. *The Mediation Process.* San Francisco: Jossey-Bass, 1986.

Morgenthau, H., and K. W. Thompson. *Politics among Nations,* 6th ed. New York: Knopf, 1985.

Morrison, A., D. Fraser, and J. Kiras (eds.). *Peacekeeping with Muscle: The Use of Force in International Conflict Resolution.* Clementsport NS: Canadian Peacekeeping Press, 1997.

Nader, L. (ed.). *No Access to Law: Alternatives to the American Judicial System.* New York: Academic Press, 1980.

———. "Controlling Processes in the Practice of Law: Hierarchy and Pacification in the Movement to Re-Form Dispute Ideology." *Ohio State Journal on Dispute Resolution.* 9:1–8, 1993.

———. "Harmony Models and the Construction of Law." In K. Avruch, P. W. Black, and J. Scimecca (eds.). *Conflict Resolution: Cross-Cultural Perspectives.* New York: Greenwood/Praeger, 1998 [1991].

Nader, L., and E. Grande. "Current Illusions and Delusions about Conflict Management, in Africa and Elsewhere." *Law and Social Inquiry* 27(3):573–594, 2002.

Nader, L., and H. Todd (eds.). *The Disputing Process—Law in Ten Societies.* New York: Columbia University Press, 1978.

Narroll, R. "Ethnic Unit Classification." *Current Anthropology* 5:282–312, 1964.

Nicholson, H. *Diplomacy,* 3rd ed. Oxford: Oxford University Press, 1963.

Niehoff, D. *The Biology of Violence.* New York: Free Press, 1999.

Nisbett, R. E. *The Geography of Thought.* New York: Free Press, 2003.

Nudler, O. "On Conflicts and Metaphors: Towards an Extended Rationality." In J. Burton (ed.) *Conflict: Human Needs Theory.* New York: St. Martin's, 1990.

Nunca Más: Report of the Argentine National Commission on the Disappeared. New York: Farrar, Straus, Giroux, 1986.

Nye Jr., J. *Soft Power: The Means to Success in World Politics.* New York: Public Affairs Press, 2004.

Ostrom E., J. Burger, C. Field, R. Norgaard, and D. Policansky. "Revisiting the Commons: Local Lessons, Global Challenges." *Science* 284:278–282, April 9, 1999.

Parsons, T. "The Distribution of Power in American Society." *World Politics* 10(1):123–143, 1957.

———. *Structure and Process in Modern Society.* New York: The Free Press, 1960.

———. "On the Concept of Power." *Proceedings of the American Philosophical Society* 107:232–262, 1963.

Patai, R. *The Arab Mind.* New York: Scribner, 1973.

Picard, C. "Learning about Learning: The Value of 'Insight.'" *Conflict Resolution Quarterly* 20(4):477–484, 2003

Picard, C., and K. Melchin. "Insight Mediation: A Learning-Centered Mediation Model." *Negotiation Journal* 23(1):35–53, 2007.

Princen, T. *Intermediaries in International Conflict.* Princeton: Princeton University Press, 1992.

Provis, C. "Interests vs. Positions: A Critique of the Distinction." *Negotiation Journal* 12 (4):305–323, 1996.

Pruitt, D. *Whither Ripeness Theory?* Arlington VA: ICAR Working Paper no. 25, 2005.

———. "Escalation and De-escalation in Asymmetric Conflict." *Dynamics of Asymmetric Conflict* 2(1):23–31, 2009.

Pruitt, D., and P. Carnevale. *Negotiation in Social Conflict.* Brooks/Cole: Pacific Grove CA, 1993.

Pruitt, D., and S. H. Kim. *Social Conflict: Escalation, Stalemate, and Settlement,* 3rd ed. Boston: McGraw-Hill, 2004.

Quinn, D., J. Wilkenfeld, K. Smarick, and A. Asal. "Power Play: Mediation in Symmetric and Asymmetric International Crises." *International Interactions* 32:441–470, 2006.

Qureshi, E. "Misreading the 'Arab Mind.'" *Boston Globe.* May 30, 2004.

Raiffa, H. *The Art & Science of Negotiation.* Cambridge: Harvard University Press, 1982.

Ramsbotham, O., T. Woodhouse, and H. Miall. *Contemporary Conflict Resolution: The Prevention, Management, and Transformation of Deadly Conflicts.* Cambridge UK and Malden MA: Polity Press, 2005.

Rapoport, A., and A. Chammah. *The Prisoner's Dilemma: A Study in Conflict and Cooperation.* Ann Arbor: University of Michigan Press, 1965.

Rawls, J. *A Theory of Justice.* Cambridge: Harvard University Press, 1971.

Reid, H. G., and E. J. Yanarella. "Toward a Critical Theory of Peace Research in the United States: the Search for an 'Intelligible Core.'" *Journal of Peace Research* 13(4):315–341, 1976.

Reisman, D. *The Lonely Crowd.* Garden City NY: Doubleday, 1956.

Renteln, A. D. *International Human Rights: Universalism versus Relativism.* Newbury Park CA: Sage, 1990.

Rice, E. *Wars of the Third Kind: Conflict in Underdeveloped Countries.* Berkeley: University of California Press, 1988.

Richmond, O. P. *Peace in International Relations.* New York: Routledge, 2008.

Ricigliano, R. "A Three Dimensional Analysis of Negotiation." In A. Schneider and C. Honeyman (eds.). *The Negotiator's Fieldbook.* Washington DC: American Bar Association, 2006.

Rigby, A. *Justice and Reconciliation: After the Violence.* Boulder CO: Lynne Rienner, 2001.

Riskin, L. "Understanding Mediator's Orientation, Strategies, and Techniques: A Guide for the Perplexed." *Harvard Negotiation Law Review* 1:7–51 (Spring), 1996.

Robben, A., and M. Orozco-Suarez (eds.). *Cultures under Siege: Collective Violence and Trauma.* Cambridge: Cambridge University Press, 2004.

Rogan, R., M. Hammer, and C. Van Zandt. *Dynamic Processes of Crisis Negotiation.* Westport CT: Praeger, 1997.

Romney, A. K., and C. Moore. "Toward a Theory of Culture as Shared Cognitive Structures." *Ethos* 26(3):314–337, 1998.

Roosens, E. E. *Creating Ethnicity.* London: Sage, 1989.

Rorty, R. "Human Rights, Rationality, and Sentimentality." In S. Shute and S. Hurley (eds.). *On Human Rights: The Oxford Lectures, 1993.* New York: Basic Books, 1993.

———. *Philosophy and Social Hope.* London: Penguin Books, 1999.

Rosch, E. "The Structure of Color Space in Naming and Memory for Two Languages." *Cognitive Psychology* 7:532–547, 1972.

———. "Cognitive Representations of Semantic Categories." *Journal of Experimental Psychology* 104:192–233, 1975.

———. "Cognitive Reference Points." *Cognitive Psychology* 7:532–547, 1976.

Rosen, L. *Bargaining for Reality: The Construction of Social Relations in a Muslim Community.* Chicago: University of Chicago Press, 1984.

Ross, M. H. *The Management of Conflict: Interpretations and Interests in Comparative Perspective.* New Haven: Yale University Press, 1993.

———. "Psychocultural Interpretation Theory and Peacemaking in Ethnic Conflicts." *Political Psychology* 16(3):523–544, 1995.

———. "Culture and Identity in Comparative Political Analysis." In M. Lichbach and A. Zuckerman (eds.). *Comparative Politics: Rationality, Culture, and Structure.* Cambridge: Cambridge University Press, 1997.

———. *Cultural Contestation in Ethnic Conflict.* Cambridge: Cambridge University Press, 2007.

Rotberg, R., and D. Thompson (eds.). *Truth vs. Justice: The Morality of Truth Commissions.* Princeton: Princeton University Press, 2000.

Rothbart, D., and K. Korostelina (eds.). *Identity, Morality, and Threat: Studies in Violent Conflict.* Lanham MD: Lexington Books, 2006.

Rouhana, N. "Group Identity and Power Asymmetry in Reconciliation Processes: The Israeli-Palestinian Case." *Peace and Conflict: Journal of Peace Psychology* 10(1):33–52, 2004.

———. "Truth and Reconciliation: The Right of Return in the Context of Past Injustice." In A. Lesch and I. Lustick (eds.). *Exile and Return: Predicaments of Palestinians and Jews.* Philadelphia: University of Pennsylvania Press, 2005, pp. 261–278.

————. "Reconciling History and Equal Citizenship in Israel: Democracy and the Politics of Historical Denial." In B. Bashir and W. Kymlicka (eds.). *The Politics of Reconciliation in Multicultural Societies.* New York: Oxford University Press, 2008, pp. 70–93.

————. "Key Issues in Reconciliation: Challenging Traditional Assumptions on Conflict Resolution and Power Dynamics." In D. Bar-Tal (ed.). *Intergroup Conflicts and Their Resolution: Social Psychological Perspectives.* New York: Psychology Press, 2011, pp. 291–314.

Rubenstein, R. E. Personal communication, July 1, 2004.

————. "Conflict Resolution in an Age of Empire." In D. J. D. Sandole, S. Byrne, I. Sandole-Staroste, and J. Senehi (eds.). *Handbook of Conflict Analysis and Resolution.* London and New York: Routledge, 2009.

Rubenstein, R. E., and J. Crocker. "Challenging Huntington." *Foreign Policy* 96:113–128 (Fall), 1994.

Rubin, J., and J. Salacuse. "The Problem of Power in International Negotiations." *International Affairs* 4:24–34, 1990.

Rubinstein, R. A. *Peacekeeping under Fire: Culture and Intervention.* Lanham MD: Paradigm Publishers, 2008.

Russell, B. *Power.* London: Allen and Unwin, 1962 [orig. 1938].

Sahlins, M. *Culture and Practical Reason.* Chicago: University of Chicago Press, 1978.

Said, E. *Orientalism.* New York: Pantheon, 1978.

Salacuse, J. "Ten Ways That Culture Affects Negotiating Style: Some Survey Results." *Negotiation Journal* 14:221–240 (July), 1998.

Salem, P. (ed.). *Conflict Resolution in the Arab World.* Beirut: American University of Beirut Press, 1997.

Samson, C. "Rights as Reward for Simulated Cultural Sameness: The Innu in the Canadian Cultural Context." In J. K. Cowan, M.-B. Dembour, and R. A. Wilson (eds.). *Culture and Rights: Anthropological Perspectives.* Cambridge, UK: Cambridge University Press, 2001.

Sandole, D. J. D. "The Western-Islamic 'Clash of Civilizations': The Inadvertent Contribution of the Bush Presidency." *Peace and Conflict Studies* 12(2):54–68, 2005.

————. "Traditional 'Realism' versus the 'New' Realism: John W. Burton, Conflict Provention, and the Elusive 'Paradigm Shift.'" *Global Society* 20(4):543–562 (October), 2006.

Sandole, D. J. D., and I. Sandole-Staroste. *Conflict Management and Problem Solving.* New York: New York University Press, 1987.

Sarat, A. "Alternative Dispute Resolution: Wrong Solution, Wrong Problem" *Proceedings of the Academy of Political Science* 37(1):162–173, 1988.

Saunders, H. "Prenegotiation and Circum-negotiation: Arenas of the Peace Process," In C. Crocker, F. Hampson, and P. Aall (eds.). *Managing Global Chaos*: Washington DC: United States Institute of Peace Press, 1996.

Scarry, E. *The Body in Pain: The Making and Unmaking of the World.* Oxford: Oxford University Press, 1985.

Schaef, A. W. *Women's Reality: An Emerging Female System in a White Male Society.* New York: Harper & Row, 1981.

Schapera, I. *A Handbook of Tswana Law and Custom.* London: Oxford University Press, 1938.

Schattschneider, E. E. *The Semi-Sovereign People: A Realist's View of Democracy in America.* New York: Holt, Rinehart and Winston, 1960.

Schecter, J. *Russian Negotiating Behavior.* Washington DC: United States Institute of Peace Press, 1998.

Scheinman, A. *From Explanation to Understanding: Toward a Hermeneutic Reconstruction of Conflict Resolution Theory.* Unpubl. Ph.D. dissertation, ICAR, George Mason University, 2008.

Schelling, T. *The Strategy of Conflict.* Cambridge: Harvard University Press, 1960.

———. *Arms and Influence.* New Haven: Yale University Press, 1966.

Schirch, L. "Linking Human Rights and Conflict Transformation." In J. A. Mertus and J. W. Helsing (eds.). *Human Rights and Conflict.* Washington DC: United States Institute of Peace Press, 2006.

Schlesinger Jr., A. M. *The Disuniting of America: Reflections on a Multicultural Society.* New York: Norton, 1992.

Schmid, H. "Peace Research and Politics." *Journal of Peace Research* 5(3):217–232, 1968.

Schneider, A. and C. Honeyman (eds.). *The Negotiator's Fieldbook.* Washington DC: American Bar Association, 2006.

Schwartz, T. "Anthropology and Psychology: An Unrequited Relationship." In T. Schwartz, G. White, and C. Lutz (eds.). *New Directions in Psychological Anthropology.* Cambridge: Cambridge University Press, 1992.

Scott, J. *Weapons of the Weak: Everyday Forms of Peasant Resistance.* New Haven: Yale University Press, 1985.

Senger, J. M. "Tales of the Bazaar: Interest-Based Negotiation across Cultures." *Negotiation Journal* 18(3):233–250, 2002.

Shweder, R., and R. LeVine (eds.). *Culture Theory: Essays on Mind, Self, and Emotion.* New York: Cambridge University Press, 1984.

Silk, J. "Traditional Culture and the Prospect for Human Rights in Africa." In A. A. An-Na'im and F. Deng (eds.). *Human Rights in Africa.* Washington DC: Brookings, 1990.

Simon, H. "A Behavioral Model of Rational Choice." *Quarterly Journal of Economics* 69:99–118, 1955.

———. *Models of Bounded Rationality.* Cambridge: MIT Press, 1982.

Skidmore, T. *Black and White: Race and Nationality in Brazilian Thought.* New York: Oxford University Press, 1974.

Slim, H. "Dealing with Moral Dilemmas." In L. Reychler and T. Paffenholz (eds.). *Peacebuilding: A Field Guide.* Boulder: Lynne Rienner, 2001.

Slyomovics, S. *The Performance of Human Rights in Morocco.* Philadelphia: University of Pennsylvania Press, 2005.

Smith, A. *National Identity.* Reno: University of Nevada Press, 1991.

Smyser, W. R. *How Germans Negotiate: Logical Goals, Practical Solutions.* Washington DC: United States Institute of Peace Press, 2002.

Snyder, S. *Negotiating on the Edge: North Korean Negotiating Behavior.* Washington DC: United States Institute of Peace Press, 1999.

Solomon, R. H. *Chinese Negotiating Behavior: Pursuing Interests through 'Old Friends.'* Washington DC: United States Institute of Peace Press, 1999.

Spiro, M. E. "Cultural Relativism and the Future of Anthropology." *Cultural Anthropology* 1:254–286, 1986.

———. "Collective Representations and Mental Representations in Religious Symbol Systems." In B. Kilborne and L. Langness (eds.). *Culture and Human Nature.* Chicago: University of Chicago Press, 1987.

Stanley, E. "Evaluating the Truth and Reconciliation Commission." *Journal of Modern African Studies* 39(3):525–546, 2001.

Starr, J., and J. Collier (eds.). *History and Power in the Study of Law.* Ithaca: Cornell University Press, 1989.

Starr, J., and M. Goodale (eds.). *Practicing Ethnography in Law: New Dialogues, Enduring Methods.* London and New York: Palgrave/Macmillan, 2002.

Staub, E. *The Root of Evil: The Origins of Genocide and Other Group Violence.* Cambridge, UK: Cambridge University Press, 1989.

Stedman, S. "Spoiler Problems in Peace Processes." *International Security* 22(2):5–53, 1997.

Stocking, G. W. *Race, Culture, and Evolution.* New York: Free Press, 1968.

Stoll, D. "To Whom Should We Listen? Human Rights Activism in Two Guatemalan Land Disputes." In R. A. Wilson (ed.). *Human Rights, Culture, and Context.* London: Pluto Press, 1997.

Stone, J. "Teaching Ethnic and Racial Relations: Some Comments on Michael Banton." *Ethnic and Racial Studies* 26:511–516, 2003.

Strauss, A. *Negotiations: Varieties, Contexts, Processes, and Social Order.* San Francisco: Jossey-Bass, 1978.

Stuhlberg, J. *Taking Charge/Managing Conflict.* Lexington MA: D.C. Heath, 1987.

Susskind, L., and J. Cruikshank. *Breaking the Impasse: Consensual Approaches to Resolving Public Disputes.* New York: Basic Books, 1987.

Tannen, D. *Gender and Discourse.* Oxford: Oxford University Press, 1994.

Taylor, A., and J. Millers (eds.). *Conflict and Gender.* Cresskill NJ: Hampton Press, 1994.

Thompson, L. *The Mind and Heart of the Negotiator,* 4th ed. Upper Saddle River NJ: Prentice Hall, 2009.

Thucydides. *History of the Peloponnesian War.* Tr. D. Grene. Chicago: University of Chicago Press, 1989.

Tibi, B. "The European Tradition of Human Rights and the Culture of Islam." In A. A. An-Na'im and F. Deng (eds.). *Human Rights in Africa.* Washington DC: Brookings, 1990.

Touval, S., and I. W. Zartman (eds.). *International Mediation in Theory and Practice.* Boulder CO: Westview Press, 1985.

Trachte-Huber, E. W., and S. K. Huber (eds.). *Alternative Dispute Resolution: Strategies for Law and Business.* Cincinnati OH: Anderson Publishing, 1996.

Triandis, H. *The Analysis of Subjective Culture.* New York: Wiley, 1972.

Trice, H., and J. Beyer. *The Cultures of Work Organizations.* Englewood Cliffs NJ: Prentice Hall, 1993.

Trujillo, M. A., S. Y. Bowland, L. J. Myers, P. M. Richards, and B. Roy (eds.). *Re-Centering: Culture and Knowledge in Conflict Resolution Practice.* Syracuse: Syracuse University Press, 2008.

Truth and Reconciliation Commission of South Africa (TRC). *Truth and Reconciliation Commission of South Africa Report.* Oxford: Macmillan Reference, 1998. See also: www.truthcommission.org/links.

Turner, V. W. *Schism and Continuity in an African Society.* Manchester, UK: Manchester University Press, 1957.

Tutu, D. *No Future without Forgiveness.* London: Rider Books, 1999.

Ury, W., J. Brett, and S. Goldberg. *Getting Disputes Resolved: Designing Systems to Cut the Costs of Conflict.* San Francisco: Jossey-Bass, 1988.

Vago, S. *Law and Society,* 7th ed. Upper Saddle River NJ: Prentice Hall, 2003.

van den Berghe, P. *The Ethnic Phenomenon.* New York: Praeger, 1987.

van der Merwe, H. "Reconciliation and Justice in South Africa: Lessons from the TRC's Community Interventions." In M. Abu-Nimer (ed.). *Reconciliation, Justice, and Coexistence.* Lanham MD: Lexington Books, 2001.

van der Merwe, H., V. Baxter, and A. R. Chapman (eds.). *Assessing the Impact of Transitional Justice: Challenges for Empirical Research.* Washington DC: United States Institute of Peace Press, 2009.

Vasquez, J. A. *The Power of Power Politics,* 2nd ed. Cambridge: Cambridge University Press, 1998 [orig. 1983].

Väyrynen, T. *Culture and International Conflict Resolution.* Manchester, UK: Manchester University Press, 2001.

Verdery, K. *National Ideology Under Socialism: Identity and Cultural Politics in Ceausescu's Romania.* Berkeley: University of California Press, 1995.

Volkan, V. *The Need to Have Enemies and Allies: From Clinical Practice to International Relationships.* New York: Jason Aronson, 1988.

———. "Transgenerational Transmission and Chosen Trauma: An Aspect of Large-Group Identity." *Group Analysis* 34:79–97, 2001.

Wagner, R. *The Invention of Culture.* Englewood Cliff NJ: Prentice-Hall, 1975.

Walton, R., and R. McKersie. *A Behavioral Theory of Labor Negotiations.* New York: McGraw-Hill, 1965.

Waltz, K. *Man, Sate, and War.* New York: Columbia University Press, 1959.

Warfield, W. "Public Policy Conflict Resolution: The Nexus between Culture and Process." In D. J. D. Sandole and H. van der Merwe (eds.). *Conflict Resolution Theory and Practice.* Manchester: Manchester University Press, 1993.

———. Personal communication, June 30, 2004.

Weaver, G. (ed.). *Culture, Communication and Conflict.* Needham Heights MA: Ginn Press, 1994.

Weber, M. *Sociological Writings.* New York: Continuum, 1994.

Wedel, J. *Collision and Collusion: The Strange Case of Western Aid to Eastern Europe 1989–1998.* New York: St. Martin's, 1998.

Weher, P., and J. P. Lederach. "Mediating Conflicts in Central America." *Journal of Peace Research* 28:85–98, 1991.

Weiss, S. "Negotiating with Romans, Part I." *Sloan Management Review* 35:51–61 (Winter), 1994a.

———. "Negotiating with Romans, Part II." *Sloan Management Review* 35:85–99 (Spring), 1994b.

White, G. M. "Culture Talk in the 90s." *Culture and Policy* 6(2):5–22, 1994.

White, R. K. *Nobody Wanted War,* rev. ed. New York: Doubleday, 1970 [orig. 1965].

Wiebelhaus-Brahm, E. *Truth Commissions and Transitional Societies: The Impact on Human Rights and Democracy.* New York: Routledge, 2010.

Wikan, U. *Generous Betrayal: The Politics of Culture in the New Europe.* Chicago: University of Chicago Press, 2002.

Wildavsky, A. "Choosing Preferences by Constructing Institutions: A Cultural Theory of Preference Formation." *American Political Science Review* 81(3):3–21, 1987.

Williams, R. *Culture.* Glasgow: Fontana, 1981.

———. *Keywords.* New York: Oxford University Press, 1983 [orig. 1976].

Wilmot, W., and J. Hocker. *Interpersonal Conflict* New York: McGraw-Hill, 2001.

Wilson R. A. (ed.). *Human Rights, Culture, and Context: Anthropological Perspectives.* London: Pluto Press, 1997.

———. "Reconciliation and Revenge in Post-Apartheid South Africa: Rethinking Legal Pluralism and Human Rights." *Current Anthropology* 41(1):75–98, 2000.

Winslade, J., and G. Monk. *Narrative Mediation: A New Approach to Conflict Resolution.* San Francisco: Jossey-Bass, 2000.

Winslow, T. "Reconciliation: The Road to Healing? Collective Good, Individual Harm?" *Track Two* 6(3–4), 1997.

Wittes, T. C. (ed.). *How Israelis and Palestinians Negotiate: A Cross-Cultural Analysis of the Oslo Peace Process.* Washington DC: United States Institute of Peace Press, 2005.

Wrong, D. *Power: Its Forms, Bases and Uses.* Chicago: University of Chicago Press 1988 [orig. 1979].

Yarrow, C. H. *Quaker Experiences in International Mediation.* New Haven: Yale University Press, 1972.

Yngvesson, B. *Virtuous Citizens, Disruptive Subjects: Order and Complaint in a New England Court.* New York: Routledge, 1993.

Zartman, I. W. "A Skeptic's View." In G. Faure and J. Rubin (eds.). *Culture and Negotiation.* Newbury Park CA: Sage, 1993.

———. "Conflict Management: The Long and the Short of It." *SAIS Review* 20: 227–325 (Winter–Spring), 200a.

———. "Ripeness: The Hurting Stalemate and Beyond." In P. P. Stern and D. Druckman (eds.). *Conflict Resolution after the Cold War.* Washington DC: National Academy Press, 2000b, pp. 225–250.

Zartman, I. W., and J. Z. Rubin (eds.). *Power and Negotiation.* Ann Arbor: University of Michigan Press, 2002.

I gratefully acknowledge the following publishers and publications where earlier versions of the essays and articles on which the following chapters are based first appeared:

Chapter 1. First published as "Culture" in *Conflict Resolution: From Analysis to Intervention,* S. Cheldelin, D. Druckman, and L. Fast (eds.). London and New York: Continuum 2003, pp. 140–153.

Chapter 2. First published as "Context and Pretext in Conflict Resolution," *Journal of Dispute Resolution* 2003(2):353–365, 2004. Curators of the University of Missouri.

Chapter 3. First published as "Culture, Relativism and Human Rights" in J. Mertus and J. Helsing, eds., *Human Rights and Conflict: Exploring the Links between Rights, Law, and Peacebuilding,* Washington DC: United States Institute of Peace Press, 2006, pp. 97–120.

Chapter 4. First published as "Constructing Ethnicity: Culture and Ethnic Conflict in the New World Disorder." *American Journal of Orthopsychiatry* 71(3):281–289.

Chapter 5. First published as "Type I and Type II Errors in Culturally Sensitive Conflict Resolution Practice." *Conflict Resolution Quarterly* 20(3):351–371. Wiley Publications, Inc.

Chapter 6. First published as "Culture Theory, Culture Clash and the Practice of Conflict Resolution," in D. J. D. Sandole, Sean Byrne, Ingrid Sandole-Staroste, and Jessica Senehi, eds. *Handbook of Conflict Analysis and Resolution.* New York: Routledge, 2008, pp. 239–253. Taylor and Francis Publishers.

Chapter 7. First published as "Toward an Expanded Canon of Negotiating Theory: Identity, Ideological and Values-Based Conflicts and the Need for a New Heuristic." *Marquette Law Review* 89:567–582; and "The Poverty of Buyer and Seller." In Andrea Kupfer Schneider and Christopher Honeyman, eds. *The Negotiator's Fieldbook,* Washington DC: American Bar Association, Section of Dispute Resolution, 2005, pp. 81–86.

Chapter 8. First published as "Truth and Reconciliation Commissions: Problems in Transitional Justice and the Reconstruction of Identity." *Transcultural Psychiatry* 47(1):33–49. SAGE Publications Ltd., http://online.sagepub.com.

Index

About the Author

Kevin Avruch is the Henry Hart Rice Professor of Conflict Resolution and Professor of Anthropology at the School for Conflict Analysis and Resolution, as well as Senior Fellow in the Peace Operations Policy Program, School of Public Policy, at George Mason University. He is the author of *Culture and Conflict Resolution*, among other works.